LEONARD PERCIVAL HOWELL
AND THE GENESIS OF RASTAFARI

LEONARD PERCIVAL HOWELL AND THE GENESIS OF RASTAFARI

– Edited by –

CLINTON A. HUTTON, MICHAEL A. BARNETT,
D.A. DUNKLEY AND JAHLANI A.H. NIAAH

THE UNIVERSITY OF THE WEST INDIES PRESS
Jamaica • Barbados • Trinidad and Tobago

The University of the West Indies Press
7A Gibraltar Hall Road, Mona
Kingston 7, Jamaica
www.uwipress.com

© Clinton A. Hutton, Michael A. Barnett,
D.A. Dunkley and Jahlani A.H. Niaah, 2015

All rights reserved. Published 2015

A catalogue record of this book is available
from the National Library of Jamaica.

ISBN: 978-976-640-549-6 (print)
      978-976-640-558-8 (Kindle)
      978-976-640-567-0 (Epub)

Cover illustration: Clinton Hutton, *The Genesis of Rastafari* (acrylic on paper, 2011).
Cover and book design by Robert Harris
Set in Minion Pro 10.5/14.5 x 27
Printed in the United States of America

For the Howellites and the Howell family

CONTENTS

List of Illustrations   *ix*

Acknowledgements   *xi*

Introduction   *1*

PART 1. ANALYSING LEONARD HOWELL

1   Leonard Howell Announcing God: The Conditions That Gave Birth to Rastafari in Jamaica   *9*
    CLINTON A. HUTTON

2   Interrogating Leonard Howell as the "First Rasta"   *53*
    MICHAEL A. BARNETT

3   "That Vagabond George Stewart of England": Leonard Howell's Seditious Sermons, 1933–1941   *69*
    JAMES ROBERTSON

4   Leonard P. Howell's Leadership of the Rastafari Movement and His "Missing Years"   *107*
    D.A. DUNKLEY

5   Leonard Howell's Philosophy of Rastafari Manhood   *130*
    JAHLANI A.H. NIAAH

6   The Process of Becoming Black: Leonard Howell and the Manifestation of Rastafari   *155*
    CHRISTOPHER A.D. CHARLES

7   Reorienting Rasta: Tracing Rastafari's Visual Roots   172
    PETRINE ARCHER

8   Social Entrepreneurship and Rastafari "Livety": Pinnacle as a Successful Social Enterprise   185
    K'ADAMAWE A.H.N. K'NIFE, EDWARD DIXON AND ALLAN BERNARD

9   Bibliographical Essay: Howell in the Studies on Rastafari   206
    LOUIS E.A. MOYSTON

PART 2. REMEMBERING LEONARD HOWELL

10 Growing Up in Pinnacle: An Interview with Monty and Billbert Howell   219
    CLINTON A. HUTTON

11 Leonard Howell versus Robert William Lyall-Grant   245
    MIGUEL LORNE

12 Leonard P. Howell: A Portrait   250
    LOUIS E.A. MOYSTON

Epilogue: The Necessity to Never Forsake or Forget Gangunguru Maragh   255
    I-NATION

Bibliography   257
Contributors   273

ILLUSTRATIONS

FIGURES

Figure 1.1.	Leonard Percival Howell	*10*
Figure 1.2.	Marcus Garvey	*18*
Figure 1.3.	Coronation of Emperor Haile Selassie and Empress Menen	*23*
Figure 1.4.	Brother Man	*37*
Figure 2.1.	Alexander Bedward	*54*
Figure 2.2.	Joseph Nathaniel Hibbert	*56*
Figure 2.3.	Archibald Dunkley	*57*
Figure 4.1.	Letter from Alexander Bustamante about Leonard Howell, 6 July 1939	*113*
Figures 7.1–7.2.	"The Mystic Signs of Ras Tafari"	*173*
Figure 7.3.	Image of Emperor Haile Selassie I sold by Leonard Howell, c. 1932	*175*
Figure 7.4.	*French Set-Girls*, Kingston, Jamaica	*179*
Figures 7.5–7.6.	"Ideographic diagrams" by Joseph Nathaniel Hibbert	*181*
Figure 10.1.	Leonard Howell and his wife, Teneth Bent	*220*
Figure 10.2.	Billbert Howell	*221*
Figure 10.3.	Monty Howell	*221*
Figure 10.4.	Destruction of Pinnacle, 1954	*241*

TABLES

Table 6.1.	Nigrescence Theory *157*
Table 6.2.	Black Identity Development of Leonard Howell, 1898–1981 *162*
Table 8.1.	Framework of the Entrepreneurial Process *193*
Table 8.2.	The Core Components of a Business Model: Foundation, Proprietorship and Rules *195*

ACKNOWLEDGEMENTS

We, the editors, would like to express special thanks to the Office of the Principal and the Special New Initiatives Grant Committee of the University of the West Indies, Mona, for providing the necessary funds to produce this ground-breaking volume. We would like to thank the Howell family and the Howellites for their support of this project. Thanks must also go to Yvonne Young-Wallace, Kadine Nickole Ferguson and Irica Grant, who helped in the preparation and assemblage of the manuscript. Lastly, we would like to sincerely thank all the contributors to this volume. Without their contributions, this book would not have materialized.

INTRODUCTION

The arrival of this cross-disciplinary volume on Leonard Howell and the early years of the Rastafari movement is a welcome addition to the growing literature on Rastafari studies. Robert Hill's 1981 article was the first academic study on Howell to be published; it was republished in 1983 in the *Jamaica Journal* and has been available since 2001 as a short monograph, *Dread History: Leonard P. Howell and Millenarian Visions in the Early Rastafarian Religion*.[1]

Other studies since then include the works written by Michael Hoenisch and Frank Jan van Dijk, published in the *Massachusetts Review* and *New West Indian Guide*, respectively.[2] In *Rastafari: Roots and Ideology*, Barry Chevannes, the noted Rastafari scholar, included a chapter, "Early Leaders and Organizations", in which, among other things, he gave sketches of the personalities and leadership and organizational styles of Leonard Howell, Joseph Hibbert, Archibald Dunkley and Robert Hinds, founders of the Rastafari movement.[3] The book *Chanting Down Babylon: The Rastafari Reader* also has a chapter titled "The First Chant: Leonard Howell's *The Promised Key*", with commentary by William David Spencer.[4]

Louis E.A. Moyston has also been publishing newspaper and online articles on Howell since the 1980s. In addition, Hélène Lee's book, the only published biography of Howell, entitled *The First Rasta: Leonard Howell and the Rise of Rastafarianism*, was originally a 1999 French publication that was republished in English in 2003.[5] These studies shed light on Howell's role as a foundational Rastafari leader and his persecution by the colonial and postcolonial states.

The next generation of studies on Howell and early Rastafari was inspired by the 2011 University of the West Indies symposium on Leonard Percival Howell to commemorate the 113th year of his birth. It is within this context that D.A.

Dunkley published two articles, one in *Caribbean Quarterly* and the other in *New West Indian Guide*.[6] The articles and other contributions in the present volume seek not only to build on this body of work, but also to provide a diverse collection of opinions about Howell published in one place.

Importantly, not only does the array of contributions – speeches, essays and an interview with Howell's sons – that has been compiled for this volume provide provocative perspectives on Leonard Howell, but it also gives us a fairly detailed glimpse of the early years of the Rastafari movement, an area in need of more attention in Rastafari studies. The present volume is therefore the product of interest in Howell and the genesis of the Rastafari movement. Also worth noting is that the volume was conceived and compiled by Rastafari scholars (three of whom are Rastafari practitioners) from a range of disciplines including politics, philosophy, sociology, history and cultural studies, thus assuring that the volume stands as an authentic representation of the Rastafari family and a cross-disciplinary contribution to Rastafari scholarship.

The volume grew out of the idea (which was broached by Michael Boyd to Clinton Hutton) of celebrating the one hundred and thirteenth anniversary of Leonard Howell's birth in a significant manner. This idea led to the planning of an elaborate symposium, the inaugural Leonard Howell Symposium, convened at the University of the West Indies, Mona, Jamaica, on 17 and 18 June 2011. This symposium was effectively the university's contribution to the celebration of the anniversary of Howell's birthday, but there were other notable activities to observe the occasion, such as a cultural celebration at the Tredegar Park School in Spanish Town on 16 June 2011. The support from within and outside of the Rastafari community for the inaugural Leonard Howell Symposium was tremendous. This particular event, which was conceptualized by Clinton Hutton, became the product of collaboration between the Faculty of Social Sciences, the Rastafari Studies Unit at the University of the West Indies, Mona, and the Leonard P. Howell Foundation. The presence of members of Howell's family was a welcome and notable addition to the symposium.

The first chapter of this volume, written by political scientist and philosopher Clinton Hutton, explores the genesis of Rastafari through the prism of Garveyism, Revivalism/Myalism, Kumina and other expressions of African Caribbean spirituality. Additional influences for this essay are the philosophy of the Morant Bay Rebellion, the knowledge system of the Haitian Revolution and the creative ethos of the African diaspora (which includes the cosmological roots of Caribbean arts, aesthetics and modes of creativity). In this chapter, Hutton positions the praxis of Leonard Howell within the trajectory of the New World's ontology of resistance. He makes the argument that Howell's ability to announce His Imperial Majesty, Haile Selassie I, as God was rooted in the ethos of the African understanding of how God is incarnated, assessed and embodied. In doing this, Hutton presents a compelling framework for the method, mode and meaning of the inner logic of the Rastafari movement at the point of its inception.

In the second chapter, sociologist Michael Barnett takes us on a departure from the notion of Howell as the first Rastafari leader. Barnett interrogates the claim that Howell was the first man in Jamaica to pronounce Haile Selassie I as God. However, Barnett does emphasize that Howell was the most influential of the early Rastafari leaders.

James Robertson's essay in chapter 3 brings readers to the Jamaica Archives in Spanish Town, St Catherine. Robertson, a historian, uses primary documents to examine Howell's proselytizing work, and shows Howell's endeavours as seen through the eyes of the colonial regime between 1933 and 1941. It was during the latter year that the state authorized the police to embark on the first of three major incursions on Howell's community, known as Pinnacle.

Historian D.A. Dunkley continues this discussion in chapter 4, presenting an analysis of Howell's leadership as a promotion of black nationalism in late colonial Jamaica. Dunkley outlines how the suppression attempts changed over the course of Howell's life, and debunks the view that Howell retreated because of these attacks on his leadership and movement.

Chapters 5 through 8 are analyses of the impact of Howell's leadership within and outside the early Rastafari movement. In the first of these chapters, cultural theorist Jahlani Niaah examines Howell's concept of black manhood as a departure from colonial characterizations. In this way, we are given an evaluation of Howell within the context of social philosophy. Niaah aims to illustrate Howell's reinvention of the black male as a father and provider, who erases the damage caused by white supremacy and offers religious, economic and political guidance.

In chapter 6, psychologist Christopher Charles looks at the production of blackness by using Howell's transition from colonial subject to anti-colonial Rastafari warrior. In this examination, Charles uses Howell's experiences and sense of self to demonstrate how in becoming a Rastafari, he was able to liberate himself and embark upon the task of helping other African Jamaicans to initiate their own redemptive processes.

Chapter 7, written by the late art historian Petrine Archer, engages with Howell's use of East Indian visual symbolism to create at least two drawings. These drawings were seized from Howell's headquarters in Port Morant in the parish of St Thomas, Jamaica, in 1937 and captioned by the *Daily Gleaner* of 18 January 1937 as "cultists' interpretation of a dream of what houses in future Abyssinia will look like". Archer, using cultural artefacts and art, argues that the Rastafari movement, through Howell's leadership, represents the creolization process through which many other aspects of Jamaican and Caribbean cultural identity have evolved.

In chapter 8, K'adamawe A.H.N. K'nIfe, Edward Dixon and Allan Bernard write from the perspectives of management and economics to consider Howell's Pinnacle community as a model of a successful social enterprise. This essay uses the framework of social entrepreneurship to show that Pinnacle became an example of an independent and self-sustaining black community. It also explains the rapid growth of the population at Pinnacle and the decision to use the police to bring about its destruction.

Chapter 9, the last chapter of part 1, is a bibliographical essay written by independent researcher Louis E.A. Moyston. The essay provides a synopsis of the scholarship on Leonard Howell that has been done within the context of Rastafari studies. Moyston's goal is to observe the treatment that Howell has received by scholars, and he implicates some of this scholarship in the undermining mission against Leonard Howell.

Chapter 10 commences part 2 of the book, with an interview with Monty and Billbert Howell, done by Clinton Hutton. Hutton conducted the interview in 2010 at his office in the Department of Government at the University of the West Indies, Mona, and it takes us through the disturbing events experienced by Howell, his family and his followers. The revelations are based on the recollections of Howell's sons – an interview filled with accounts of cruelty and trauma, but which will help us to gain first-hand knowledge of the campaign against Howell that took place during the colonial and postcolonial periods.

For chapter 11, Rastafari practitioner and attorney-at-law Miguel Lorne contributes a commentary on the 1934 trial of Leonard Howell at the Morant Bay courthouse in the parish of St Thomas. At this trial, Howell faced the serious charge of sedition and at its conclusion was sentenced to two years at hard labour. His compatriot, Robert Hinds, was also tried. He, however, was sentenced to one year at hard labour. Lorne observes that the trial represented the first public attempt by the colonial regime to undermine the Rastafari movement. The charges brought to light at the trial are vital to showing the determination of the state to destabilize Rastafari's early leadership, but they also reveal the confidence and mental agility displayed by Howell and Hinds in defending their struggle against white oppression.

Chapter 12 is adapted from a presentation given by Moyston at the second annual Leonard Howell Symposium in 2012. Moyston considers Howell's sense of purpose and vision, and goes on to describe the Rastafari leader using an optic that encourages us to view him as someone with a sociological and anthropological understanding of the fight for black liberation.

The final chapter is a short commentary written in "Rasta talk", reminding readers of Howell's importance to Jamaica and the world. It is written by a Rastafari practitioner, Kirk Scarlett, who has appropriated the name I-Nation, which exemplifies his argument that there is power in Leonard Howell's message. Scarlett's decision in choosing his name is a reflection of his identification with Howell and the Rastafari movement as a whole.

Ultimately, the intention of this edited volume is to balance the scales by examining Howell as a key contributor to the genesis of the Rastafari movement and to modern Jamaica, and thus to black consciousness and African modality in Jamaica and the wider African diaspora. While this volume does not offer an exhaustive treatment of Leonard Howell, it does provide important and insightful material that should stimulate discussion and further research on Howell, not only as a father and patriarch of the Rastafari movement, but also in terms of his vision and his legacy.

The editors, September 2014

Notes

1. Robert A. Hill, "Dread History: Leonard P. Howell and Millenarian Visions in Early Rastafari Religion in Jamaica", *Epoché: Journal of the History of Religions* 9 (1981): 30–71; Robert A. Hill, "Leonard P. Howell and Millenarian Visions in Early Rastafari Religion in Jamaica", *Jamaica Journal* 16, no. 1 (February 1983): 24–39; Robert A. Hill, *Dread History: Leonard P. Howell and Millenarian Visions in the Early Rastafarian Religion* (Chicago: Research Associates School Times Publications and Frontline Distribution International, 2001).
2. Michael Hoenisch, "Symbolic Politics: Perceptions of the Early Rastafari Movement", *Massachusetts Review* 29, no. 3 (Fall 1988): 432–49; Frank Jan van Dijk, *Jahmaica: Rastafari and Jamaican Society, 1930–1990* (Utrecht: ISOR, 1993); Frank Jan van Dijk, "Sociological Means: Colonial Reactions to the Radicalization of Rastafari in Jamaica, 1956–1959", *New West Indian Guide* 69, nos. 1–2 (1995): 67–101.
3. Barry Chevannes, *Rastafari: Roots and Ideology* (Syracuse, NY: Syracuse University Press, 1995).
4. Nathaniel Samuel Murrell, William David Spencer and Adrian Anthony McFarlane, eds., *Chanting Down Babylon: The Rastafari Reader* (Kingston: Ian Randle, 1998).
5. Hélène Lee, *The First Rasta: Leonard Howell and the Rise of Rastafarianism* (Chicago: Lawrence Hill, 2003).
6. D.A. Dunkley, "Leonard P. Howell's Leadership of the Rastafari Movement and His 'Missing Years'", *Caribbean Quarterly* 58, no. 4 (December 2012): 1–24; D.A. Dunkley, "The Suppression of Leonard Howell in Late Colonial Jamaica, 1932–1954", *New West Indian Guide* 87, nos. 1–2 (January 2013): 62–93.

Part 1

ANALYSING LEONARD HOWELL

1

LEONARD HOWELL ANNOUNCING GOD
The Conditions That Gave Birth to Rastafari in Jamaica

CLINTON A. HUTTON

God lives within I and I live within God.
 –*Herman "Woody" King, Rastafari elder*

Ethiopia is the Succeeding Kingdom of the Angl[o] Saxon Kingdom. Our philosopher is the Angl[o] Saxon Philosopher's (Successor), a wide awake Universal Master Mind.
 –*Reverend Fitz Balintine Pettersburgh*, The Royal Parchment Scroll of Black Supremacy

On **2 November 1930,** Ras Tafari Makonnen was crowned Haile Selassie I, emperor of Ethiopia, with titles such as King of Kings, Lord of Lords, Light of Saba, the Conquering Lion of the Tribe of Judah. This was witnessed by world leaders or their representatives and stirred the ontological and imaginative strivings and hopes of people of African descent the world over, for freedom, justice, sovereignty and redemption with catalytic agential force. In Jamaica, the response to the coronation was unique. It led to the birth of an anti-colonial pan-Africanist movement centred on the divination of Emperor Haile Selassie I.

Leonard Howell Announcing God

The first recorded public expression of the deification of Haile Selassie occurred in January 1933, according to Leonard Percival Howell, who initiated this public display of divination in Kingston, Jamaica.[1] Howell had lived abroad some twenty years, having migrated to Panama and the United States, and returned home from the latter in December 1932. The first public expression of deification, at "Redemption Ground" in Kingston, was described by P.A. Thompson, one of the attendees, as Howell's first meeting.[2] In any event, Howell's Kingston meeting was not successful, and in February, he took his Ras Tafari meeting to the southeastern parish of St Thomas. On 18 April 1933, Howell addressed some two hundred persons at a meeting in Trinity Ville, St Thomas. The police who were present took notes and later submitted a report to the clerk of the courts of statements allegedly made by Howell, which they considered to be of a seditious nature. According to one of the police corporals,

Figure 1.1. Leonard Percival Howell. Courtesy of the *Gleaner*.

> I heard Leonard Howell, the speaker, said [sic] to the hearers: "The Lion of Judah has broken the chain, and we of the black race are now free. George the Fifth is no more our King. George the Fifth has sent his third son down to Africa in 1928 [sic] to bow down to our new King Ras Tafair. Ras Tafair is King of Kings and Lord of Lords. The Black people must not look to George the Fifth as their King anymore – Ras Tafair is their king." . . . He said "The negro is now free and the white people will have to bow to the Negro Race." At the end of the meeting, he said "You must sing the National Anthem, but before you start, you must remember that you are not singing it for King George the Fifth, but for Ras Tafair our new king."[3]

As sympathetic as the crown solicitor and the attorney general might have been with pressing charges of sedition against Howell, they were concerned that taking such a measure would prove beneficial to "a ranter who would revel in the advertisement of a prosecution".[4] The prosecutor's method of suppressing Howell might not be prudent, stated a police report. It would be better, perhaps, if he were guided on a path to "the Lunatic Asylum".[5] Support for the lunatic asylum model for suppressing Howell was implied in the crown solicitor's statement: "The man is a stupid ranter who puts forward an imaginary being or person who he calls 'Ras Tafari' and whom he describes as Christ as well as King of Ethiopians. I think we can leave Howell unadvertised so far as the annex statements are concerned."[6]

The attorney general was on the same page: "I should treat those statements as his ravings [and let them] go unnoticed."[7] The preferred method of dealing with Howell in the meantime was to spy on him or "to keep a strict eye on him", as directed by the inspector general of police to the island's constabulary in a memo.[8] At a meeting at Port Morant, St Thomas, on 13 September 1933, the police from the area whom Howell had invited to attend reported that his "meeting was opened with the singing of hymns. He amused himself by taunting the clergymen of different denominations and told people not to go to church because the ministers were liars."[9] The police also reported that Howell talked about slavery and how "the White man stole Africa from Africans, and that Black people should think that Africa is their home, not Jamaica".[10] On 8 October 1933, Howell made another speech at a public meeting in Port Morant, where it was noted that

> he chiefly in his speeches abuses the Parsons by calling them thieves and robbers and that they should be driven out of the Churches and the Churches locked up. He also abuses the white men calling them rascals and scoundrels and that they are robbing the people and keeping them down, but their eyes are now opened to everything and that they can live independently without white men. He urges to support his movement for the Negro King Ras ta Fari is doing great things for them and they will be taken to Africa next year August by ships provided for the purpose.[11]

On 10 December 1933, Leonard Howell and Robert Hinds addressed a public gathering of some three hundred at Seaforth, St Thomas. One month later, Howell and Hinds were arrested and charged for sedition because of speeches they had made at that meeting. Rasta had now entered the first stage of the suppression of its leaders by the state. It had begun with Robert Hinds and three others, who were arrested for sedition on 13 November 1933 while they were having a public meeting in a cane field in Stokes Hall.[12] On 16 December 1933, six days after the 10 December meeting which eventually led to the arrest of Leonard Howell, Hinds was again arrested for disorderly conduct at a public meeting in Trinity Ville. Joseph Hibbert, another pioneering leader of the Rastafari movement, who was present at that meeting along with others, freed Hinds from the police. However, John Ross, a vigilante plantocrat – who had mobilized to his cause the Reverend M.C. Surgeon, a Methodist minister of Morant Bay and Seaforth; Ronald Robinson, justice of the peace from Port Morant; and Thomas Warfinger of the Port Morant branch of the Jamaica Producers Association – joined forces with the police and rearrested Hinds, along with Hibbert and six of their supporters.[13] At Howell's trial for sedition at the Morant Bay courthouse on 13 March 1934, the *Daily Gleaner* noted that

> the small courtroom was packed with anxious spectators when Leonard Howell was called up to answer charges of sedition preferred against him. He pleaded not guilty to an indictment charging him with uttering, on the 10th of December last year, in the presence of H.M.'s liege subjects a seditious speech, in which he abused the Sovereign, the Queen, Queen Victoria, the Governor of Jamaica and both the governments of Great Britain and this island, "thereby intending to excite hatred and contempt for His Majesty the King, and of those responsible for the Government of this island, and to create disaffection among the subjects of His Majesty in this island and to disturb the public peace and tranquillity of this island".[14]

The *Daily Gleaner* reported that "[Howell,] an athletic figure in black, with a beard not dissimilar to that worn by the King of Abyssinia, whose photograph and name figured largely in the evidence, was undefended by council". Howell defended himself. The newspaper report further noted that Howell "wore a rosette of yellow, green and black similar to that worn by a large number of men and women who accompanied him to court". Howell, according to the *Daily Gleaner*, "took with him into the dock sheaths of documents and a few books of unusual proportions".[15]

Howell Defends Haile Selassie as God in the Colonial Court

Leonard Howell made history in the Morant Bay courthouse, the historical and symbolic site of elite power and the battle site of the Morant Bay Rebellion of 1865, by becoming the first to declare and defend in the court of British colonialism that Ras Tafari was "the Messiah returned to earth". He was sentenced to two years' imprisonment for sedition by the chief justice of Jamaica, Robert William Lyall-Grant. The *Daily Gleaner* of 17 March 1934 announced the news thus: "DENOUNCED as a fraud by the Chief Justice, Leonard Howell, self-made disciple of Ras Tafari, King of Abyssinia, and exponent of the doctrine that Ras Tafari is The Messiah returned to earth, was given a two-year term of imprisonment yesterday in the St Thomas Circuit Court at Morant Bay."[16]

Between 18 April and 16 December 1933, an average of one Rastafari meeting was held per month, mostly in the parish of St Thomas. Most of them were addressed by Leonard Howell. But this "stupid ranter who puts forward an imaginary being or person whom he calls 'Ras Tafari' [the] Christ", as the crown solicitor contemptuously termed Howell and his thoughts, was meeting with much success in St Thomas.[17] The idea of Rastafari as an anti-colonial alternative became popular in that parish and frightened the ruling local elites to their core. Howell, for them, was inciting the black masses to rebel in a parish which had been the location of the Morant Bay uprising sixty-eight years before. The Morant Bay Rebellion became an enduring spectre in the imagination of the elite classes, especially those in St Thomas.

From the beginning, persons such as John Ross insisted that Howell should be stopped and that those who were susceptible to the terrible ideas of Rastafari should be quarantined. It was the activism of the elite classes and their allies that helped the authorities to move from their policy to "leave Howell unadvertised", to deny him any means of revelling in "the advertisement of a prosecution", to charging him for sedition and sending him to prison.[18] Indeed, the chief justice himself, Lyall-Grant, left his jurisdiction in Kingston and travelled to Morant Bay to prosecute the case against Howell and Hinds to ensure that they were imprisoned. Lyall-Grant's presence as prosecutor in the case was an indication of the serious political importance that the colonial authorities attached to the threat of Rastafari and their determination to kill it in its infancy. But the die was already cast. While in prison, Leonard Howell put down his thoughts about the existential dimension and role of Haile Selassie in Rasta's first tract, *The Promised Key*. With respect to the news of the coronation of Ras Tafari, Howell interpreted it to mean that "the glory that was Solomon greater still reigns in Ethiopia. We can see all the Kings of the earth surrendering their crowns to His Majesty Ras Tafari the King of Kings and Lord of Lords Earth's Rightful Ruler to reign forever and ever."[19]

This being the case, there was no need to obey the authority of the British monarchy in Jamaica, since the British king, like all other kings, surrendered his crown to the emperor. In this context, the British monarch had no authority, for "upon His Majesty Ras Tafari's head are many diadems", including that of George V.[20] Moreover, in Haile Selassie's existential dimension, he was not just the "Elect of God" or "the Messiah returned"; he was God Almighty Himself, the Mighty Redeemer and the Mighty Liberator: "His Majesty Ras Tafari is the head over all men for He is the Supreme God. His body is the fullness in all. Now my dear people let this be our goal, forward to the King of Kings must be the cry of our social hope. Forward to the King of Kings to purify our social standards and our way of living and rebuild and inspire our character."[21]

The black prophetic metaphorical destruction of the power, authority and legitimacy of the British Empire in particular, and global white supremacy in general, what Anthony Bogues called "the successful challenge of the colonial symbolic order", had real existential meaning for identity, agency and socio-political mobilization in Jamaica and beyond.[22] The year 1933 – the first year that Howell announced the emperor to be the returned Messiah to receptive ears and minds in public meetings across St Thomas – was a crowning success for the nascent Rastafari movement, despite the determined efforts by elite forces in the media, church and state to destroy it.

African Diasporic Artistic Methods of Creating Rastafari

What conditions and permissive contexts could have conspired to produce the gestational materials and creative process that would become ontological flesh in constituting an anti-colonial pan-Africanist movement centred on the deification of Ras Tafari as earth's rightful ruler? The understanding of this creative process and of the ethos which in the space of one year overthrew the epistemic, ontological and psychological culture of a critical core of black peasant-labourers is key in making sense of this rare response to the coronation of Ras Tafari. The ontological construction of such a movement organized around the deification of Ras Tafari and the inversion of European imperial power is captured in an insightful essay by Robert Hill. This essay, "Leonard Howell and Millenarian Visions in Early Rastafari", was published in *Jamaica Journal* in February 1983. This truly cornerstone narrative of the cosmological roots of Rastafari was republished in 2001 as a monograph called *Dread History: Leonard P. Howell and Millenarian Visions in the Early Rastafarian Religion*. The present chapter seeks to extend Hill's article with a conceptual and methodological mode of probing, analysing and constructing meanings rooted in the cultural, aesthetic and creative agential traditions of the African diaspora. The rationale is the construction of a conceptual and methodological frame of reference in which to locate and probe Howell. This is congruent with an African diasporic mode of thought and creation, rooted in the aesthetic culture and agency of the artist.

I have taken this approach for a number of reasons: first, the African diasporic artistic traditions were critical to enslaved Africans and their descendants coping with slavery, resisting it and creating diasporic communities;[23] second, the cosmological roots of African diasporic art are the same as those of African diasporic spirituality and freedom;[24] third, artistic traditions have often invoked expressions, such as spirit possession, which were or are deemed to be artistic expressions and are articulated as such in African diasporic cosmology and culture;[25] fourth, the act of putting back together or reconfiguring shattered lives, cultures, epistemologies, ontologies and communities, as Howell was endeavouring to do in consequence of slavery and colonialism, must necessarily be an act of recreation, resurrection and redemption, or as Prince Buster puts it in his song "Creation", "It takes creation to build a nation";[26] and fifth, there is a rich culture of the creative arts, their methodologies and modes of creative thinking in the African diaspora that we can use to help us to explain the making of Rastafari in Jamaica in the 1930s.

There is also a sixth reason for my approach. This has to do with my own experience as a visual artist and as a person who has studied the creative methods of LeRoy Clarke, Trinidad and Tobago's master painter; Philip Moore, the late Guyanese painter and sculptor; Jamaican popular music masters Bob Marley, Lloyd Knibb and Lee "Scratch" Perry; as well as the methods of dub construction and the making of African Caribbean altar art, masquerade and other African ancestral artistic creations. Thus, it is not difficult for me to visualize Leonard Howell as an artist and Rastafari as his artistic creation, as I have visualized LeRoy Clarke, the painter, and his pantheon of breathtaking paintings imploring us to embrace the apotheosis of self; or Bob Marley, the composer/musician and lyric poet, whose works are seductive metaphorical monuments of freedom and being; or Lee "Scratch" Perry and his extemporaneous sonic canvases, brimming with spiritual aliveness. From the days of slavery, when Africans ritually repossessed themselves through sacred nocturnal ceremonies, thereby temporarily transforming their commercialized bodies – bodies possessed and desecrated by slave-makers – into bodies exorcized, (re)created, (re)textured and (re)possessed by ancestral spirits and deities, all the way to post-slavery, their struggles to be(come) were necessarily modes of reinventing or recreating themselves, requiring the tools and aesthetic compass and agency of the artist. The making of Rastafari was no different.

Based on my extensive research, I have concluded that a pervasive tradition in artistic construction methodology, guided by its own episteme, existed in the aesthetic culture of the African diaspora. It can be described as "the method and philosophy of assemblage aesthetics",[27] or what Chevannes referred to as "an open-ended adventure of imagination".[28] My reference to LeRoy Clarke's style of image-making as "the gathering and choreographing of fragments to create a redemptive universe or redemptive whole" falls into the above category of artistic construction methodology and aesthetic logic that could easily be used to denote Howell's creative ethos in the making of Rastafari.[29] The description of a few examples of creation, done on the basis of the principle of gathering and choreographing fragments to create a redemptive universe, may give us some insight into the method of constituting Rastafari. In 1789, Stephen Fuller described in his *Reports to Lords of Committee* that the thatch roof and walls of an old woman's house in Jamaica were "stuck with" the "rags, feathers [and] bones of cats", adding that

> a large earthen pot or jar, close covered, was found concealed under her bed.... It contained a prodigious quantity of round balls of earth or clay of various dimensions, large and small, whitened on the outside, and variously compounded, some with hair and rags and feathers of all sorts, and strongly bound with twine; others blended with the upper section of the skulls of cats, or stuck round with cat teeth and claws, or with human or dog's teeth, and some glass beads of different colours; there were also a great many egg shells filled with a viscous or gummy substance... and many little bags stuffed with a variety of articles.[30]

Fuller was describing an Obeah woman's kit, which seems to have been conceptually and structurally rooted in the method and philosophy of assemblage aesthetics. So too do the decorated graves in John Michael Vlach's description of African American funerary tradition:

> Black graves are made distinct by the placement of a wide variety of offerings on the tops of the burial mound. Most of these items are pottery or pressed-glass containers, but many different objects are encouraged, including cups, saucers, bowls, clocks, salt and pepper shakers, medicine bottles, spoons, pitchers, oyster shells, conch shells, white pebbles, toys, dolls' heads, bric-a-brac statues, light bulbs, tureens, flashlights, soap dishes, false teeth, syrup jugs, spectacles, cigar boxes, piggy banks, gum locks, razors, knives, tomato cans, flower pots, marbles, bits of plaster, toilet tanks. These

objects, when arranged on a group of graves, constitute a visual environment which in Afro-American tradition is seen as the world of the spirits, often the ancestors.[31]

Another example of this African diasporic mode of creation is evident in Alfred Métraux's description of the Vodou altar:

> A vodun altar is a veritable bric-a-brac display of ritual objects: jars and jugs for the deities and for the dead, plates consecrated to twin-spirits, vessels for initiated priestesses, thunderstones, swimming in oil, playing-cards, ritual rattles and emblems of the gods, as well as bottles of wine and liquor offered to the deities.... Chromolithographs are pinned to the walls. Near the Sword for Ogun, driven into the earth, one still finds, in some shrines, assein, those curious supports in iron which are still to be bought in the market of Abomey in Africa.[32]

This mode of creation, the gathering, orchestrating and choreographing of a multiplicity of fragments to constitute a redemptive universe, is central to LeRoy Clarke's artistic creation and to the making of the Revival tables in Jamaica.

Michael Veal's compelling narrative of dub music reveals the use of the same kinds of principles employed in the constitution of the Obeah woman's kit in the eighteenth century, the making of Vodou altars and Revival tables, the decoration of African American graves and the paintings of LeRoy Clarke and Philip Moore. Dub, according to Veal, is "a style built around fragments of sound over a hypnotically repeating reggae groove". It is a "fragmented and collaged-sounding" Jamaican song, with "emphasis on repetitive rhythmic structures (which have often been stripped of their harmonic elements)", leaving their elemental drum and bass core.[33] It is around this core, by means of filtering, erasure, reverberation/delays, splicing and other modes of sonic texturing, spacing, deconstruction and reconfiguration that a redemptive sonic universe called dub is constructed. Veal's summary of the elemental construction of dub and its aesthetic corpus is worth noting because the making of Rastafari in the 1930s, though not a work of art in the sense of the examples of African diasporic art cited above but rather a social movement, employed principles similar to those used in artistic creations. According to Veal, "One good analogy for the dubmixer is that of an 'action painter' of sound. Operating upon a continuously unfolding 'canvas' of drum and bass, the engineer throws up a brief snatch of piano, a few seconds of organ, a bit of guitar, and a dash of singing, modulating and blending the 'colors' (frequencies) through the use of reverb, equalization, and other sound processing."[34]

If we were to use the analogy of dub-making to grasp the principles of the making of Rastafari, Howell would be likened to a divinatory dub mixer. His role: the gathering, incorporating, deconstructing and reconfiguring of fragments of an assemblage of ontological materials from various forms of Ethiopianism, as well as Myalism (Myaalism), elements of East Indian cosmology, the Church of God and Saints of Christ, Masonic beliefs and symbols, and de Laurence publications on occulticism/mysticism and black Marxism, to create an anti-colonial, pan-African redemptive universe called Rastafari. Ethiopianism in its various manifestations includes Garveyism, Balintinism, Athlyianism and the Israelites (the Black Jew movement), while Myalist expressions include Revivalism (Zion, Poko, Bedwardism), Bongo/Convince, Obeah and Kumina.

The Logic of Garveyism in the Deification of Ras Tafari

Figure 1.2. Marcus Garvey. Drawing by Clinton Hutton.

At the time of Haile Selassie's coronation in Ethiopia in 1930, Marcus Garvey had been back in Jamaica some three years, having been deported from the United States in November 1927 after spending time in prison on made-up charges. He arrived in Jamaica in December 1927 and launched the People's Political Party on 9 September 1929. It was "the first time that a political party defending the interests of the masses . . . had been launched on the island". The party's first convention was held at the end of September 1929 in Edelweiss Park and was attended by some five thousand persons.[35] That year was one of "intensive political activity" in Jamaica. The massive outpouring of support Garvey received on his route back home (New Orleans, Panama and Kingston) must have lifted him to persistent political activity in Jamaica. On his landing in Kingston, the *Daily Gleaner* reported that "Mr Garvey's arrival . . . was perhaps the most historic event that has taken place in the metropolis of the island", and "no denser crowd has ever been witnessed in Kingston".[36]

In the first speech that Garvey made on his arrival in Jamaica, he told an audience at the Ward Theatre, to "thunderous applause", that "you shall find no coward in me. You shall find a black man ready and willing to represent the interests of the black people of this country and the black people of the world without any compromise."[37] What seemed self-evident in this statement by Garvey on the occasion of his return to Jamaica, seemingly in consequence of the response of the black masses to him on his departure from New Orleans, his stop in Panama and his arrival in Kingston, as well as his position as global leader of African peoples, was Garvey's assumption of the role of national, regional and international leader of black people. This position, which was rooted to a great extent in extant historical reality, would also become a key part of the logic behind the elevation of the emperor by some Jamaicans (including some Garveyites) over Garvey as universal leader in the tender years of the 1930s, when decline and disintegration set in in Garvey's Universal Negro Improvement Association (UNIA). This decline was also due to Garvey's evolving negative attitude towards Haile Selassie.

The editorial response of Garvey's newspaper, the *Blackman*, to the coronation of Ras Tafari was quite positive. It was published on 8 November 1930, six days after the coronation events commenced:

> The Psalmist prophesied that Princes would come out of Egypt and Ethiopia would stretch forth her hands unto God. We have no doubt that the time is now come. Ethiopia is now really stretching forth her hands. This great kingdom of the East has been hidden for many centuries, but gradually she is rising to take a leading place in the world and it is for us of the Negro race to assist in every way to hold up the head of Emperor Ras Tafari.[38]

Garvey also sent a telegram on behalf of the UNIA giving due recognition and support to this historical event. This editorial statement recognized the coronation of Ras Tafari as a prophetic historical juncture in black people's struggle for freedom, sovereignty and redemption, but it also stipulated that this Psalmist prophecy required the leadership, tutelage and guidance of Garvey and the UNIA to endow it with epistemic, ontological and agential flesh, by assisting "in every way to hold up the head of Emperor Ras Tafari", the apparent head of this new historical reality.[39] But, as history would have it, men and women spawned and cultured, to some extent, in the realm of Garveyism would come to the belief that the emperor would have no need for anyone to hold up his head, since he was the Godhead himself.

In the Ethiopianist conception of history, the *Blackman*'s editorial interpretation of the coronation of Ras Tafari as prophecy was spot on, given the particular global context in which it took place and the prophetic culture in which many people of African descent were socialized to expect the coming redemption. The prophetic Psalmist creed, "Princes shall come out of Egypt, Ethiopia shall stretch her hands unto God", and the culture it engendered through a multiplicity of rituals performed by generations of Africans, reached its zenith under the Garvey movement and spawned a number of pan-African Ethiopianist texts and Garveyite circles, associations and leaders, two of whom would figure prominently in the epistemic and ontological composition of Rastafari.

Balintine and Rogers: Proto-Rastas and Their Ethiopianist Texts

Two prophetic texts of note, *The Royal Parchment Scroll of Black Supremacy* (1926), by the Reverend Fitz Balintine Pettersburgh, and *The Holy Piby* (1924), by the Anguillan Robert Athlyi Rogers, preceded the coronation of Ras Tafari by some four to six years. These two publications, brimming with Psalmist forecasts of the certainty of an African resurrection, became textual compasses and canonical signatures of the birthing of Rastafari and the articulation of the movement in its infancy.

In the prophetic language of these texts, Pettersburgh writes to his "dear inhabitants of this world", "we are the foundation stones of the resurrection of the Kingdom of Ethiopia", a resurrection made necessary because Africa, "that Rich National Woman" who "has Charmed the Men of Nations to Lie With Her", was left broken down and persecuted. He notes that "SLAVE TRADERS WENT INTO AFRICA AND DAMAGED her Seeds, beyond any EARTHLY CURE." This, in Pettersburgh's logic, provided the basis for resurrection (recreation) by deifical agency but, alas, by human agency as well. Because Africa "HAD TOO MUCH SYMPATHY FOR WILFULL IDLERS of Various Nations", Pettersburgh asserted, "THEY WENT INTO HER AND ROBBED her Lands, Money, and took her seeds, to be slaves. That to-day she and her children have no Power in Her own Land [sic], nor ABROAD."[40] Consequently, "All the African is to do now, [is] Build a New", build anew in tandem with the agency of the God of Ethiopia to deal with that damage which is "beyond any EARTHLY CURE". He or she must "get out a New Dictionary & a New Bible & a New Board of Education, & a New Money Mint" to seal this resurrection, this "NEW OUTFIT [WHICH] SHALL BE CALLED BLACK SUPREMACY".[41]

For Fitz Balintine Pettersburgh, African recreation or resurrection was only possible if its would-be recreators embraced a new dictionary, a new Bible and a new language – that is, a new episteme, pedagogy and ontology in which the apotheosis of self was rooted in the realm of a black Almighty – and an economy or "money mint" in which the African was decidedly sovereign.

Nevertheless, the 6 June 1927 *Daily Gleaner* took a contemptuous swipe at *The Royal Parchment Scroll of Black Supremacy*: "The grammar is like the sense, which seems to us to be indistinguishable from nonsense, and the whole concoction is so putrid that we wonder what class of people could ever take such rubbish seriously."[42] By October 1933, one elder, W.E. Barclay of the Church of God, wrote to Inspector Adams of the Morant Bay police, warning of and protesting the activity of "L. Howell and Valentine [i.e., Balintine]". Barclay wrote,

> The Ras Tafari gang [sic] are defying British law by proclaiming that their kingdom is Africa. . . . Two men, L. Howell and Valentine [sic], are holding meetings and teaching several practices contradictory to the laws of our country. . . . They are acquiring money on false pretenses, claiming themselves ambassadors of this African king, by collecting funds from the people and promising them free transportation to Africa if they pay a certain sum. This man denounces ministers, myself included, and has the audacity to call us thieves and vagabonds at his open air meetings. . . . They make ignorant people believe that this man [Selassie] now crowned is Christ, and that he has come to redeem the negro race. . . . Enclosed you will find one of their tracts.[43]

Hélène Lee, citing the "Pinnacle Papers" of the Jamaica National Archives in Spanish Town, notes that "this is the first documented link between Howell and the Ethiopianist preacher Balintine". Furthermore, "the 'tract' is a digest of Athlican theory. Three of ten verses are extracted from [Robert Athlyi Rogers's] *The Holy Piby*", thus:

> Woe be unto a race of people who seek not their own foundation. Their wives shall be servants to the wives of other men, and their daughters shall be the wives of poor men and vagabonds – and there shall be tears of deprivation.

> I strongly appeal to you to seek and learn of your own foundation. Woe be unto a race of people who forsake their own doctrine for another. They shall be slaves of the people thereof.

> O people of Ethiopia boast not the progress of the white race, believing that you are part of the project. You shall be cast over the bridge of death both body and soul.[44]

When the *Daily Gleaner* disparaged Fitz Balintine Pettersburgh's text, wondering aloud "what class of people could ever take such rubbish seriously", and contemptuously characterized *The Holy Piby* as "weird doctrine", its editors did not know that six years later these two texts would become foundational creative materials for the making of Rastafari, and that the class of people who would take such "rubbish" seriously would include the owners and editors of the *Daily Gleaner* and persons like Elder Barclay and John Ross.[45]

For those who embraced Rastafari, its Balintinean and Athlyian (Athlican) roots were not the rubbish and weird doctrine that became the spectre haunting the minds and existential foundations of the ruling classes; they were profoundly liberating. And the triune recreationist agency that the fearful elder W.E. Barclay reported to the police that he saw in Howell and Balintine as they preached the divinity of Ras Tafari in St Thomas, aided by the extracts from *The Holy Piby* which they distributed, would become Rasta's first text, *The Promised Key*. Howell wove this text from *The Holy Piby* and *The Royal Parchment Scroll of Black Supremacy*, as well as from his 1933 speeches, while serving two years in prison following his conviction for sedition in 1934.

The Promised Key

The deification of Ras Tafari, to an important degree, seems to have been possible only because, in terms of his international status as an African leader, he appeared to have superseded the one person in the world whom he could be measured against, Marcus Garvey. The emperor became global African leader (God), denoting a shift in the world order in which Europe was metaphorically turned on its head, as Howell's logic would have it in *The Promised Key*. It was not Marcus Garvey before whom the Duke of Gloucester, representing his father, the British king, "fell down on bending knees" and declared his father's servitude to forever; it was Ras Tafari. To surpass Garvey's status was to enter the realm of divinity, and Howell's interpretation of the response of the world's governments to the coronation of Ras Tafari, especially the British response, suggested that the entry into the realm of divine leadership on earth had commenced. Put another way, anyone who superseded Garvey's quality and global leadership status, as seemed to true for Ras Tafari, must be God.

In chapter 1 of *The Promised Key*, Howell, in articulating the emergence of a new realm in global political relations, noted the demeanour of the son of the

Leonard Howell Announcing God   23

Figure 1.3. Coronation of Emperor Haile Selassie and Empress Menen. *National Geographic*, June 1931.

British king, who represented his father at the coronation. It was the ontology of the surrender of an almost transcendental type of global order to an emerging one that Howell saw in his representation of the Duke of Gloucester on the one hand and Ras Tafari on the other.

> In 1930, the Duke of Gloucester undertook one of the most interesting duties he had been called upon to execute up to this date. The occasion was the Coronation of His Majesty Ras Tafari the King of Kings and Lord of Lords the Conquering Lion of Judah, the Elect of God and the Light of the World. The Duke was to represent his father the Anglo-Saxon king. The Duke handed to His Majesty Rastafari the King of Kings and Lord of Lords a sceptre of solid gold twenty-seven inches long, which had been taken from the hands of Ethiopia some thousand years ago.

The Duke fell down on bending knees before His Majesty Ras Tafari, the King of Kings and Lord of Lords and spoke in a loud tone of voice and said, "Master, Master, my father has sent me to represent him sir. He is unable to come and he said that he will serve you to the end Master."[46]

Here, the coronation of Ras Tafari was the simultaneous surrendering of the crowns of all the kings of the earth to Haile Selassie. The epoch of a new global order had begun. As far as Howell was concerned, in this coronation, a global realm upon which the sun was not supposed to set surrendered to an emerging other realm, led by the King of Kings. Having described the spiritual aesthetic grandeur[47] in which this Ethiopianist prophecy manifested itself, Howell wrote,

> The glory that was Solomon greater still reigns in Ethiopia. We can see all the kings of the earth surrendering their crowns to His Majesty Ras Tafari the King of Kings and Lord of Lords Earth's Rightful Ruler to reign forever and ever.
>
> Upon His Majesty Ras Tafari's head are many diadems and on His garments a name written King of Kings and Lord of Lords oh come let us adore him for He is King of Kings and Lord of Lords the Conquering Lion of Judah, the Elect of God and the Light of the World.
>
> His Majesty Ras Tafari is the head over all men, for He is the Supreme God. His body is the fullness of Him that filleth all in all. Now my dear people, let this be our goal, forward to the King of Kings must be the cry of our social hope. Forward to the King of Kings to purify our social standards and our way of living, and rebuild and inspire our character. Forward to the King of Kings to learn the worth of manhood and womanhood.
>
> Forward to the King of Kings to learn His code of Laws from the mount demanding absolute Love, Purity, Honesty, Truthfulness. Forward to the King of Kings to learn His Laws and Social Order, so that Virtue will eventually gain the Victory over our body and soul and that truth will drive away falsehood and fraud. Members of the King of Kings, arise for God's sake and put your armour on.[48]

Howell's interpretation of the coronation was a profound triumphalist rejection of the prevailing global order built on the imperial superstructure of white supremacy and Christianity. It pointed to the emergence of a new order in which African peoples the world over, especially those from the Western Hemisphere, would have to put on their battle armour to defend themselves and to vanquish the agency of the old order. Howell had no doubt as to who would prevail.

> Dear inhabitants of the Western Hemisphere, the King of Kings' warriors can never be defeated, the Pope of Rome and his agents shall not prevail against the King of Kings' host warriors, you must all stand up, stand up for the King of Kings.

All ye warriors of the King of Kings lift high King Alpha's Royal Banner, from Victory to Victory King Alpha shall lead His army till every enemy is vanquished.⁴⁹

Garvey the Mighty Revealer, Selassie I the Mighty Redeemer

Marcus Garvey and the UNIA's impressive royal ceremonies ritualizing Africa's future under black sovereignty, with which Leonard Howell was familiar, were no match for the aesthetic grandeur of the stately coronation of Ras Tafari. Nor were global leaders or their representatives bowing down to Garvey in surrender, in the logic of *The Holy Piby*. Indeed, global leaders were plotting his destruction and that of the UNIA. Garvey's work and steadfast defence of African peoples around the world, against all odds, had made him the most revered leader of global Africa, "an apostle of the Lord God for the redemption of Ethiopia and her suffering posterities", according to Robert Athlyi Rogers, who declared him such in *The Holy Piby* in 1922, eight years before the coronation of Ras Tafari.⁵⁰

Emperor Haile Selassie, for some, especially those who saw him as divine, replaced Garvey as global leader. For Rastafari, only God could supersede Garvey's leadership and render him as number two, or the emperor's forerunner, John the Baptist or Moses in Rasta cosmology. In this respect, in Rogers's description of Garvey as "an apostle of the Lord God for the redemption of Ethiopia", Garvey was preparing the path for God to enter the realm. Reports of the coronation of Ras Tafari undermined the global leadership position of Garvey, even as his standing was being undermined by the decline of the UNIA. At the same time, Haile Selassie became the international front-page agenda item in major world and local media. Unlike Garvey, he was head of a state, an African state with a biblical, prophetic name and certitude, denoting a prophetic, epochal, historical and agential mission of reassigning the global order. Ethiopia was the only true sovereign African state, the only one to have thwarted the colonial scramble for Africa by defeating Italy and its Berlin mandate in the battle at Adwa in 1896.

Reports of the majestic events that took place during the ten days of coronation, along with the attendance of world leaders or their representatives, enlaced in diplomatic symbolism, seem to have signalled a global recognition of Ethiopian sovereignty. It was these reports, crowned by the June 1931 *National Geographic* features on the coronation – "Modern Ethiopia: Haile Selassie the

First, Formerly Ras Tafari, Succeeds to the World's Oldest Continuously Sovereign Throne" and "Coronation Days in Addis Ababa" – which captivated so many persons of African descent and incited and orchestrated Howell's imagination and agency towards a pan-Africanist redemption centred around the deification of Ras Tafari.[51] Howell's tract, *The Promised Key*, reflected his interpretation and cinematic dramatization of the news of the coronation carried in *National Geographic*, woven into the language and the meaning of royalty, God and freedom for African redemption seen in the Ethiopianist tracts of Robert Athlyi Rogers and Fitz Balintine Pettersburgh. And that Athlyian-Balintinean language and spirit in which Howell spoke of the coronation of Ras Tafari in *The Promised Key* is exemplified by Robert Athlyi Rogers's articulation of his vision of a liberated Africa: "And there appeared a light matchless in its beauty. Straightway the whole celestial host shouted and there appeared millions of Angels dancing in the light singing, 'Behold! Behold Ethiopia! The bride of the master. Her day has come at last! The Lord has received her hand. Her night has forever passed.'"[52]

The coronation of Ras Tafari spawned a whole set of Ethiopianist associations, organizations and sentiments in Jamaica and in global black spaces. And when Ethiopia was once more invaded by Italy, five years into the reign of the emperor, it spawned even more support for Ethiopia and its emperor.[53] Post-1930 Ethiopianism was rapidly becoming post-Garvey pan-Africanism.

Garvey's Criticisms of Haile Selassie Backfire

Marcus Garvey's criticisms of Emperor Haile Selassie for his handling of Ethiopia's response to the Italian war of conquest severely undermined his global standing and appeal as well as the viability of the UNIA, which had been going through a process of decline since the mid- to late 1920s, after Garvey's imprisonment and deportation to Jamaica from the United States. Initially, Garvey, like his followers, "denounced Mussolini as 'a barbarian, compared to Haile Selassie', whom Garvey at the time saw as a 'sober, courteous and courageous gentleman'".[54] However, not long into the fascist Italian invasion of Ethiopia in October 1935, Garvey argued that Italy's war on Ethiopia "affords only another example of what unpreparedness means to a people".[55]

The implication here is that the handling of the war was not the only example of unpreparedness in the country headed by Haile Selassie. From this point,

Garvey stepped up his criticisms of the emperor, who, after the summer of 1936, went into exile in Britain:

> He kept his country unprepared for modern civilization, whose policy was strictly aggressive. He resorted sentimentally to prayer and to feasting and fasting, not consistent with the policy that secures the existence of present-day freedom for peoples whilst other nations and rulers are building up armaments of the most destructive kind as the only means of securing peace ... and protection.... The results show that God had nothing to do with the campaign of Italy in Abyssinia, for on the one side we had the Pope of the Catholic Church blessing the Crusade, and the other, the Coptic Church fasting and praying with confidence of victory.... It is logical, therefore, that God did not take sides, but left the matter to be settled by the strongest human battalion.[56]

One of the ways that Haile Selassie could have prepared his country for war (and transformed Ethiopia into a modern, developed state), Garvey suggested, was to mobilize African peoples from around the world "to protect it from any foe". If Haile Selassie had negotiated the proper relationship with the hundreds of millions of black people outside of Abyssinia, in Africa, South and Central America, the United States, Canada, the West Indies, and Australia, he could have had an organization of men and women ready to do service not only in the development of Abyssinia, as a great Negro nation, but on the spur of the moment to protect it from invasion.[57]

Looking back at the UNIA's statement on the coronation, it would seem that Garvey's expectation of UNIA's role, "to hold up the head of Emperor Ras Tafari" so that Ethiopia's "rising to take a leading place in the world" was ensured, came to naught as a result of Emperor Haile Selassie's poor handling of the Italian invasion and of the modernization of Ethiopia. Garvey's assessment was that Ras Tafari was not pan-Africanist enough and that consequently he neglected to sufficiently mobilize and make use of the tremendous global pan-African resources to counteract the forces of Italian aggression – resources that were largely mobilized under the UNIA a good decade before the coronation of Ras Tafari.

Garvey withdrew his support from Haile Selassie, citing, in addition to the above claims, that the Ethiopian monarch had sold out to white people. Garvey's stand would prove catastrophic for him and for the UNIA. Even though there was a good measure of truth in his assessment and criticism of the emperor's handling of Italian aggression and of national development, to do it in the way

Garvey did, and especially to withdraw his support for His Majesty when his was the most capable global voice to mobilize pan-African solidarity to protect the viability of the Ethiopian state, seemed insensitive and incomprehensible to many of Garvey's supporters.

Hill notes that "after Haile Selassie took up exile in England, Garvey was denouncing him and blaming him for the Italian invasion, claiming that he 'allowed himself to be conquered, by playing white'". Hill further notes that

> Garvey's new stance led to a significant number of his remaining followers to repudiate him and leave the UNIA to join the other organizations that had been formed to come to the defence of the African nation. A woman follower wrote to Garvey from New York to protest his "unjust criticism of Emperor Haile Selassie" and to inform him that she felt "like a lot of others that you have been quite unfair in your writing on Ethiopia". "You who have done so much for the race", she declared, "surprise the entire race for saying the Emperor has outlived his usefulness and should seek asylum in a monastery. For your own prestige and the high esteem which the race holds for you, it would mean a lot if you would retract those statements and resume the place of honour and confidence which our hearts hold for you."[58]

Moreover, according to Hill,

> Repeated attempts by the national representative of the UNIA in the U.S., Samuel A. Haynes, to persuade Garvey "to issue a ringing proclamation in the 'Blackman' [Black Man] calling upon all Garveyites, and the Negro People of the World, to go to the immediate defence of Ethiopia against Italy, by raising defence funds and medical supplies, etc.", proved in vain, despite the severe hemorrhage of loyal supporters that the UNIA was suffering.[59]

Italy's invasion of Ethiopia and the evacuation of the emperor to Britain constituted the first major test of the viability of the unique Ethiopianist movement that had emerged in the wake of the coronation of Ras Tafari. Italy's military successes against Ethiopia put the existence of the nascent Rastafari movement in jeopardy. How can man defeat God?

In addition to the multitudes of blacks around the world protesting against Italy and expressing political and material support for Haile Selassie and Ethiopia, it was faith, to an important degree, that saved Rastafari. It was a faith not rooted so much in conventional Ethiopianism as it was in a complex of African Jamaican ancestral beliefs and ritual practices (including the realm of magic) regarding healing, protection, guarding, tying, binding and the culturing of perseverance and fortitude associated with Myalism: Revival (Poko, Zion), Kumina, Obeah and others.

The Culturing of Faith in Rasta Ontology: Revival and Kumina Roots

In this complex of faith construction, belief in the power of His Majesty to orchestrate secret superior military forces, invoke ancestral warrior spirits (*dopi*) and commandeer apocalyptic creatures to defeat the forces of colonialism played an important role in the culturing of faith in Rastafari. Hill notes that it was, to some extent, "belief in the power of magic that sustained the faith of Rastafari followers of Howell against the reality of Ethiopia's defeat in 1936".[60] As an example of this, Hill points to the published report that one Rudolph Williams made regarding Howell and his followers.[61] Williams stated that followers of Rastafari rejected the idea that "Abyssinia is no longer an independent state, but a part of the Italian Empire, [and that] Rastafari is for all practical purposes no longer Emperor of Ethiopia but an ex-monarch in exile":[62]

> Ras Tafarites of Jamaica . . . say no to these facts. They say that in truth the King of Kings has a great navy hidden in the interior of Abyssinia on a lake, a navy that anytime it sails out will make the navies of England, Italy, Germany, America and Japan look like poor little undersized boats; that there are armament factories in the uplands of Abyssinia in huge caves turning out tons of ammunitions daily; that there are airplanes and submarines galore at the disposal of the Rasses of Ethiopia. They also declare that such forces, when the time is ripe, will be augmented by sinister influences; that the Ethiopians slain in battle will rise up and become an invisible army that will march upon the foe when commanded by Ras Tafari.
>
> They say that the King of Kings has a stronger army, consisting of fierce man-eating beasts – tigers, leopards, lions, waiting to bound out of hiding at dead of night, raid Italian camps and feed on the invaders as soon as the word comes from the Emperor; snakes, caterpillars, scorpions and all sorts of poisonous reptiles and insects are said to have been conscripted and regimented for war service so that they may be ready when Ethiopia calls.[63]

This, of course, was not just a belief in the power of magic. The belief that informed the statement above was similar to the one that announced Ras Tafari as the Supreme God to whom the king of England and, indeed, all monarchs surrendered their crowns. Despite being the biggest, most powerful colonial empire-building state in history, Britain could not prevent some of its African

Jamaican subjects from believing that Emperor Haile Selassie was King and God of all the earth, based on Howell's interpretation of Western news reports of the coronation, any more than it could have caused the collapse of the Rasta deification story by arguing that Howell's rationale for it could not be sustained by belief in stories about the emperor's secret military complexes and his ability to mobilize warrior duppies (*dopi*) and fierce man-eating beasts to defeat any imperial power.

The bigger question is, in a belief system which held that "belief kill and belief cure", what constituted the cultural, ontological and epistemic bases for the Rasta creation story and the faith that was cultured to sustain it?[64] And what of the founding figures of Rastafari, especially Howell? What factors would have moved Howell from the Ethiopianist position that God was black to announcing Haile Selassie as God? Hill rightly points to the crossroads cultural dimensions of Howell's ontological ethos, which, for me, would constitute the foundations of his creative ethos and hence his ability to make the leap from God being black to Ras Tafari being God.

Just about the same year that Ras Tafari was crowned Haile Selassie and a decade after Alexander Bedward, the best-known Revival leader, was arrested, tried and sentenced to the lunatic asylum,[65] an upsurge of Revivalism spread across Jamaica. Bedward died in this institution on 8 November 1930, six days after the coronation of Ras Tafari. Some Bedwardites in short order would become an important socio-cosmological foundation of Rastafari.

Following 1865, there was a constant effort from above to silence Revivalism, as well as a determination among Revivalists to prevent this.[66] The social electricity that Bedward generated in the first decade of the twentieth century was similar to that produced by the Great Revival and Paul Bogle in the 1860s. In the 1920s, one man who had witnessed both periods told American folklorist Martha Beckwith, "I remember the St Thomas rebellion and the revival in 1860. It was taken up by the whole world. Now today there is Bedward."[67] This electricity became an upsurge in the 1930s and was a key factor in the birth of Rastafari and in the evolution of Revivalism itself.

Coming at the time that it did, the Revivalist upsurge helped significantly to constitute the gestational site for Rastafari. While Marcus Garvey condemned this movement in racist language similar to that used by the colonial state and church, Howell embraced it. Garvey apparently viewed Revivalism as a fettering agency to the development of the kind of African necessary to carry out the UNIA's vision for a free sovereign Africa and his People's Political Party's programme for national development in Jamaica.

From the standpoint of Garvey, the Revivalist upsurge reflected one of the sources of degeneration that had been seen in the decline of the UNIA. Thus, it was a threat to pan-African black consciousness and rationalist secularism which Garvey, in a Weberian manner, associated with the established churches. In "Religious Fanatic", one of his editorial columns published in his newspaper, *New Jamaican*, dated 11 August 1932, Garvey noted that "a large number of the people are leaving the established churches to join these religions – religions that howl, religions that create saints, religions that dance to frantic emotion".[68] He returned to that theme on 19 October 1932, declaring that "the various revival cults are driving a large number of [our people] crazy".[69]

Garvey's epistemological construct had clearly intersected with the occidental epistemic construction of the African outside the realm of Europe's civilizing mission. On 25 January 1933, he declared that "Bedward attempted to fly some years ago and the people were so ignorant as to have sold nearly everything they had to go with him to Heaven on the flight. The same kind of ignorance and superstition has its grip on the people now."[70]

And Charles James, one of the visiting delegates to the August 1934 convention of the UNIA in Jamaica, told the *Daily Gleaner* in an interview, published on 22 August 1934, that "one alarming condition that seems ridiculous to me is that one hundred years after Emancipation in this country, cults and religious fanaticism are still having a grip on the island, and which forces one to pause to know that such ideas could prevail in a civilized community".[71] James also deplored the fact that "there is not enough effort on the part of the intelligentcias [sic] to stomp out such evil".[72]

The harm of religious "fanaticism" figured prominently at the UNIA convention. This body passed seven resolutions on religion, and the delegates enacted "legislation" on the subject to ensure that "fanaticism and silly and impossible conceptions and interpretations should not form a basis of any religious cult that would tend to destroy the higher principles of religion", the *Daily Gleaner* noted.[73]

Whatever these "higher principles of religion" were, the "revival cults", in the UNIA's estimation, were a threat to them.[74] So too was Rastafari, whose principals held public meetings throughout the parish of St Thomas in 1933, garnering mass support for ideas that the UNIA deemed to be fanatical, silly, evil and antithetical to the development of civilization.

Rastafari became a part and progeny of the Revivalist upsurge of the 1930s. The seed produced by the coronation of Ras Tafari found optimum socio-cosmological and political conditions for reproduction in this religious climate, as the Great Revival (a renewed interest in Christianity and Myalism) of the early 1860s had produced fertile ground for the birth of Revivalism in two manifestations, Poko (Pukkumina) and Zion.[75] Both religious upsurges were reflective, in the final analysis, of grassroots social movements which led to new religious formations as well as to the development of revolutionary campaigns, in particular those of 1865 and 1938. In both cases, these campaigns matured first in St Thomas – the Morant Bay Rebellion in Stony Gut in 1865 and the labour rebellion at Serge Island estate in 1938.[76]

The Revivalist upsurge (Kumina must be added to it) was part of a more general multidimensional mobilization of masses of people across the island into shoots and offshoots of activism, organization and movement as well as social, cultural, ideological and political fermentation, leading to a flood of strikes, civil disobedience and turmoil which had never been seen before. Against the backdrop of the Great Depression, thousands of Jamaicans who had migrated to Panama, Costa Rica, Cuba, the United States and Canada returned home with various kinds of social, political, organizational and cosmopolitan experiences, especially in the 1930s. These included Hugh Clifford Buchanan (a black nationalist, regarded as Jamaica's first Marxist), who came back from Cuba in the late 1920s, Marcus Garvey in 1927, Leonard Howell in 1932, Joseph Hibbert in 1931 and Alexander Bustamante in 1934. Others included St William Grant, Arthur Henry, Lionel Lynch and W.A. Domingo.

The formation of a plethora of social, political and religious organizations characterized the period. These included the People's Political Party, the Jamaica Workers and Transport Union, the National Reform Association, the King of Kings Mission, the Jamaica Progressive League (an organization formed in New York by Jamaicans which played a significant role in the development of Jamaican nationalism), the Darliston Literary Society, the Frankfield Citizens Association, the Ink and Quill Club of Port Maria and the Ethiopian Salvation Society. Persons such as Una Marson, U. Theo McKay, W.A. Domingo, Alexander Bustamante, St William Grant, Kenneth Hill, Leonard Howell, Archibald Dunkley, Robert Hinds, Marcus Garvey and Walter Adolphe Roberts made their views known by way of writing, speaking and preaching.

Also in the mix were a number of American churches. Of these, the principal of Calabar College, E.P. Price, noted in 1930, "Proximity to America makes the little island the happy hunting ground of . . . queer denominations. Seventh Day Adventists, Millennial Darwinists, Seven Keys, Pentecostal Holiness Missions and other strange inventions are welcomed by groups of unbalanced and disgruntled people."[77]

The Importance of St Thomas to the Genesis of Rastafari

Hélène Lee states that "Howell found fertile ground for his new ideas in St Thomas parish in southeastern Jamaica".[78] At the same time, she notes that "this remote agricultural parish was notoriously the most backward on the island, and its mentality was deeply colonial". Lee does not explain this statement; she does not describe the parish's state of backwardness, nor indicate why it was so deeply colonial in mentality, nor detail the features or cultural expressions of this mentality.

Howell certainly "found fertile ground for his ideas in St Thomas", but was this so because of a colonial mentality?[79] Or could it be that his ideas were well received because the mentality of that parish was dominated by, as Garvey had contemptuously claimed, religions which howled, created saints, danced to frantic emotion and drove large numbers of people crazy?

What was this deep colonial mentality that Lee identifies? Was it reflective of the centrality of the epistemology and ontology of white superiority as certitude and the internalization of such by the black masses as their path to freedom from themselves, from their primitive ontologies? Or was it the expression of "fanaticism" which tended "to destroy the higher principles of religion", as the UNIA elites, or more so, the European colonizing church and state estimated? Lee does not say.

To be sure, historically, the European churches, the main agency of occidental cultural colonialism in Jamaica, had less influence in St Thomas than in any other parish in Jamaica. This was so during the Great Revival of the 1860s and again during the 1930s. I have referred to Myalist traditions in the Great Revival which played a central role in the development of a revolutionary mood in Jamaica and exploded in Morant Bay, St Thomas-in-the-East, in 1865, as "various kinds of African retentions, which at that time, were experiencing one of their periodic flows";[80] I also noted that "historically, the African-Jamaican revolt usually coincided with an increase in the practice of African (religious) retentions by the black masses".[81]

Historically, St Thomas had a more unfettered system of the practices of African Jamaican religion and spirituality known as Myalism. Myalism is a pan-African/Jamaican designation for various expressions of African ancestral religions and spiritualities. The locating in St Thomas-in-the-East (now called St Thomas with the former parish of St David added to it) of most of the Kongolese people who were brought to Jamaica as indentured labourers in the early 1840s allowed for the flow of African cosmological blood into the religious and spiritual practices of African Jamaicans in the parish. Kumina, the name given to this relatively recent flow of African spirituality into Jamaica, would play a major ontological role in the making of Rastafari and in the evolution of Revivalism. Indeed, Kumina adherents would become the core of Leonard Howell's Rastafarian movement, the Ethiopian Salvation Society at Pinnacle, St Catherine, Jamaica, when they were driven out of Port Morant, St Thomas, in 1937. Kumina cosmology, rituals and other cultural expressions would play a significant role in shaping the identity of Rastafari.[82]

Further, the cultural and cosmological presence of East Indians who were brought to Jamaica as indentured labourers shortly after the arrival of the Kongolese was felt in St Thomas-in-the-East, where a significant number of them were located. The Revivalists would incorporate various East Indian elements into their ritual practices, as they had done with Christianity decades before the emergence of Rastafari. And Leonard Howell would use the East Indian presence in St Thomas in the framing of the Rastafari creation story.

Those who engaged in the suppression of the Morant Bay Rebellion or in framing the justification for its brutal suppression had no doubt about the role of African ancestral religious beliefs and agency in its making. In this regard, Colonel Francis Hobbs, one of the British military officers involved in the suppression of the uprising in St Thomas-in-the-East, said the following:

> If ever there was anything calculated to endear a man to the Established Church (or, indeed, to any recognized and regular kind of religion), it is a week's campaign in St Thomas-in-the-East, Jamaica. The place swarms with Native Baptist "chapels"; their ministers are the leading rebels (unable in many cases to read or write), who rant, excite, and poison the minds of their flocks against the powers that be. At the door of these wolves in sheep's clothing lies the responsibility of all this rebellion.... Let those who doubt this statement visit "Somerset", "Mount Lebanus", "Mount Pisgah" – the

hotbed of the rebellion – and account for this, in a province of wealth, in any other way than fanaticism; and it is the fact of this being the case that has from the first made me take a graver view of the rebellion than those who considered it a question of mere discontent about local wages.[83]

The Native Baptist "chapels" which, according to Hobbs, swarmed the parish of St Thomas-in-the-East were, "with few exceptions", noted missionary historian William Gardner in 1873, "associations of men and women who, in too many cases, mingled the belief and even the practice of Mialism with religious observances [Christian rituals], and who perverted and corrupted what they retained of these: among them sensuality was almost entirely unrestrained".[84]

It was this linking of the uprising at Morant Bay to the agency and expressions of African-derived religious "fanaticism" which inspired the questioning of the Stony Gut resident James Taylor about revivals at Paul Bogle's chapel, by one of the royal commissioners mandated to enquire into the causes and suppression of the rebellion:

22,511. What did you do at the revivals? – I never do anything but sing hymns.
22,512. Did you eat? – No, never eat.
22,513. Did you drink there? – No.
22,514. Did you smoke there? – No.
22,515. Did you dance there? – No.
22,518. Did you ever pray? – Me sir?
22,519. Yes, you – Yes, sometimes me pray.
22,520. Out loud I mean? – Yes.
22,521. Did you ever see visions? – No, I never saw any signs, I never worked at that myself.[85]

Sixty-eight years later, the practice for which James Taylor was given one hundred lashes would shape the consciousness and identity of an important contingent of the social forces which would provide fertile ground for Howell's new ideas to become flesh. Howell's first meeting in the creative cause of Rastafari took place at "Redemption Ground" in Kingston, according to P.A. Thompson, who was present at the event.[86] At that meeting, said Thompson, many "old-time Bedwardites" whom Howell had "made contact with . . . were on his platform that evening".[87] It was from the ranks of the old-time Bedwardites that Howell would find partnership with Robert Hinds, one of the foundational leaders of the Rastafari movement. Hinds was a Revivalist preacher and a disciple of

Alexander Bedward, long before the coronation of Ras Tafari. It was Howell who introduced Hinds to the concept of Emperor Haile Selassie as Christ.

In his cross-examination of Robert Hinds on 16 March 1934, assistant to the attorney general H.M. Radcliffe, KC, sought to clarify Howell's role vis-à-vis Hinds's in the genesis of Rastafari, 1933–1934.

> *Mr. Radcliffe (cross-examining):* You say King Tafari is Christ?
> *Hinds:* Yes, sir.
> *Radcliffe:* When was it you first heard that was so?
> *Hinds:* Not until L.P. Howell came, sir (*laughter*). But I read of the King of Kings in the Bible.

Answering further, Hinds said that he had seen photographs of Ras Tafari before Howell came. He had seen a man from Cuba with one, and he had also seen a magazine with pictures of the coronation:

> *Radcliffe:* Did Howell tell you that you are a Jew?
> *Hinds:* No, sir. It was not Howell who tell us.
> *Radcliffe:* How you knew?
> *Hinds:* We found it in the Bible. The brethren, who could write, search the Bible and use dictionary and we find out that [we] were Ethiopians.
> *Radcliffe:* You go around with Howell, don't you?
> *Hinds:* Yes, sir.
> *Radcliffe:* You preached before Howell came
> *Hinds:* Yes, sir. Long before.
> *Radcliffe:* You didn't preach about Ras Tafari before?
> *Hinds:* No, sir. But I found ou[t] afterward.
> *Radcliffe:* You preached that Ras Tafari was the king above all other kings. Didn't you think he was the only person [to] whom tribute or taxes should be paid?
> *Hinds:* No, sir.[88]

Revivalists were among the earliest adherents and supporters of Rastafari, but Revivalism also brought some persons to Rastafari in a more direct way. To investigate one example of this, I went down to the Junction in St Mary in 2005 to interview the eighty-three-year-old Rastafari elder Brother Man. He was seven years old when Ras Tafari was crowned in 1930. That same year, Marcus Garvey visited his school, and it had a profound impact on his life.

Poko and Kumina Declare Ras Tafari God

Brother Man was born in the parish of St Elizabeth in 1923 and came to live in Kingston in 1940, when he was seventeen years old. I asked him to tell me about the time he manifested, or became Rasta, after coming to Kingston. His answer was quite unexpected. He told me that when he came to Kingston he was already a Rastafarian. I asked him to explain how that happened, and he explained that the Poko church in his community in St Elizabeth declared His Imperial Majesty Emperor Haile Selassie God when news came about his coronation.

Some five years before I interviewed Brother Man, Robert Hill noted that the Kumina people referred to Emperor Haile Selassie "as Nzambi Mpungu . . . , the supreme deity of the Bakongo religion".[89] Hill states that in the early 1930s, "the Ethiopianists . . . [those] radical militant Black Christians . . . could

Figure 1.4. Brother Man. Photograph by Clinton Hutton.

not make the leap from Haile Selassie as king, to deifying him". However, the Bakongo people, he notes, "transferred the divinity of their Supreme God, to Selassie".[90] He continues, "It was only after the Bakongo people made that link [that the] Ethiopianists could now appropriate him, because on their own they couldn't do it."[91] Here Hill makes a critical discovery, the ontological key to the deification of Ras Tafari.

How did Revival and Kumina enable persons to make the leap from seeing Haile Selassie as king to deifying him? The answer can be found in the cosmological complex and ritual practices of Revivalism and Kumina, which allowed adherents to communicate with their gods, ancestors and other spirits through spirit possession or riding, also called Myal or Myal dance, as spirit possession is often referred to in Jamaican. Revivalists and Kumina adherents did not only worship God or gods or spirits; they became God or gods or spirits by being temporarily possessed by them. In the African Jamaican/Caribbean cosmological system, a person becomes God or spirit by being possessed by God or spirit. It was in this tradition and culture of spirit possession, in the rare historical moment presented by the coronation of Ras Tafari, that Haile Selassie made the leap from being king to being God.

The following is a description of spirit possession or Myal that Moravian pastor J.H. Buchner gave in 1854. This practice was widespread in Jamaica during and after slavery.

> As soon as the darkness of evening set in, they [African Jamaicans] assembled in crowds in open pastures, most frequently under large cotton trees, which they worshipped, and counted as holy; after sacrificing some fowls, the leader began an extempore song, in a wild strain which was answered in chorus; the dance followed, grew wilder and wilder, until they were in a state of excitement bordering on madness. Some would perform incredible evolutions while in this state, until, nearly exhausted, they fell senseless to the ground, when every word they uttered was received as a divine revelation.[92]

This was precisely the picture that the royal commissioner, in his questioning of James Taylor, had been seeking to paint of the Native Baptist or Revivalist rituals performed in Bogle's chapel before the 1865 Morant Bay uprising as proof that such rituals were an important source of inspiration for the rebellion. Possession rituals were an essential African diasporic therapeutic and identity-constructing device for the communal weaving of the psychic, psychological and general metaphysical or existential corpus of black personhood.

Africans, who were held for generations in a dystopian landscape of enslavement by Europeans who imposed countless acts of ownership on them to "crush the race of blacks by a contempt so great that whoever descends from it even to the sixth generation shall be covered with an indelible stain",[93] performed rituals of (re)possession like the one described above by Buchner to reclaim themselves from the ontological desecration of their black bodies. Possession rituals were a profoundly important foil for the propertification of the black body: "These ritual performances transformed commercialized bodies, merchandized bodies, bodies possessed and desecrated by slave holders into bodies exorcized, (re)consecrated, (re)textured and (re)possessed by African spirits and deities."[94]

In African Caribbean metaphysics, to be (re)possessed by the spirit, or to be in Myal, meant that the possessing spirit was temporarily occupying or dancing in the head or corporeal abode normally occupied by the person's own spirit, since in the episteme of this belief system, a person is made up of two versions in one: the visible physical person who eventually dies, and the invisible spirit person who does not die.[95] This tradition of Myal can be found in Kumina, Revivalism and Bongo in Jamaica, Vodou in Haiti, Lukumi and Mayombe in Cuba, Kumfa in Guyana, Candomblé in Brazil, Orisha and the Spiritual Baptist tradition in Trinidad and Tobago, and constitutes a key ontological difference with European Christianity as well as Ethiopianist (pan-African) Christianity, in which God was often denoted as black.

The critical thing to note here is that in the culture of (re)possession rituals in which Howell's new ideas found traction, people became God or spirit as a result of Myal, albeit temporarily. Thus, it was not impossibly hard or particularly strange for persons within Revivalism and Kumina to imagine and embrace Emperor Haile Selassie as God. Neither was it strange for them to hear and to imagine that, with the appropriate rituals, *dopi* could be summoned to fight in black peoples' wars of liberation, as Rastas stated the emperor would have done as part of his strategy to defeat the Italian invaders. The belief that death enhanced the power of the dead, ancestors or the living dead was commonly held among Africans in the Americas.

Death can be defined as the permanent exiting or withdrawal of the spirit person from his or her corporeal abode or physical, visible, finite body, whose existence ceases to be. With the enhanced power of the spirit, a consequence of death in this belief system, the living developed ways of utilizing that power for the benefit of the living by establishing a reciprocal relationship with the community of the dead through various kinds of rituals – libation, feasting rituals, blood rituals/sacrificial rituals (forms of feasting rituals), memorial rituals, communication rituals, rituals of contract (oath-taking rituals) and so on. It was within this context that Africans in the Americas enlisted the living dead or ancestors to march into war with them against slave-makers and colonial oppressors.[96] It was within the rubric of this belief system that Rastafari asserted, among other things, in the 1930s, that "the Ethiopians slain in battle will rise up and become an invisible army that will march upon the foe when commanded by Ras Tafari".[97] "Although it sees itself as Christian", Chevannes notes, "Revival has more in common with native African-Christian religions ... than it has with the traditional Christian religions that came from Europe."[98] According to Chevannes, all of these religions

> recognize a supreme, omnipotent force, but also personalized forces whose powers are limited and specific, with whom human beings enter into relationships or become familiar with through libation, blood sacrifice, appeasement and possession. God, the

Supreme Being, they do not worship in cultic or ritualistic ways; he exists, but is "far away". The lesser deities, however, are part of the everyday lives of humans. Besides, the spiritual world is seen as pure power, which human beings can manipulate in the way we manipulate electricity. Such manipulation is done in a variety of ways, namely through fetishes, amulets, prayer, ritual, masks and sacrifice.[99]

It is within this context that "Revival conceptualizes the relationship between the material and spiritual worlds", notes Chevannes. He writes, "God is identified as the Supreme Being, the Omnipresent and Almighty Creator, but unlike in Christian religions, he is not worshipped; his spirit is not invoked. The lesser spirits, like River Muma (a water spirit), the Indian Spirit, the Archangel Gabriel, and the Prophets Jeremiah and Isaiah, are integral to the ritual life of Revival, and to whom the seals or sacred spots are dedicated."[100]

From Revival and Kumina perspectives, when Emperor Haile Selassie was declared to be God, his position was that of Supreme Being. Thus, he was not central to the day-to-day concerns and needs of Kumina and Revival adherents, as the lesser spirits were. He was treated as the Almighty, far removed from the daily existential concerns of mortals, thus leaving a pantheon of lesser spirits to meet those concerns. As Supreme Being (God or Father God or Massa Gaad or Nzambi Mpungu), Haile Selassie would not have been worshipped or invoked in the same personal and familiar ritualistic ways (including feasting, libation, blood rituals and invocating art) as the lesser spirits.

Almighty God Is a Living Man

It would take the followers of Rastafari to reverse that process, (re)assigning the portfolio of the lesser spirits to the Supreme God, thereby making the Supreme God central and immediate to the daily existential concerns of the people and simultaneously making the role, and perhaps the existence, of the lesser spirits redundant in Rasta cosmology and cultural practices.[101] The position of Emperor Haile Selassie in Rastafari is unlike the position he was assigned in Revivalism and Kumina after the coronation when he was declared God. Rather than being a faraway Supreme Being, God (Haile Selassie) lives in man, and man lives in God. Put another way, "Almighty God is a living man", to cite the song "Get Up, Stand Up", written by Peter Tosh and Bob Marley. In this explicit expression of monotheism, God alone "in the person of Haile Selassie is the object of Rastafari adoration".[102]

The belief that "Almighty God is a living man", that God lives within the person, who in turn lives within God, reflects in Rastafari the cosmic artistic realization and articulation of the power of the sovereignty of being and agency in imagining and creating a free, redemptive universe of man (God). In his assessment of Howell's logic of the existence and agency of God and its meaning for society, Bogues notes that "his key argument was that if God is a living man, then any ritual which puts God outside of both human affairs and the world worships the wrong God". This, Bogues argues, was obviously "a radical criticism of some of the central aspects of Christian doctrine".[103] The belief that "Almighty God is a living man" is a profoundly Garveyite Ethiopianism ontologically, and yet it took the agency, the belief and the ritual (re)possession complex of Revivalism and Kumina to give it ontological flesh in the rare alignment of circumstances sparked by the coronation of Ras Tafari.

Revival Symbols in Rastafari

The symbols, signatures and agency of Revivalism were pretty much established in Howell's metaphysicality, political association and modes of activity. The presence of Revivalism as an ontological constructing material of Rastafari was obvious. It was observable in the name of the pioneering Rastafari organization, the King of Kings Mission; in the fact that Howell "made contact with many of the old-time Bedwardites", who "were on his platform", at his first meeting;[104] and in what seemed to be a sort of leadership team he established with the Bedwardite preacher Robert Hinds in 1933, until they were sent to prison for sedition in 1934.[105] It was also observable in the presence of the "revival preacher who was working the crowd" at the 10 December 1933 public meeting in Seaforth, before handing over the podium to Leonard Howell to address the gathering of over three hundred,[106] and in the title of Howell's tract, Rastafari's first text, *The Promised Key*.

The title of *The Promised Key* might have conceptually referred to a Revivalist or Seven Keys[107] method of realizing an Ethiopianist prophecy. Moreover, the symbology of the key was ever present in Revivalist ritual spaces. Today, the key is quite pervasive in the semiological terrain of Revivalism across Jamaica. It is used as a motif in drawings, paintings and sculptures both inside and outside the structure of the Revivalist church. It is printed on fabric tablecloths to be used in feasting rituals and on garments worn by Revival adherents. It is fashioned from wood or metal and, in the manner of a staff or crucifix, attached to garments, waist bands, necklaces and head wraps. The key, like the cutlass, sword, axe, saw, scissors and flag, became a symbol of that ritual in Revivalism called "cut and clear", cutting and clearing the path away from unwanted spirits, or from the stumbling block of oppression, ignorance and social and spiritual impediments and opening the door, the pathway, to truth, wisdom, freedom, imagination, creativity, redemption.

Like the cutlass, the scissors and the flag, the key has become the symbol of the spirit of the crossroads, the guardian of all pathways, all doorways, the god messenger, the revealer: Legba, Eshu, Eleggua, (Kwaku) Ananse, Agwu. The symbol of the key in Revivalism and early Rastafari has been generally replaced today in the Rastafari cosmology and ritual complex by the drum and the "holy herb", or ganja (cannabis), a ritual or invocating device to reveal the power of insight, consciousness, imagination, wisdom, knowledge and reasoning.

The Promised Key, then, was the long-awaited prophetic path-opener to African freedom, to redemption, and the closer of the global order of white supremacy. The title bore the Revivalist symbology of the key along with the prophetic Ethiopianist designation "promised", and Howell's ritual East Indian name, G.G. Maragh, was used to designate the tract's authorship – another testimony to the creative methodology employed in the making of Rastafari, namely the gathering and choreographing of fragments of spirituals from diverse spaces where they were shattered or scattered to (re)create a redemptive universe.

Elements of East Indian Cosmology

Hill notes that "in his role as prophet, Howell assumed a ritual personality separate from his secular identity". This ritual identity, according to Hill, "was expressed through the use of the separate name 'G.G. Maragh', which was the name Howell employed in his putative role as author of *The Promised Key*". "Everybody know him and call him Gangunguru Maragh", one of Howell's early followers, Japhet Wilson, told Hill. Wilson continued, "When we say Mr Howell, he say no, Gangunguru Maragh, and everybody would say, 'Yes, Gong.'" Gong "was the abbreviated form that was most popularly used to refer to Gangunguru Maragh", notes Hill.[108]

Hill further states that Howell's ritual name appeared to be "a combination of three Hindi words, *gyan* (meaning wisdom), *gun* (meaning virtue or talent), and *guru* (meaning teacher)". According to Hill, "The English translation of the three conjoined words is 'teacher of famed wisdom', corresponding to the names that Hindu leaders customarily adopt to suggest wisdom or enlightenment. Howell's use of the surname 'Maragh', which in Hindi means 'great king' or 'king of kings', was also consistent with the significance of the first set of names; in fact, Brahmin holy men and priests are addressed frequently by the name 'Maharaj'."[109] Thus, for Hill, "the cult name 'Gangunguru Maragh' suggests a quest by Howell for mystical status, which probably confirmed the mental picture that he had of himself as well as the attitude that his followers held of him as a religious prophet".[110]

In African Caribbean ontology and cosmology, royalty as a metaphor of knowing and being was and is quite widespread in cultural artistic expressions and rituals of the sacred and secular realms, one example being the performance of royal ancestral courts and of priestly kings and queens in Revivalism, Kumina, Orisha, Vodou and Lukumi and in the masquerade traditions in Cuba, Haiti, Jamaica, Guadeloupe and the Bahamas. Howell was informed by this cultural, ontological or even cosmological tradition in constructing what Hill calls his "ritual personality", a tendency that is firmly established in the culture of Rastafari today. East Indian cosmology, ritual practices and other forms of cultural expression, through their incorporation in Revivalism, became part of the ontological fabric of Jamaica, and they remain so to an important degree today.

During the course of its development, starting in the nineteenth century following the abolition of slavery and the importation of East Indians as indentured labourers, Revivalism/Myalism incorporated elements of East Indian cosmology and culture into its realm, a consequence of the evolving social, cultural and familial relationship between East Indians and African Jamaicans.[111] These include East Indian spirit dance movements, music, ritual language and forms of dress. The madras became one of Revivalism's iconographic symbols; the Indian Spirit was incorporated into the pantheon of Revival spirits; and East Indian cuisine (especially vegetarian) became a part of the tradition. Revivalists can be possessed by the Indian Spirit, a spirit which has been rendered its own feasting rituals, its own seals or altars, ritual house and ritual night (Indian Night). There are Revivalists who "robe" according to the Indian Spirit, since that spirit has become their personal Angel.[112]

Howell's "ritual personality" would have been shaped in Revivalism's incorporation of East Indian elements as well as in relationships between East Indians and African Jamaicans outside of Revivalism. It was also shaped by his own personal relationships and encounters with East Indians. The relative weakness of European cultural penetration in St Thomas would have benefited the East Indian and African Jamaican communities of that parish, as it would the Revivalist community and the nascent Rastafari movement.

It was Howell's direct relationship with one East Indian in particular, a man remembered as Laloo, who was said to be "one of Howell's direct bodyguards", which shaped the "ritual personality" and agency of the founder of Rastafari with respect to the weaving of East Indian elements into the ritual composition of early Rastafari. Hill notes that the "mysterious" prayer that formed "a pivotal part of all Ras Tafarian ceremonies", according to one reporter from the *Daily Gleaner*, seemed to contain "a curious blend of several words that appear to be derivations from original Hindi, Urdu, and Bengali words". The *Daily Gleaner* reporter observed that "after each incantation, the cultists are thrown into a fanatical frenzy not far removed from the throes of pocomania".[113]

Even two drawings reproduced in the *Daily Gleaner* of 18 January 1937 bore the signature of East Indian influence. Captioned "A cultists' interpretation of a dream of what houses in future Abyssinia will look like", these ritual architectural drawings, which were seized from Howell's headquarters in Port Morant, seemed to be influenced by East Indian aesthetics – lineal and architectural. But in all of this, the creative methodology, which was similar to that employed by Revivalists, was rooted in principles central to the making or remaking of the African diaspora: an open-ended adventure of imagination, or the gathering, orchestrating and choreographing of a multiplicity of fragments to constitute a redemptive universe. For many persons in Jamaica and across the Caribbean as well as around the world, Rastafari has become that redemptive universe.

Notes

1. At his trial for sedition in 1934, Leonard Howell told the court in Morant Bay that he started to preach about Ras Tafari as the Messiah returned in Kingston, Jamaica, in January 1933. See Hélène Lee, *The First Rasta: Leonard Howell and the Rise of Rastafarianism* (Chicago: Lawrence Hill, 2003), 78.
2. Robert A. Hill, *Dread History: Leonard P. Howell and Millenarian Visions in the Early Rastafarian Religion* (Chicago: Research Associates School Times Publications and Frontline Distribution International, 2001), 45.

3. Ibid., 29.
4. Ibid.
5. Lee, *First Rasta*, 65.
6. Ibid.
7. Ibid.
8. Hill, *Dread History*, 29.
9. Lee, *First Rasta*, 66–67.
10. Ibid., 67.
11. Ibid.
12. Ibid., 69.
13. Ibid., 70.
14. "Leonard Howell Being Tried for Sedition in St Thomas", *Daily Gleaner*, 14 March 1934, 21.
15. Ibid.
16. "Chief Justice Denounces Leonard Howell as a Fraud", *Daily Gleaner*, 17 March 1934, 1.
17. Lee, *First Rasta*, 65.
18. Ibid., 71.
19. G.G. Maragh [Leonard Percival Howell], *The Promised Key* (1935; repr., Kingston: Headstart, n.d.), 5.
20. Ibid., 5.
21. Ibid.
22. Anthony Bogues, *Black Heretics, Black Prophets: Radical Political Intellectuals* (New York: Routledge, 2003), 160–61.
23. For more, see Clinton Hutton, "The Creative Ethos of the African Diaspora: Performance Aesthetics and the Fight for Freedom and Identity", *Caribbean Quarterly* 53, nos. 1–2 (March–June 2007): 127–49.
24. See Hutton, "Creative Ethos", as well as Clinton Hutton, "Esclavage et origines cosmologiques de l'art afro-caribéen" ("Slavery and the Cosmological Roots of African Caribbean Art"), in *Art contemporain de la Caraïbe: Mythes, croyances, religions et imaginaires*, ed. Renée-Paule Yung-Hing (Paris: HC Éditions, 2012), 14–21 or 356–58.
25. See also Clinton Hutton, "La splendeur ésthetique du Revivalisme: L'art liturgique des festins chez les ancêtres et les esprits" ("The Aesthetic Grandeur of the Revival Table: Invocational Art and Feasting with Ancestors and Spirits"), in Yung-Hing, *Art contemporain*, 66–73.
26. "Creation" can be found on the 1998 album *Prince Buster Record Shack Presents the Original Golden Oldies*, vol. 1, Prince Buster Record Shack, Jet Star Phonographics, DRPBCD10.

27. Hutton, "Creative Ethos", 140.
28. Barry Chevannes, *Betwixt and Between: Explorations in an African-Caribbean Mindscape* (Kingston: Ian Randle, 2006), 77.
29. Clinton Hutton, "Leroy Clarke: Des yeux pour voir derrière le zéro des choses et apprendre à reconstruire les ruines" ("Leroy Clarke's Art: Eyes to See Behind the Zero of Things to Reinvent the Self and Rechart the Ruins"), in Yung-Hing, *Art contemporain*, 391.
30. Maureen Warner-Lewis, *Central Africa in the Caribbean: Transcending Time, Transforming Cultures* (Kingston: University of the West Indies Press, 2003), 173–74.
31. John Michael Vlach, *The Afro-American Tradition in Decorative Arts* (Athens, GA: Brown Thrasher Books, University of Georgia Press, 1990), 139.
32. Robert Farris Thompson, *Flash of the Spirit: African and Afro-American Art and Philosophy* (New York: Vintage, 1984), 184.
33. Michael Veal, *Dub: Soundscapes and Shattered Songs in Jamaican Reggae* (Middletown, CT: Wesleyan University Press, 2007), 2, 9, 39.
34. Ibid., 77–78.
35. Rupert Lewis, *Marcus Garvey: Anti-Colonial Champion* (London: Karia Press, 1987), 209.
36. Ibid., 209, 197–98.
37. Ibid., 205.
38. Ibid., 168.
39. Ibid.
40. Fitz Balintine Pettersburgh, *The Royal Parchment Scroll of Black Supremacy* (Kingston: Headstart, 1996), 5, 74.
41. Ibid., 75.
42. Quoted by Miguel Lorne in the prologue of the 1996 republication of *The Royal Parchment Scroll of Black Supremacy*. See Pettersburgh, *Royal Parchment Scroll*, xvii.
43. Lee, *First Rasta*, 68.
44. Ibid.; Robert Athlyi Rogers, *The Holy Piby* (Chicago and Kingston: Research Associates School Times Publications and Headstart, 2000), 68.
45. Miguel Lorne cited the 17 May 1927 issue of the *Daily Gleaner* in the introduction to the 2000 edition of *The Holy Piby*. See Rogers, *Holy Piby*, 13.
46. Howell, *Promised Key*, 1–2.
47. Howell noted, among other things, that "it was a brilliant ceremony.... The Ethiopians were brilliant in special robes, having discarded their precious white robes, and wore jewels of great value. The men's swords [were] heavily ornamented with gems. On their heads they wore gold braided hats, in which the covered lion's manes were to be seen. In contraction then were the solar note struck by the women who were heavily veiled, and wore heavy cloaks. His and Her Majesty King Alpha and Queen

Omega the King of Kings drove to the Cathedral in a coach drawn by six white Arab horses." See Howell, *Promised Key*, 2-3.
48. Howell, *Promised Key*, 5.
49. Ibid., 6.
50. Rogers, *Holy Piby*, 55.
51. See *National Geographic*, June 1931, 679–746.
52. Rogers, *Holy Piby*, 61.
53. See Hill, *Dread History*, 20–22; Robert A. Hill, introduction to *The Marcus Garvey and Universal Negro Improvement Association Papers*, vol. 10, *Africa for the Africans, 1923–1945* (Berkeley: University of California Press, 2006), 100.
54. Hill, *Marcus Garvey*, 100.
55. Lewis, *Marcus Garvey*, 172.
56. Ibid.
57. Ibid., 173.
58. Hill, *Marcus Garvey*, 100.
59. Ibid.
60. Hill, *Dread History*, 43.
61. Rudolph Williams (Mas Ran), a cultural artistic figure in the Garvey movement, became one of Jamaica's leading and most revered personalities in theatre, satire and the articulation of Jamaican culture.
62. Hill, *Dread History*, 43–44.
63. Ibid., 44.
64. "Belief kill and belief cure" is an aphorism commonly used by older Jamaicans.
65. For more on Bedward's arrest and trial, see Veront Satchell, "Colonial Injustice: The Crown v. the Bedwardites, 27 April 1921", in *The African-Caribbean Worldview and the Making of Caribbean Society*, ed. Horace Levy (Kingston: University of the West Indies Press, 2009), 46–67.
66. See Brian L. Moore and Michele A. Johnson, *Neither Led nor Driven: Contesting British Cultural Imperialism in Jamaica, 1865–1920* (Kingston: University of the West Indies Press, 2004).
67. Joseph M. Murphy, *Working the Spirit: Ceremonies of the African Diaspora* (Boston: Beacon Press, 1994), 124–25.
68. Hill, *Dread History*, 24.
69. Ibid., 24.
70. Ibid.
71. Ibid., 25.
72. Ibid.
73. Ibid., 56–57.
74. Ibid., 25, 56–57.
75. The Great Revival started out as a Christian mission across Jamaica, primarily to

convert black souls by exposing Africans (and wayward Europeans) to the light of God through Jesus Christ, a main basis for civilizing Africans in European epistemology and ontology. This Christian revival upsurge became the spark and mask (cover) for a Myalist upsurge, resulting in Revivalism (Zion, also called 60, denoting the year of its genesis, 1860, and Poko or 61, since it emerged in 1861). Pukkumina (Poko) deals primarily with ground spirits, while Zion deals more with heavenly spirits. "Native Baptism", like "Revival", was used as a generic name to include all spiritual expressions and religious practices that were deemed by Europeans to be African, although one stream of Native Baptism was more in the tradition of the black church in the United States.

76. In 1865, the uprising from below was contained in St Thomas-in-the-East and Portland, while in 1938, it spread across the island.
77. Diane J. Austin-Broos, *Jamaica Genesis: Religion and the Politics of Moral Orders* (Chicago: University of Chicago Press, 1997), 75.
78. Lee, *First Rasta*, 63.
79. Ibid., 63.
80. Ibid., 166.
81. Ibid., 168. For more on the role of the African ancestral religious upsurge and the making of the Morant Bay Rebellion, see Clinton Hutton, "'Colour for Colour, Skin for Skin': The Ideological Foundations of Post-Slavery Society, 1838–1865 – The Jamaican Case" (PhD thesis, University of the West Indies, 1992), 164–75.
82. See Kenneth Bilby and Elliot Leib, "Kumina, the Howellite Church and the Emergence of Rastafarian Traditional Music in Jamaica", *Jamaican Journal* 19, no. 3 (1986): 22–28; and Clinton Hutton, *The Logic and Historical Significance of the Haitian Revolution and the Cosmological Roots of Haitian Freedom* (Kingston: Arawak Publications, 2005).
83. *Report of the Jamaica Royal Commission, 1866, Part II: Minutes of Evidence and Appendix* (1866; Shannon: Irish University Press, 1966), 1122. Hobbs used the term "Native Baptist" in a generic sense, to denote the range of African Jamaican–derived religion and spirituality, from the Myalist orders to the Native Baptist Church founded by George Liele and other African American preachers in the eighteenth century. Moreover, the English Baptist Church in Jamaica made it known that it was not to be confused with the Native Baptists. Edward B. Underhill, who spoke for the English Baptists, made it clear that "in the district to which the outbreak been confined, there are no Baptist missionaries, nor any congregations connected with them. . . . The Baptists spoken of by Governor Eyre are Native Baptists. They originated in the preaching of an American negro about 1783, thirty years before the Baptist Mission sent any agents to Jamaica, and with whom no union of any kind has taken place." See Hutton, "Colour for Colour", 164.
84. Murphy, *Working the Spirit*, 123.

85. *Report of the Jamaica Royal Commission*, 447. James Taylor was arrested for being a drummer by Alexander Barclay during the suppression of the people of St Thomas-in-the-East and Portland, following the uprising in Morant Bay on 11 October 1865. He was given one hundred lashes. The questions that Taylor was asked by the royal commissioner appeared to have been motivated by a desire on the part of the latter to find out if the Morant Bay Rebellion was inspired by the African ancestral rituals practised at Paul Bogle's chapel in Stony Gut. Perhaps their practices included feasting rituals denoting compacts with the ancestors (*Did you eat there?/Did you drink?*); cleansing the air to invite or to clear the way for the spirit to enter into feasting/blood rituals (*Did you smoke?*); spirit possession or Shakerism/eroticism (*Did you dance there?*); invoking/summoning/commanding (shouting out) God (*Did you ever pray? Out loud I mean?*); or receiving messages/seeing signs, getting visions from the spirit world as to how to act in society (*Did you ever see visions?*).
86. Hill, *Dread History*, 45.
87. Ibid.
88. *Daily Gleaner*, "Chief Justice Denounces Leonard Howell", 6. It was quite clear that the chief justice, Sir Robert William Lyall-Grant, was seeking to weaken the nascent founding leadership of the Rastafari movement by sentencing Howell to two years and Hinds to one year. In sentencing Hinds, he stated his reason in court: "Unfortunately, his [Howell's] evil doctrine has got into your brain and you want to put it into others. I have seen the consequences of it in other countries, and the result has been serious rioting. In view of your ignorance, I am going to pass a comparatively light sentence on you, in the hope that in future you will reflect before saying anything against the Government which is calculated to make people rebel against it. You will be imprisoned for twelve months." When he said he had seen the consequences of "evil doctrine" in other countries, Lyall-Grant was almost certainly referring to Nyasaland (Malawi), where in 1915 a nationalist uprising against white rule, led by John Chilembwe, was put down by the British. Lyall-Grant, who was appointed to the Nyasaland Legislative Council on 21 May 1909, played a leading role in using the courts to pronounce execution and imprisonment on the freedom fighters who were not killed during the uprising. Chilembwe, the leader of the movement, developed a nationalist doctrine based on the weaving of Christianity with elements of African spirituality. He was killed on 3 February 1915, during the uprising.
89. Hutton, *Logic and Historical Significance*, 90.
90. Ibid.
91. Ibid. Robert Hill made these remarks on *The Breakfast Club*, the Jamaican radio talk show programme on Hot 102 (FM radio), on 28 March 2000. The noted Jamaican poet Mutabaruka and the University of the West Indies life sciences professor Ajai Mansingh also participated in that discussion on Rastafari. Hill had done fieldwork

on the link between Rastafari and Kumina in St Thomas and St Catherine, Jamaica. It was while he was doing this fieldwork that he learned from elder Kumina adherents that Emperor Haile Selassie was declared the earthly manifestation of Nzambi Mpungu, the Bakongo Supreme Being, by the Kumina or Bongo people in Jamaica when news came of his coronation. It should be noted that the invocations that launched the Haitian Revolution in August 1791 at Bois Caïman and Lenormand de Mézy were chanted to Mbùmba, another name for Nzambi Mpungu. Mbùmba, the creator and warrior god, was depicted as a snake and was a patron god of the Haitian Revolution.

92. Murphy, *Working the Spirit*, 118.
93. Hilliard d'Auberteuil, one of the eighteenth-century voices of slave-making, supported the rituals of owning and possessing Africans as necessary, for "policy and safety require that we crush the race of blacks by a contempt so great that whoever descends from it even to the sixth generation shall be covered with an indelible stain". See J.A. Rogers, *Sex and Race: A History of White, Negro, and Indian Miscegenation in the Two Americas*, vol. 2, *The New World* (St Petersburg, FL: Helga M. Rogers, 1994), 99.
94. Hutton, *Logic and Historical Significance*, 84.
95. Clinton Hutton, "From Douens to El Tucuche: Becoming and the Meaning of Being in LeRoy Clarke's Art", in *LeRoy at 70: The Art, the Poetry, the Man*, ed. Trinidad and Tobago National Commission for UNESCO (Port of Spain: Trinidad and Tobago National Commission for UNESCO, 2011), 548–49.
96. Hutton, *Logic and Historical Significance*, 62–81.
97. Hill, *Dread History*, 44.
98. Barry Chevannes, "Ships That Will Never Sail: The Paradox of Rastafari Pan-Africanism", in *Critical Arts* 25, no. 4 (December 2011): 570.
99. Ibid., 571; also see Chevannes, *Betwixt and Between*, 221; Barry Chevannes, *Rastafari: Roots and Ideology* (Kingston: University of the West Indies Press, 1995), 17–28; Murphy, *Working the Spirit*, chapter 5; and Dianne M. Stewart, *Three Eyes for the Journey: African Dimensions of the Jamaican Religious Experience* (New York: Oxford University Press, 2005), 106– 20.
100. Chevannes, "Ships That Will Never Sail", 571.
101. A group of second-generation Rastafari belonging to the group known as Youth Black Faith waged a campaign against Revivalist ideas, symbols and sentiments in Rastafari. These young Rastas came out against the burning of candles and "other powers" used by first-generation Rastas such as Downer and Hibbert. They also attacked the Revivalist organizational structure employed by first-generation Rastas. See Barry Chevannes, "The Origin of the Dreadlocks", in *Rastafari and Other African-Caribbean Worldviews*, ed. Chevannes (New Brunswick, NJ: Rutgers University Press, 1998), 80, 83. This group was led by Bongo Wato. See John P. Homiak, "Dub

History: Soundings on Rastafari Livity and Language", in Chevannes, *Rastafari*, 159–60.
102. Chevannes, "Ships That Will Never Sail", 572.
103. Bogues, *Black Heretics*, 161. Also see Bogues's critique of *The Promised Key*, 162–65.
104. Hill, *Dread History*, 45.
105. *Daily Gleaner*, "Chief Justice Denounces Leonard Howell", 1, 6.
106. Lee, *First Rasta*, 69.
107. The origin of the key in Revivalist cosmology, rituals and cultural practices and its use as in the title of Howell's tract existed for some time before the 1930s. However, it might have been the Church of God and Saints of Christ, an Ethiopianist African American church founded by Prophet Crowdy in the last decade of the nineteenth century, that bore some ontological significance for Rastafari and perhaps Revivalism. According to Erna Brodber, in a previously unstated source of Rastafari, the "'Seven Keys' are an often-mentioned concept in the Church of God and Saints of Christ. These are the keys to the church given to Prophet Crowdy by the Lord in a vision. There are Bible passages found in Corinthians, Leviticus, Matthew, John, Romans and Revelation. The blessings and curses of Deuteronomy 28 are not unknown and very important to establishing the connection between God and the Africans of the Diaspora." See Erna Brodber, "The Church of God and Saints of Christ: African American/African Jamaican Cooperation and Incorporation before Marcus Garvey's UNIA" (unpublished essay, 2010), 18.

This American black church was established at the corner of North and Regent Streets, Kingston, Jamaica, in 1931, under the leadership of the American evangelist Howard L. Chase. However, it was not the Church of God and Saints of Christ that figured in the accounts of several informants who talked to Barry Chevannes on what they knew about Africa. They talked about a religious sect known as "the Seven Keys", founded by a street preacher called "the Seven Keys man", who was described as being "from foreign" and a "tall, strapping man, him mout' red, big hand, big lip, big nose". Chevannes was told that this man shouted out while preaching one day on Oxford Street, Kingston, "Take seven keys to breathe God's word, Deuteronomy to seal!" In this ceremony, he taught the people about Africa, "where the living God is". See Chevannes, *Rastafari*, 89. Based on this and other information about the Seven Keys man, Chevannes concluded that he was a Revivalist. However, Brodber was able to conclude fifteen years later that the Seven Keys man was unlikely to have been a Revivalist but rather was Howard L. Chase of the Church of God and Saints of Christ – who brought that church to Jamaica before 1931, if a statement made by the Calabar College principal about American churches in Jamaica, which mentions the Seven Keys, was indeed made in 1930, a year before the stated inauguration of that church in Jamaica. See Diane J. Austin-Broos, *Jamaica Genesis: Religion and the Politics of Moral Orders* (Chicago: University of Chicago Press, 1997), 75. Brodber notes that Robert Hinds "had his meeting place at 82 North Street and later at 6 Laws Street". Either way, he "was close enough to the Church of God and Saints of Christ and their functioning to have copied their externals". See Brodber, "Church of God", 19. One of these externals could have been the wearing of rosettes by Rastafarians, including Howell's wearing of one to his sedition trial at the courthouse in Morant Bay, backed up by supporters also wearing their green, black and yellow rosettes. All female members of the Church of God and Saints of Christ wore rosettes to church. This was part of their uniform. For more on this, read Brodber, "Church of God".

108. Hill, *Dread History*, 38–39.
109. Ibid., 39.
110. Ibid.
111. See a description and assessment of this in Ajai Mansingh and Laxmi Mansingh, "Hindu Influences on Rastafarianism", in *Caribbean Quarterly Monograph: Rastafari*, ed. Rex Nettleford (repr., Kingston: Caribbean Quarterly, 2000), 43–66.
112. It is a commonly held belief across Jamaica that the Indian Spirit (Coolie Duppy) is one of the most aggressive spirits – fitting the description of "Kali, the black, terrifying earth mother of Indian mythology, [who] is believed to be the most destructive form of divine energy which is invoked for lifting sagging spirits and feelings of desperation and helplessness, as the Goddess is expected to destroy the evil". See Mansingh and Mansingh, "Hindu Influences", 50. By the way, Kali is one of the names given to the "holy herb" in Rastafari. My study (including extensive photographic documentation) of Revivalism across Jamaica over the last fourteen years has revealed a multiplicity of East Indian elements in Revivalism.
113. Hill, *Dread History*, 40–42.

2

INTERROGATING LEONARD HOWELL AS THE "FIRST RASTA"

MICHAEL A. BARNETT

Leonard Howell, Joseph Hibbert, Robert Hinds and Archibald Dunkley formed a four-man foundation for Rastafari and were essentially the first generation of leaders for the movement. Leonard Howell is widely considered to be the first Rasta by many Rastafari studies scholars, as he clearly rose to a greater level of prominence and visibility than any of the other leaders did during the 1930s and 1940s (the embryonic stages of the movement). However, the question still remains as to who out of the foundation elders actually started to publicly preach first about the divinity of Haile Selassie. This would be the person who could be most fittingly referred to as the "first Rasta".

This chapter intends to shed more light on the early history of the movement, particularly in regard to the early preaching of the divinity of Haile Selassie I in Jamaica, and along these lines to establish a critical basis on which to discern which of the first generation of Rastafari leaders, regardless of popularity or following, was the first Rasta.

According to Robert Hill, Leonard Howell was born on 16 June 1898 in the village of May Crawle, near Crooked River in the Bull Head mountain district of upper Clarendon. He was the oldest of ten children. His father, Charles Theophilus Howell, was an independent peasant cultivator and a tailor, and his mother, Clementina Bennett, was an agricultural labourer. Howell became a seaman and was part of a Jamaican contingent sent to Colón, Panama, during the First World War. He travelled back and forth between New York and Panama a few times before settling in the former in 1918. He remained there for several years, becoming a member of Garvey's Universal Negro Improvement Association (UNIA) and noting Garvey's organizational techniques. He then returned to Jamaica in 1932, whereupon he started preaching the divinity of His Imperial Majesty, Haile Selassie I.[1]

Howell's Precursors and Contemporaries

Significantly, soon after Howell started preaching that Haile Selassie I was the manifestation of God in the flesh upon his return to Jamaica, he joined forces with the notable Bedwardite and Garveyite Robert Hinds. Not only did Hinds have the distinction of being a staunch lieutenant of Howell during the early years of Rastafari in the early 1930s, when the parish of St Thomas became the crucible for the movement, but he also represented the important link between the rich Revivalist tradition in Jamaica and the emerging Rastafari movement.[2] Prior to his espousal of the divinity of Haile Selassie I, Hinds had been a devout disciple of Alexander Bedward, the legendary Revivalist leader from August Town who effectively led the Native Baptist Church from 1895 to 1921, at which time he was incarcerated in the Bellevue lunatic asylum.[3] (For more on Alexander Bedward, see appendix to this chapter.) Hinds took part in Bedward's final march, in the spring of 1921. When the police halted the marchers and arrested them, Hinds was one of the participants who was arrested. Notably, when the marchers were tried at the Half Way Tree Courthouse, Hinds, by his own admission, was fortunate, because although he was actually committed to Bellevue along with Bedward, the doctors there determined that he was not mad, and he was subsequently

Figure 2.1. Alexander Bedward. Courtesy of the National Library of Jamaica. Restored by Clinton Hutton.

discharged.⁴ In stark contrast, Bedward remained confined at Bellevue until he died on 8 November 1930, no longer a force or an influence on the peasantry in Jamaica. (Legend has it, however, that Bedward died a happy man, after receiving news of the coronation of His Imperial Majesty [HIM] Haile Selassie I in Ethiopia, believing this to be a sign that the redemption of African people was at hand, and that his work in the physical realm was now well and truly over.)

In addition to Hinds, many others among Howell's first followers were old-time Bedwardites.⁵ The possibility of religious convergence clearly existed in the parish of St Thomas, and thus the early Rastafari preachers (Howell and Hinds specifically) were able to find ready converts there. In fact, St Thomas had proven to be a good recruiting ground for Rastafari adherents, as this was not only a parish where many Revivalists were based, but also one in which there were numerous Kumina practitioners, many of whom were descendants of nineteenth-century Central African immigrants to Jamaica.⁶ Interestingly, in a conversation in 2012 with one of this volume's editors and contributors, Clinton Hutton, I was told that a Rastafari elder by the name of Brother Man said that when he came to Kingston from St Elizabeth in 1940, he was already Rastafari, and that this was because the Revivalist church in western Jamaica, which he had been a part of, had declared Haile Selassie I as God Almighty soon after his coronation in 1930.⁷

This is extremely valuable ethnography, as it alludes to the possibility of additional flashpoints for the emergence of Rastafari in Jamaica other than the preaching by Howell, Hinds, Hibbert and Dunkley. Additionally, Dr Hutton told me that he had learned from other respondents, who had been formally part of the Revivalist tradition in St Thomas, that the Pukkumina church in St Thomas had declared Haile Selassie I as Nzambi, a supreme deity in Kongo cosmology. The fact that this Kongo cosmology was most strongly expressed by the Kumina practitioners of St Thomas is proof that a significant convergence of religious belief systems had in fact taken place in that parish. One might ask why is this significant. The answer is that in St Thomas, the particular strain of Revivalism known as Pukkumina, which had been influenced by the Kumina practitioners with their strong sense of ancestor worship, as well as the usage of much of the Kongo cosmology, had gone on to embrace a key tenet of Rastafari – that is, the assertion that Haile Selassie I was divine. This was very likely the key reason that Howell had much greater success in preaching to the St Thomas population than to the communities of Kingston during the early 1930s.

Figure 2.2. Joseph Nathaniel Hibbert. Painting by Clinton Hutton.

Joseph Nathaniel Hibbert was another of the early preachers of the divinity of Haile Selassie I. He was born in Jamaica in 1894, but travelled to Costa Rica with his adoptive father in 1911.[8] In 1924, Hibbert joined the ancient Mystic Order of Ethiopia, a Masonic society based in Panama, which did not become formally incorporated until 1928. Hibbert became a master Mason of this order before he returned to Jamaica in 1931, which was notably months before Leonard Howell's return. In fact, Ras Sekou Sankara Tafari, in the preface to the 2001 republication of Robert Hill's "Dread History" article, argues that Hibbert was already teaching the divinity of Haile Selassie I in Jamaica before the return of Howell to the island in 1932.[9] Leonard Barrett also alludes to the distinct likelihood that Hibbert started to preach that Haile Selassie I was divine, at Benoah, in the district of St Andrew, before Howell returned to Jamaica.[10] Therefore, it could quite easily be argued (controversial as it may be) that Hibbert was the first Rastafari preacher, and thus the "first Rasta", not Howell. Whether or not one chooses to entertain this postulation, what cannot be refuted is that Howell was a much more effective propagandist than was Hibbert and was thus able to garner a much larger following.

According to Barry Chevannes, Hibbert was something of a mystic, that is, a leader who built his organization along the lines of "occultism".[11] He professed that there were hidden secrets in the books of the Maccabees as well as in the publications of Lauron William de Laurence on occult and spiritual topics. Many of Hibbert's congregants were awed by his reputed powers and were desirous of learning his magical secrets. According to Chevannes, what led to the decline of Hibbert's organization was a combination of two things. First, he was unwilling to impart his innermost secrets to his initiates; second, he did not tolerate anyone or anything that challenged his leadership.[12] A prime example is that of the Ethiopian World Federation (EWF), which came to Jamaica in 1939 through the initiative of Paul Earlington. In an effort to establish a charter, which required a minimum of twenty-five dues-paying members, Earlington first appealed to Hinds, then to Dunkley and finally to Hibbert, as the other aforementioned Rastafari leaders had turned him down flat. Hibbert, interestingly enough, agreed to lend his support to the initiative, assuming that he would inherit a strong leadership role for the charter. However, after learning that the position that was being offered to him was as far down as third vice president, he ordered all of his members out of this local branch of the EWF.

Figure 2.3. Archibald Dunkley. Photograph by Robert Hill.

Archibald Dunkley was another early proponent and preacher of Rastafari. He had been a Jamaican seaman on the Atlantic Fruit Company's boats, until he quit the sea on 8 December 1930, when he landed at Port Antonio off the SS *St Mary*. Upon his arrival at Kingston from Port Antonio, Dunkley studied the Bible for two and a half years on his own to determine whether Haile Selassie I was the returned Messiah. Ezekiel 30, Revelation 17 and 19, and Isaiah 43 finally convinced him. In 1933, Dunkley opened his mission, preaching Ras Tafari as the King of Kings, the Root of David and the returned Messiah. A key point of consideration is that Dunkley arguably made a stronger effort than the other three leaders did to incorporate the entire Bible when preaching about Rastafari. Thus, in this author's opinion, we could argue that Dunkley can be conceived of as a leader with a more distinctly Christianized approach to Rastafari and could therefore be considered to have provided a theological foundation for the Twelve Tribes of Israel mansion of Rastafari, which was to be founded some thirty-five years later.

Contextualizing Howell's Significance

By all accounts, whoever was the first to start preaching that the newly crowned emperor of Ethiopia, Haile Selassie I, was divine – which arguably could well have been Hibbert and not necessarily Howell – the fact remains that Leonard Percival Howell was the most effective of the early Rastafari preachers. A content analysis of the then colonial newspaper, the *Daily Gleaner*, during the early 1930s reveals a much greater degree of attention being paid to Howell and his lieutenant at the time, Hinds, than to Dunkley or even Hibbert. Interestingly, on 16 December 1933, the *Daily Gleaner* reported that Howell was selling photographs of HIM Haile Selassie I in St Thomas for one shilling each. On 5 January 1934, the *Daily Gleaner* reported on Howell's arrest at Port Morant. The trial of Howell and Hinds was well publicized in the editions of the *Daily Gleaner* published on 15 and 17 March 1934. Leonard Howell, considered by chief justice Sir Robert William Lyall-Grant as the main perpetrator of sedition, was sentenced to two years in prison with hard labour, while Hinds, being recognized as Howell's lieutenant, received a one-year sentence which also included hard labour.[13]

Of interest is that during sentencing, the chief justice remarked to Howell, "I consider that you are a fraud, that you pretend you have been to Ethiopia, when you have never been near the place." And to Hinds, the chief justice said,

> I take into account in your case, that to a considerable extent, you were led [astray] by Howell who is a fraud; who knows nothing about Ethiopia. I have spent a long time in Africa and at one time was quite near Ethiopia.... Unfortunately his [Howell's] evil doctrine has got into your brain and you want to put it into others. I have seen the consequences of it in other countries and the result has been serious rioting. In view of your ignorance, I am going to pass a comparatively light sentence on you, in the hope that in future you will reflect before saying anything against the Government which is calculated to make people rebel against it. You will be imprisoned for twelve months.[14]

These words from the chief justice are actually very revealing, as prior to being a judge in Jamaica, he had in fact had the distinction of being a judge in Nyasaland, Africa (now Malawi), where he had tried many of the followers of the freedom fighter John Chilembwe for rebelling against the colonial order. So in reality, this was no ordinary judge. He was a man who had been rewarded with a knighthood for his contribution towards countering a colonial rebellion in Africa. Thus, it stands to reason that he would have been very much motivated to contribute his efforts to quell any threat of colonial rebellion or insubordination in Jamaica. This is discussed further in Miguel Lorne's chapter in this volume.

Now, it should also be noted that the police, who were the first layer of defence for the colonial order in Jamaica at the time, proved to take their jobs very seriously, as in late 1934, with Howell and Hinds temporarily silenced, they turned their attention to the other two early Rastafari preachers, Dunkley and Hibbert. On 11 September 1934, the police charged Dunkley with disorderly conduct while he was holding a meeting at the corner of Bond Street and Spanish Town Road in Kingston.[15] Shortly after this, Dunkley was sent to jail for thirty days on a similar charge when he was holding a meeting in Morant Bay, St Thomas. On 20 February 1935, he was placed in the Half Way Tree lock-up and from there moved to the Bellevue asylum, where he remained for almost six months.[16] Joseph Hibbert was himself arrested three times in 1935, once in Port Morant, where he had gone in an attempt to capitalize on the void that had been left by Howell's incarceration, and twice in Kingston.[17]

All said, however, history has shown that it was Howell who was the most persecuted among the first generation of Rastafari preachers, having throughout his lifetime been incarcerated in jail or the Bellevue asylum for a total period that far exceeded the incarceration period of the other three first-generation Rastafari preachers put together. This is one of the likely reasons why Howell was conspicuously absent from the public arena during the historic visit of Haile Selassie I to Jamaica in 1966. Why was Leonard Howell the most persecuted of the early Rastafari leaders? I posit that this was because he was the most charismatic and most effective among them, and therefore posed the greatest threat to the colonial government of Jamaica.

The Mission and Impact of Rastafari's Early Leaders

Not only was Howell able to incorporate many of Garvey's organizational techniques in his mobilization efforts, but he was also able to carve out a distinctive ideological, theological and cosmological orientation for his followers when he synthesized aspects of Robert Athlyi Rogers's *The Holy Piby*[18] with Reverend Fitz Balintine Pettersburgh's *The Royal Parchment Scroll of Black Supremacy*[19] to produce the document known as *The Promised Key*. This pamphlet essentially declares Haile Selassie I to be the Supreme God and notably takes issue with Roman Catholicism, which Howell depicts as a false, hypocritical religion, headed by the Pope of Rome, whom he castigates as "Satan the devil".[20] Additionally, Howell reiterates the conception of "Black Supremacy" as an antidote for white supremacy that Reverend Pettersburgh discusses in his *Royal Parchment Scroll of Black Supremacy*, and echoes Pettersburgh's disdain for the practice of Obeah. In this regard, we see that much of the conceptions and ideas of Robert Athlyi Rogers and (especially) Reverend Pettersburgh, synthesized by Howell in *The Promised Key*, still remain key tenets of the Rastafari movement today, particularly in the Nyabinghi and Bobo Shanti mansions. As a result of the many foundational pillars that Leonard Howell was able to effectively impart to Rastafari, many scholars accord him the title of father of the movement. However, the implicit assumption here is that the other early Rastafari preachers had little to no lasting impact on the movement as a whole and were relatively unsuccessful as leaders.

Notably, Chevannes departs from this position, arguing that it was Robert Hinds who ultimately proved to be the most effective and successful of the early Rastafari leaders. According to Chevannes, "Hinds was undoubtedly the most successful of all early Rastafari in terms of membership."[21] He goes on to state that Hinds, at the height of his career, with his King of Kings organization, led over eight hundred listed members and had a turnout of over two hundred at regular functions. Chevannes argues that Hinds's success was due to the fact that he was the most experienced religious leader out of the four first-generation Rastafari leaders, having been a staunch lieutenant of Bedward during the 1920s, when the latter was a Revivalist preacher, and then going on to be a steadfast preacher of Rastafari during the early 1930s, when the Rastafari movement was in its embryonic stage. For Chevannes, Hinds was a man who had once defended the old, but who had now seen the light of the new.[22] In fact, the religious career of Hinds is one of the strongest examples of the clear Revivalist roots of Rastafari. Here, we have a man whose religious origins are strongly embedded in Revivalism, and who makes a seemingly non-conflictive and non-contradictory transition into Rastafari.

Chevannes adds that Hinds separated himself from Howell when he was released from prison in 1935 by setting up his own organization, the King of Kings Mission, first at 82 North Street, Kingston, and then at 6 Law Street, Kingston.[23] The mission was organized along the lines of a Revival group, with the leader, or the "shepherd", being Hinds himself. Beneath him were the secretaries, two chaplains, an armour-bearer, twelve male officers and twelve water-mothers. The secretaries were the recording officers. They were literate, which was common among the peasantry back then. Thus, in addition to handling general written correspondence, for matters both internal and external to the organization, they were responsible for reading lessons at the meetings. The chaplains, water-mothers and officers were indispensable at the baptism rituals which took place twice a year to mark the reception of candidates into full membership. Baptisms were usually held at the Ferry River, on the border of St Andrew and St Catherine.

According to Leo Erskine, it was in Hinds's King of Kings organization that the Revivalist spirit was the strongest. Additionally, it was because Hinds was able to skilfully merge Revivalism with Rastafari that his organization held such a wide-scale appeal.[24] The carry-overs of Revivalism were very much evident in the King of Kings Mission. You had feasts, fasts and of course baptism. Along with these carry-overs, Hinds also introduced new practices and beliefs, such as the celebration of the Passover to remind his congregation that they were exiles in Babylon who sought to return to Ethiopia, as well as the introduction of Haile Selassie I as the messianic figure who would redeem black people all over the world from the shackles of colonialism and poverty.

A notable similarity between Hinds's and Howell's individual organizations was the relatively large number of women that they had in their congregations. This, arguably, was an outcome of the high Revivalist influence that was part and parcel of both Rastafari followings. According to Erskine, a key feature of Revivalism is the preponderance of women in the congregations, and this characteristic was clearly transferred into the Rastafari organizations of both Howell and Hinds. Not only were women very much visible in Howell's Pinnacle community and Hinds's King of Kings Mission, but they were also important players, sharing in key responsibilities for these Rastafari organizations along with the men.

All said, although Hinds was successful as a Rastafari preacher, with a congregation numbering almost a thousand, it should be noted that Leonard Howell had a membership of several thousand when he established his Pinnacle community in St Catherine in 1940. The huge, vibrant and independent Rastafari community that Howell was able to establish at Pinnacle essentially trumped the accomplishment of Robert Hinds when he broke out on his own.

Critically Reviewing the Process by Which the Rastafari Movement Emerges

What is crucial in regard to this critical analysis of the emergence of the Rastafari movement is the key assertion that three of its early preachers – Archibald Dunkley, Joseph Hibbert and Leonard Howell – independently came to the conclusion that Haile Selassie I was divine. Robert Hinds is, in fact, the only prominent early Rastafari preacher who went on record to say that it was Leonard Howell who convinced him of Haile Selassie's divinity. Just like Leonard Howell, both Hibbert and Dunkley had the notoriety of being worldly, well-travelled individuals. Leonard Barrett writes that Hibbert, upon returning to Jamaica in 1931 from Costa Rica, started his own Ethiopian Coptic ministry in Benoah, St Andrew, whereupon he commenced to preach that Haile Selassie was divine.[25] It was only when he went to Kingston in early 1933, in an attempt to broaden his following, that he met Leonard Howell, who himself was preaching that Haile Selassie was divine.

Beyond this similarity, there are critical doctrinal differences in the teachings of Howell and Hibbert. While Howell developed an ideological and theological orientation inspired by both Robert Athlyi Rogers and Reverend Fitz Balintine Pettersburgh, Hibbert, contrastingly (largely as a consequence of his immersion into the ancient Mystic Order of Ethiopia), introduced a version of Rastafari teachings that was based on Freemasonry, in addition to an interpretive analysis of an Ethiopic version of the Bible.[26] In this regard, although there are specific occasions in which Hibbert accompanied Howell to some of the latter's early meetings, in no way can Hibbert be considered a lieutenant for Howell, contrary to what Hélène Lee suggests in her book *The First Rasta*.[27] Certainly, there were instances of cooperation and collaboration between the two men, but this should not be confused with the significantly different scenario of Hibbert being a follower, a disciple or a lieutenant of Howell. Chevannes notes that one of Hibbert's shortcomings was that he did not take kindly to any challenges to his leadership. His unhesitant withdrawal from the initial branch of the EWF that was set up in Jamaica in 1938, upon realizing that he was not going to be the leader of the branch, was a key example of this.[28] In this regard, as a preacher in his own right, a master Mason and a man with his own distinct ideological bent, it is hard to conceive of Hibbert following anyone, even the charismatic Leonard Howell.

Then there is the case of Archibald Dunkley, whom Lee also documents as a follower of Howell, consistent in her belief that nobody other than Howell was able to conclude independently that Haile Selassie I was divine.[29] Lee does concede, however, that Dunkley endured persecution for being a Rastafari preacher just as Howell and Hinds did. In this regard, Lee writes, "What happened to Archibald Dunkley, the Bible-reading sailor who compiled all the scriptural references that identified Haile Selassie as the Lion of Judah? He was arrested several times in 1934–35 and eventually spent six months in an asylum."[30]

Dunkley, who took at least two and a half years to read through the entire

King James version of the Bible upon his return to Jamaica from Panama in December of 1930 (which is somewhat akin to a tradition later introduced to the Twelve Tribes of Israel mansion by Vernon Carrington), did not come to the conclusion that Haile Selassie was divine until about the middle of 1933.[31] This was at a time when, notably, Hinds, Hibbert and Howell were already preaching about the divinity of Haile Selassie. However, the key point is that Dunkley came to this conclusion independently and went on to forge his own separate Rastafari organization.

There is also the case of David and Annie Harvey, who, upon their return to the island in 1930, founded a religious sect in Jamaica known as the Israelites. They were a Jamaican couple who had also travelled extensively, first meeting in Costa Rica, where they got married; after leaving Costa Rica in 1920, they travelled to Panama, Cuba and then the United States.[32] They returned to Jamaica in 1924 but only stayed for a few months, suddenly becoming inspired to go to Ethiopia to live. They lived there for almost six years, observing the coronation of Haile Selassie I in 1930, before returning to Jamaica again. Importantly, they brought back with them the picture of Haile Selassie I that Leonard Howell ended up copying and using as postcards for his own purposes, according to Archibald Dunkley.[33] In an interview with Hill, Dunkley, who dubbed this photo "the Prince of Peace photo", claimed that Howell went directly to the Israelites' headquarters at Paradise Street in Kingston after he came back from New York and took hold of one of the photos of Haile Selassie. Dunkley further argued that "if they [the Harveys] did not believe in Ras Tafari, I do not think that they would bring the photograph of him and teach the people them of Africa", insinuating that it was the Harveys who were in fact the first preachers of the divinity of Ras Tafari, and not Howell.[34] This matter raised by Dunkley is not something that should be considered lightly, and the Harveys could very well be serious contenders for the mantle of first Rasta.

Conclusion

When we ask the question of who should be dubbed the first Rasta, there are several candidates. We have the Harveys, who founded the Israelite sect in Jamaica in the early 1930s. Additionally, we have the possibility that some of the Revivalist churches in Jamaica may have declared Haile Selassie I as God or divine shortly after his 1930 coronation. And then we have the case of Joseph Nathaniel Hibbert.

Hibbert is the strongest candidate, I feel, by the mere fact that after being so deeply immersed in the ancient Mystic Order of Ethiopia while in Costa Rica, and becoming a master Mason as well as being highly familiar with the Ethiopic version of the Bible, it is highly likely that he would have believed Haile Selassie I to be divine in an independent fashion shortly after the grand coronation, as opposed to a couple of years or so after the event. Thus, it would not be too hard to imagine Hibbert, after arriving in Jamaica, notably just a few months after the coronation, preaching to a congregation about this, albeit a small one. The other possibility, which is that after arriving in Jamaica in 1931, Hibbert did not conceive of Haile Selassie as divine, but instead remained in a relatively dormant, uninspired state until he met Howell in 1933, seems far more remote, in my opinion.

This, however, in no way takes away from Leonard Howell being the most successful and most prolific of the first generation of Rastafari leaders. His eventual following, especially when he got to Pinnacle, definitely trumps that of the other early leaders, even that of Hinds, whom Chevannes credits as the most successful among them.

Appendix: The Native Baptist Movement and the Subsequent Development of Revivalism in Jamaica

The Native Baptist movement in Jamaica was a branch of Christianity that most effectively empowered the black population of the island. It is essentially a blending of Christianity with Myalism or a syncretic Africanized Christian belief system. It dates back to George Liele, a slave who migrated to Jamaica in 1783 and founded the first Baptist Church, which he named the Ethiopian Baptist Church.[35] Interestingly, in Jamaica, along with the establishment of the Native Baptist movement came the first strands of Ethiopianism. In fact, so far as the Jamaican context is concerned, the two traditions are inextricably tied.

The Native Baptist movement is characterized by drumming, dancing and handclapping, clearly comprising an African dimension and clearly incorporating Myal. Other prominent Native Baptist leaders were George Lewis, George Gibb and Moses Baker. From the time that George Liele arrived in Jamaica in 1783, he started to interpret Christianity from an African perspective instead of a European perspective. Other Native Baptists followed suit, including George Gibb and Moses Baker. What allowed this movement to strengthen was that the Native Baptists existed in a relatively autonomous state, unfettered by European regulation, at least until about 1814, when the first Baptist missionaries arrived from Great Britain. This means that for about twenty-eight years, the first Native Baptists were able to develop and establish a theology that valued blackness and empowered and emboldened the slaves, rather than pacifying them.

According to Leo Erskine, it is quite clear that the arrival of the British missionaries in 1814 did not slow down the Africanization of Christianity along Myal lines among the slaves at all. There were cultural barriers to communication, for one thing, but more importantly there was a clear preference among the slaves for Africanized religious celebration. As a result, many of them rejected Baptist orthodoxy for native-led forms of expression. Because the Native Baptist movement in Jamaica was started by black leaders and because it was essentially an Africanized form of Christianity, replete with spirit possession, it provided the basis for black resistance to European oppression as well as for some of Jamaica's most well-known rebellions. There was the famous Sam Sharpe Rebellion of 1831–32, for instance, also known as the Baptist War. Sam "Daddy" Sharpe, a Native Baptist leader, was able to inspire thousands of slaves to revolt. According to Erskine, more than twenty thousand slaves were involved in the rebellion.

Many historians consider it to have been the critical event that brought slavery to an end in Jamaica.

Then there was the famous rebellion of 1865, led by another charismatic Native Baptist leader, Paul Bogle. Despite the emancipation of slaves in 1838, the actual living conditions for black Jamaicans were still wretched almost thirty years later. Instead of freedom and self-betterment, African Jamaicans found themselves landless, homeless, penniless and disenfranchised overall. These social conditions laid the groundwork for Paul Bogle's Morant Bay Rebellion of 1865.

Further into the nineteenth century, Revivalism or the Revival Church developed as an outgrowth of the Native Baptist movement. Revivalism did not represent a revival of Christianity; rather, it represented a resounding rejection of orthodox Christianity and a revival of the African *force vitale*.[36] One of the pivotal leaders of Revivalism was Alexander Bedward. He emphasized black pride and black dignity and taught that blacks should seek to resist and challenge white colonial rule. With his teachings and his leadership, he essentially laid the spiritual and ideological foundation for the Rastafari movement in Jamaica, which emerged a little over a decade after he was imprisoned in Bellevue.

The strong linkage between Revivalism and Rastafari is probably most clearly epitomized by Robert Hinds, who was a staunch follower of Alexander Bedward before he met Leonard Howell and became a Rastafari leader in his own right.

Notes

1. Robert A. Hill, *Dread History: Leonard P. Howell and Millenarian Visions in the Early Rastafarian Religion* (Chicago: Research Associates School Times Publications and Frontline Distribution International, 2001), 21, 22, 25.
2. Noel Leo Erskine, *From Garvey to Marley: Rastafari Theology* (Gainesville: University Press of Florida, 2005), 65.
3. Ibid., 27, 30.
4. "Chief Justice Denounces Leonard Howell as a Fraud", *Daily Gleaner*, 17 March 1934, 6.
5. Hill, *Dread History*, 45.
6. Ibid., 46.
7. Interview with Clinton Hutton, University of the West Indies, Mona, Jamaica, 15 April 2012.
8. Leonard E. Barrett, *The Rastafarians* (Boston, MA: Beacon Press, 1997), 82.
9. Hill, *Dread History*, 5.

10. Barrett, *Rastafarians*, 82.
11. Barry Chevannes, *Rastafari: Roots and Ideology* (Syracuse, NY: Syracuse University Press, 1994), 124.
12. Ibid., 125.
13. *Daily Gleaner*, "Chief Justice Denounces Leonard Howell", 6.
14. Ibid.
15. M.G. Smith, Roy Augier and Rex Nettleford, *Report on the Rastafari Movement in Kingston, Jamaica* (Kingston: Department of Extra-Mural Studies, University of the West Indies, 1988), 8.
16. Ibid.
17. Ibid.
18. *The Holy Piby*, otherwise known as *The Blackman's Bible*, was written and published by Robert Athlyi Rogers of Newark, New Jersey, in 1924. Rogers was born in Anguilla and migrated to the United States at an early age. On 15 April 1917, Rogers produced the "Negro Map of Life" and founded the United Home and Bank of the Negroes in the state of New Jersey. In 1921, he travelled throughout Central and South America, as well as the Caribbean, preaching about the greatness of Ethiopia. Rogers returned to the United States a year later and met Marcus Garvey when they both gave addresses to a gathering of the Newark division of the UNIA in 1922. Rogers was so impressed with Garvey that he declared him "an apostle of the Lord God for the redemption of Ethiopia and her suffering posterities" when he came to write *The Holy Piby*. After publishing this book in January 1924, Rogers established the Afro-Athlican Constructive Gaathly with its headquarters at Kimberley, South Africa, in August 1924. It is *The Holy Piby*, in fact, which provided the foundation for this church.

The Jamaica branch of the Afro-Athlican Constructive Gaathly went under the name of the Hamitic Church and was established jointly in 1925 by Grace Jenkins Garrison and Reverend Charles Goodridge. According to Hélène Lee, the cornerstone of the Hamitic Church was laid in Kingston at 7 Elgin Street, Smith Village, on November 1925. Goodridge, a co-founder of this church, started disseminating *The Holy Piby* in Jamaica as early as 1924, just a few months after it was published. According to Miguel Lorne, Rogers was something of a dramatic character, and in 1927, having remained in Jamaica for two years after founding the Jamaica branch of his church, he cut his veins and caused his blood to spill, using it to draw a symbolic line between Athlyians/Athlicans and other peoples of the earth. Then, four years later, in 1931, while still living in Jamaica, feeling that he had accomplished his mission on earth and no doubt being aware of the coronation of Haile Selassie in Ethiopia, Rogers committed suicide by going out to sea and drowning himself. See Hill, *Dread History*, 18; Hélène Lee, *The First Rasta: Leonard Howell and the Rise of the Rastafarianism* (Chicago: Lawrence Hill, 2003), 41, 42, 43; and Miguel

Lorne, introduction to Robert Athlyi Rogers, *The Holy Piby* (Chicago and Kingston: Research Associates School Times Publications and Headstart, 2000), 7–9.

19. *The Royal Parchment Scroll of Black Supremacy* was published in Jamaica in 1926 by Reverend Fitz Balintine Pettersburgh. According to Lee, Pettersburgh had also lived in the United States, just as Robert Athlyi Rogers and Leonard Howell did. However, Pettersburgh returned to Jamaica in 1924. Hill informs us that Pettersburgh referred to his book variously as "Ethiopia's Bible-Text" and a "supreme Book of Royal Rules for the Ethiopian Western Repository". Hill further argues that this book was plagiarized "extensively" by Leonard Howell in his own work *The Promised Key*, published in 1935. The *Daily Gleaner*, while on one hand stating that Pettersburgh's *Royal Parchment Scroll of Black Supremacy* was complementary to *The Holy Piby*, also notably rubbished and dismissed Pettersburgh's text, writing that "the grammar is like the sense, which seems to us to be indistinguishable from nonsense, and the whole concoction is so putrid that we must wonder what class of people could ever take such rubbish seriously". See Lee, *First Rasta*, 48; Hill, *Dread History*, 18; and "A New Religion", *Daily Gleaner*, 6 June 1927, 12.

20. G.G. Maragh [Leonard Percival Howell], *The Promised Key* (1935; repr., Kingston: Headstart, n.d.), 4.
21. Chevannes, *Rastafari*, 127.
22. Ibid.
23. Ibid.
24. Erskine, *From Garvey to Marley*, 66.
25. Barrett, *Rastafarians*, 82.
26. William David Spencer, *Dread Jesus* (London: The Society for Promoting Christian Knowledge, 1999), 14.
27. Lee, *First Rasta*, 21, 70.
28. Chevannes, *Rastafari*, 126.
29. Lee, *First Rasta*, 59.
30. Ibid., 207.
31. Nettleford, Smith and Augier, *Report on the Rastafari Movement*, 6.
32. Hill, *Dread History*, 27.
33. Ibid.
34. Ibid.
35. Erskine, *From Garvey to Marley*, 9.
36. Ibid., 26.

3

"THAT VAGABOND GEORGE STEWART OF ENGLAND"
Leonard Howell's Seditious Sermons, 1933–1941

JAMES ROBERTSON

When Leonard Howell started preaching about Ras Tafari in 1933, his audiences soon included policemen with open notebooks. In July of that year, he called on the inspector in charge of the Detective Office in Kingston to protest "that the Police attended his meetings and made notes", but received a brisk answer "that this is one of the duties of the Police and he should make no complaint at all".[1] The inspector was accurate. Jamaica's police had been attending political meetings and compiling reports for at least the preceding decade.[2] These official auditors' surviving notes, along with the testimony that they and other hostile witnesses prepared, shed fresh light on how Howell's arguments developed during what has been described as the incubation period of Rastafarianism (see appendices A, B and D to this chapter).[3]

The colonial-era police files on Howell have not survived. Individual police reports drew on far more extensive surveillance data than ever reached the colonial secretary, the head of the island's civil service. In 1937, a memo by the acting inspector general of police could even quote the meagre three-pence-halfpenny total the Rastafarians had received in the collection plate after a sermon.[4] However, the police did send notes from some of Howell's sermons across to the colonial secretary. His office's surviving files, now at the Jamaica Archives, include one entitled "Sedition in St Thomas", recording some of Howell's early speeches as well as other material on Howell and the early Rastafarian movement.[5] The files retain summaries of several speeches, which illuminate the style and changing substance of Howell's delivery, along with a description by a white detective corporal of a meeting with Howell in June 1941 (appendix E, no. 1). This record of Howell as the leader of his mountaintop settlement at Pinnacle, near Spanish Town, offers more striking images than those provided by any visiting journalists. Yet, full as these official texts appear, they remain selective accounts. When giving evidence at Howell's trial in 1934, Corporal Isaac Brooks stated that upon attending a speech of Howell's, "he did not take down all that Howell said; but only those parts of the speech which he considered seditious".[6] There would be gaps in these transcriptions; the advice Howell offers in his *Promised Key*, for example, not to "follow the Court House and Doctors [as] they will fake you to death", meaning that paying professionals' fees would swallow a poor family's savings, was so mainstream that anyone struggling to keep up while scribbling into a notebook might skip it.[7] None of the summaries compiled by police or, later, journalists note his criticisms of lawyers or physicians. With this caveat, the policemen's notes still record arguments Howell presented which, against all the expectations of the colonial establishment, not only attracted auditors to his meetings but could convince them, too.

The surviving texts cluster in three periods between 1933 and 1941. Several records from 1933 report early speeches given by Howell in Kingston and Port Morant in St Thomas. This file remains full because the colony's crown solicitor and attorney general decided not to use these texts to prosecute Howell – they dismissed him as "a ranter" and feared that a trial would only give him publicity – so they left the accumulated evidence on file.[8] Despite this dismissal by the colony's law officers, the police maintained their watch while the colonial secretary had a report compiled on Howell and in March 1934 sent a copy to Britain's domestic security service, MI5, which had responsibility for colonial security.[9] The administration continued to observe Howell's activities with foreboding.

These notes tend to highlight elements of continuity in Howell's message. Police auditors were listening for material to use in a trial, and even after the passage of emergency defence regulations in 1939, the basic legal grounds for initiating prosecutions for public orators hardly changed. Howell's speaking style left him open to accusations of sedition, an offence that the island's attorney general defined as exciting "discontent and hostility between different classes of the King's subjects", or in the words of the prosecuting counsel in 1934, disturbing "the peace of the community, to bring the Sovereign into contempt, to bring the Government and those administering it into hatred, to put class against class and stir up discontent among the public".[10] The reports show areas where Howell's criticisms of colonial Jamaican society developed, even though they omit other factors that helped to shape his beliefs.[11]

1933–1934: Speeches in Kingston and St Thomas

Within a couple of months of his return to Jamaica from New York on 17 November 1932, the thirty-four-year-old Howell was preaching on the steps of the Methodist Coke Chapel on the north side of Kingston's main square, a traditional venue for public speakers.[12] By 14 June 1933, one of his late-evening meetings had a police observer (appendix A). The report is sketchy and unsympathetic but indicates the presence of several themes in Howell's discourse: he mentions two international issues, with praise for Haile Selassie and comments on current racial politics in America, and several domestic topics, with criticisms of Jamaica's churchmen, jeers at the police and the British governor, along with invocations of a higher black loyalty to Ethiopia as a justification for his audience to reject established symbols of imperial loyalty. The report also notes that Howell already had an audience of two hundred, with more joining them, and that he was selling postcards of Selassie.[13] Despite Marcus Garvey's refusal to allow Howell "to sell the Emperor's pictures at Edelweiss Park", there was progress. Howell had already moved beyond such religious cranks as the preaching atheist "No God Smith", who shared these steps.[14]

In parallel with cultivating an audience in Kingston, Howell was also speaking in Port Morant in St Thomas, a port that housed the United Fruit Company's main depot on Jamaica's south coast, where he spoke in "a booth" in the yard of the house where he lodged. On 30 May 1933, an evening meeting was attended by the police corporal and two constables stationed in the town. These officers were not the experienced shorthand experts of Kingston's Crime Investigation Division, nor did they have the political awareness of one of those officers, who, although he heard "a hell of a lot of subversive things" in the public meetings he was sent to observe, because "they were black people saying what [he] wanted to say", "doctored the speeches when they were dangerous".[15] At the Port Morant meeting, the corporal took longhand notes (appendix B, no. 1), from which he composed a statement summarizing the sermon (appendix B, no. 2). Statements by the two constables both described the same speech (appendix B, nos. 3 and 4).

The texts we have were compiled by policemen. As a result, they prioritized potential crimes, such as whether Howell was dishonest in selling for a shilling postcards of Haile Selassie that had cost a penny or a penny-halfpenny to print – so at either a 12:1 or an 8:1 profit margin.[16] Then they listened for points which reflected negatively on the colonial status quo. Here, insults to the governor or the monarch earned entries in their notebooks, as did comments that Jamaicans should give their reverence to the green, yellow and red of the Ethiopian flag, or that "God Save the King", the imperial national anthem sung at the end of Howell's meetings, was to be dedicated to the Ethiopian monarch, His Imperial Majesty Haile Selassie I, rather than to George Stewart (George V) in England. Howell's dismissals of the colonial establishment went further, with a claim that the arguments presented to his audience in small-town St Thomas would be "too deep" for the island's governor to comprehend. This comment flattered his auditors and encouraged them to ponder his arguments – though making this claim was not legally actionable.

In Port Morant, all the policemen's accounts noted Howell's assertion that a government that demanded taxes from its people was inherently corrupted – an appealing argument during a prolonged depression.[17] This verdict led on to his statement that Jamaica was burdened with too many police. Wherever Howell spoke, the police in attendance always recalled his dismissive comments about the Jamaica Constabulary. He criticized both the institution and the men who served in it. In 1933, he claimed that every night, African Jamaican policemen had to bleach their complexions, and that they were obliged to "tell lies on their own colour" as a part of their job. In later speeches, he added reports of the bad ends that befell individual officers who testified against him. Then, as working-class Jamaican auditors, the policemen registered in their notes Howell's frequent use of "vagabond", "low" and "dirty" as adjectives describing the colony and empire's elites. These dismissals were not only striking reversals of the language of imperial patriotism – with the king disparaged as "that vagabond George Stewart of England" – but they were likely to resonate with the poor in Howell's audiences, who were liable to receive such insults themselves.

When it came to the religious and millenarian elements of Howell's sermons, these notes simply recorded his comments about how foolish it was to believe in a God in heaven, while here on earth the Ras Tafari was the true God. This distinction underlay subsequent Rastafarian assertions that "the English ... invented the idea that God is a spirit in Heaven that men cannot see. Since white men have given no proof to support this belief, it can only be regarded as a racket." This view was extrapolated from Howell's rejection of belief in "a dead God" who allegedly resided in heaven and sent children to earth, rather than believing in Rastafari, "the living God" in Africa – but when it came to Howell's further claim that "You are God and every one of you is God", this novel theology prompted no comment in the police notes.[18] Instead all the policemen recorded the immediate anticlerical focus of Howell's sermons, which described clergymen's dependence on donations from their congregations as corruption: ministers were skimming off their congregations' resources to support their own families. Howell proposed a radical solution: the island's churches should be closed and the clergy chased away. Then, to top off all these claims, there were promises of passage to a new home in Africa in the ships that Haile Selassie was sending.

The theme of a return to Africa was not new. Enslaved Africans had also believed that they would return to Africa when they died.[19] More recently, Marcus Garvey and his Universal Negro Improvement Association had brought Africa back to the centre of the diaspora's pride and hopes.[20] Then, in 1930s Jamaica, the language of repatriation proved increasingly current as the Great Depression led to Cuba and several Central American nations forcefully repatriating West Indians who had been working there. Between January 1930 and December 1934, 12,103 Jamaicans were sent home, along with around 3,000 of their children born abroad, while another 15,500 individuals paid their own passage back.[21] More continued to arrive for the rest of the decade. The resonances of repatriation extended further: Jamaica had only recently ceased transporting time-served indentured labourers back to India. The last returning "coolie ship" had left for India in 1929, though the option remained under consideration for a few more years – with the colonial government finally deciding not to charter a ship when one sailed from Trinidad in 1935.[22]

So why not extend the same policy to African Jamaicans? Groups who appealed to the governor of Jamaica during the 1930s for "a Free Deportation to Africa, the land of my sires" as belated justice and "Racial Rights" expected to find undeveloped land when they arrived, but then expected to work it.[23]

In contrast, the passages to Africa that Howell offered not only bypassed the colonial government – where all the other would-be returnees' applications ran aground on persistent official refusals to allocate funds for this project – but also offered the beneficiaries of Haile Selassie's bounty freedom from labour when they disembarked. The three police witnesses left Howell's Port Maria sermon with a cluster of ideas that had strong contemporary resonances. His audiences were offered plenty to consider, even if the island's elite chose to dismiss his message as "bosh and twaddle".[24]

Early Reactions: Hostile Auditors' Responses

Controversial doctrines provoked contention. Howell arrived in Trinity Ville, a rural crossroads community in St Thomas, on 18 April 1933, after Robert Hinds and two more of his followers had been arrested there as "disorderly and assaulting constables", prompting official fears of "further trouble".[25] In the event, Howell not only provoked a local crowd's anger, but laid himself open to a prosecution for sedition. Four people swore out statements recalling his words:

> Howell repeatedly said to the audience "George the Fifth is no longer King of the Negro race for the Negroes have now a King in Africa – called King Ras Tafari who is the Lord of Lords and King of Kings which is the fulfillment of prophecy. He is the Lion of Judah which shall break every chain for the Negroes are now under a greater oppression than during the years of slavery. You must no longer look upon George the Fifth as your King, but to Ras Tafari as your Majesty the King, for the white people have now to bow down to the Negro Race."[26]

However successful his message's appeal might be in Port Morant or Kingston, in Trinity Ville individual audience members protested Howell's rejection of King George V. By September 1933, shifts of emphasis in Howell's teaching had become apparent. The local agent for the banana-exporting Standard Fruit Company in Port Morant, who was also a justice of the peace, obtained a printed flyer proclaiming Howell's rejection of the white preachers' heaven-centred religion (appendix C), and complained that "he has told the people not to work for the white man".[27] When Howell held a meeting there later that month – where he made a point of inviting the Port Morant police to attend – the speech they recorded engaged with the legacy of slavery and "how the White man stole Africa from the Africans". After urging his audience to think of Africa rather than

Jamaica as their home, he ended "by telling the people that in 1934, there will be Politicians coming from Africa and there will be a Convention in Jamaica, such as was never seen before, and there will be ships here, waiting to take Black people back to Africa, those who want to go".[28]

By October 1933, a local minister reported that Howell was "promising . . . free transportation to Africa" in exchange for cash, while a further report on his sermons indicated that he had specified that the ships would arrive in August 1934.[29] With the approaching centenary of the abolition of slavery on 1 August 1834, millenarian claims were potent. Howell's convention invoked the forthcoming international conference in Kingston on emancipation that Marcus Garvey and the Kingston UNIA were organizing for August 1934, for which they sent formal invitations to African and other colonial delegates.[30] Howell's image of ships arriving to take people back to Africa took on an independent life. After he was sent to jail in March 1934, his followers' hopes adjusted. Rastafarians reportedly believed that "on a certain day they would walk on the sea from Jamaica to Abyssinia, and that their beards were to part the sea so as to give them easy passage".[31] In the event, incarceration offered Howell an alibi when the ships he had promised failed to arrive.

The police reports from a further tendentious sermon made on 10 December 1933 now only survive in quotations published in newspapers' trial reports, where Howell was described as leading his congregation in singing a four-verse psalm with the chorus "Day by day I see what Leonard Howell is doing for my soul". In this instance, the police's original notes were transferred to the colony's legal officers and no longer survive.[32] Journalists' reports on the trials of Howell and his associate Robert Hinds for sedition – because Howell had allegedly abused "the Sovereign, the Queen, Queen Victoria, the Governor of Jamaica and both the governments of Great Britain and this island" – gave the Rastafarian doctrines their first island-wide exposure.[33] Afterwards, Howell received a sentence of two years' imprisonment.

Out of Jail Again: Glimpses of Leonard Howell between 1936 and 1938

On completing this sentence, Howell returned to a very different situation from the one he had left in 1934. In jail, he had missed the Italian invasion of Ethiopia in October 1935, the seven-month Italo-Ethiopian War and the public protests by

West Indians along with their efforts to volunteer for the kingdom's defence.[34] Reports in the *Daily Gleaner* and other rumours had led to some Jamaicans writing to the colonial secretary to ask about enlisting for the Ethiopian cause, prompting an official lawyer's disapproval: "As the British Empire is not a participant in the conflict between Italy and Ethiopia, the enlistment of British subjects in the armies of either of the belligerents is a breach of international law and cannot be countenanced."[35] This naysaying failed to prevent West Indians' passion for the Ethiopian cause from seeking outlets in mass meetings that sent telegrams to the British monarch or, occasionally, in attacks of Catholic priests and nuns.[36] Police reports claimed that after his release later in 1936, Howell had trouble re-establishing himself, as "owing to the result of the War between Italy and Ethiopia his followers have lost confidence in him", while there had also been splits in his congregation when "some others who saw the possibility of easy living started branches of their own".[37]

The reports on Howell forwarded to the colonial secretary during the later 1930s remain sparse, not only through Howell's two years in jail, from 1934 to 1936, but also from his release until he was certified insane and committed to Bellevue asylum on 15 February 1938.[38] Several contemporaries disagreed with this assessment – with good cause, as this period saw the establishment of further Rastafarian congregations.[39] In January 1936, a letter to the secretary of state for the colonies in London protested the "pernicious and demoralizing" Rastafarian cult. The letter's Kingston-based authors objected to "the kind of teachings . . . disseminated at the Street corners . . . night after nights", while also noting the "frequent disorder at these Meetings due to Interruptions from persons of other faith and belief". The following April another letter, directed to the permanent undersecretary responsible for Britain's West Indian colonies, offered more specific complaints, describing "a public demonstration with drum and fife and emblems", in Kingston, besides street preachers there claiming "ere long Jamaica will have its own war and every negro must come to their colours and fight for their rights! A black Governor! A black Colonial Secretary! A black Judge! A black Inspector General!", all alongside assertions that "if Britain has taken Africa from them then they must have Jamaica".[40] However, the inspector general of police's official responses after these letters were passed to him for comment was far cooler: "As regards the Ras Tafari Sect, this is rapidly falling away, and at the present time is almost broken up. The followers have lost confidence in their leader, the result being that meetings are very poorly attended and the collection taken up, on which their leader subsists, is extremely small." He concluded, "I do not think the Ras Tafari element need to be any longer seriously regarded."[41] He judged mass unemployment a greater threat.

Our knowledge of Howell's activities actually increases after he was locked up in Bellevue and his wife made contact with him there, as he was able to undertake some correspondence. This included exchanges with George Padmore, a London-based African Trinidadian activist, which drew the renewed interest of Britain's MI5, who were intercepting Padmore's mail.[42] Hélène Lee points out that Howell's committal occurred five weeks after the strike at the Serge Island estate in St Thomas, which proved to be the opening exchange in the labour unrest that wracked Jamaica in 1938 and led to the transformation of the island's politics. Given Howell's earlier activities in the parish, Lee's suggestion that this timing may not have been coincidental may be correct. With the Serge Island strikers singing "the white man has the money and the black man has the labour" during a protest march, race was at issue, though the strike had begun over the rates per tonne to be paid for harvested cane and then escalated when strike-breakers were driven in from neighbouring parishes.[43] However, other issues may have worried the government more. The imminent centenary of "full free", the end of the transition status of apprenticeship on 1 August 1838, prompted stories of extensive land grants falling due to the ex-slaves' descendants. The administration ordered extra guns and barbed wire from Britain, while shipping lines manoeuvred to schedule their ships away from Kingston on 1 August.[44] Howell's preaching might well have appeared a further incendiary threat to neutralize. Incarcerating him at Bellevue kept him out of Jamaica's political and social transformations.

A Catalyst for Domestic and International Contention: From Howell's Release from Bellevue to His Move to Pinnacle

Howell therefore missed the riots of 1938 and the subsequent establishment of the Bustamante Industrial Trade Union. After his release, he soon clashed with the new union. On 25 June 1939, a meeting held at the same Port Morant premises as before prompted a hostile demonstration after claims "that Howell spoke against the Labour Union".[45] Two weeks later, Alexander Bustamante, the new union's president, wrote to the colonial secretary, warning of "trouble brewing at Port Morant . . . owing to the mischievousness of a man whose name is Howell, Leader of the terrible thing that is called 'Rastafari'". Bustamante's expressions of fear that Howell's endeavours "to put one group against another group" would aggravate the conflict appear disingenuous, seeking to shift onto Howell the blame for any further heckling or stone-throwing undertaken by his union's members.[46] These comments also reflected the continuing appeal of Howell's message, which had been reinforced in January 1939 by the legal incorporation of his congregation as the Ethiopian Salvation Society under the island's Friendly Societies Act, an action subsequently marked by a procession "through the streets" of Kingston and a jubilee celebration at the UNIA's Liberty Hall on 3 and 4 April. Over the next few months, the society established its Bond Bakery, with a headquarters and depot at 25 Oxford Street, Kingston, and eleven branches. The profits from this enterprise not only allowed Howell to scatter occasional coins in front of the bakery's door but also to equip himself with all the proper accoutrements of colonial commercial success: a Yorkshire tweed suit, spats and a gold watch and chain.[47]

Official complacency about Howell ended abruptly in the early months of the Second World War. Even though the first few months of "phony war" remained indecisive, Howell's speeches already offered a millenarian commentary on Britain's plight. Hitler's European successes offered the instrument for one of the core prophecies in Howell's *The Promised Key*: that "Ethiopia is the succeeding Kingdom to the Anglo-Saxon Kingdom". This war, in Howell's view, would end white rule. A report compiled by the commissioner of police in January 1940 observed that Howell "has again begun to hold meetings in St Thomas", though now employing the Ethiopian Salvation Society name, and described a meeting in Port Morant on New Year's Eve which around five hundred people attended, each paying two shillings – money that went to Howell. "He told the crowd that the white man's time was ended and that soon black men would sit on the throne of England; further that Hitler was in charge of Europe and that all European powers will be overthrown in 1947, which, according to Ethiopia's reckoning, means 1940 and at the end of this War the white nation shall be utterly exterminated."[48]

These calculations, by the Ethiopian calendar, also served to make 1933 – the eve of the 1834 centenary – the year of Jamaica's return to Ethiopia, suggesting the continuing resonances of emancipation within Howell's own vision. His message apparently had a broad appeal, as a week after the meeting described above, he held another meeting, with "five hundred persons being again present".

A policeman compiled a one-page summary of Howell's speech on 7 January (appendix D). Even though these meetings were held on private land – which proved a sticking point for the attorney general, as the colony's newly passed defence regulations "were made to prevent 'a disturbance of *public* order'" – the commissioner of police not only claimed that the speeches could be heard from the road but considered "that the words used by Howell are of themselves sufficient to cause a disturbance of Public Order during wartime, and to promote disaffection". The commissioner felt that "if Howell is allowed to continue, he will stir up racial feeling which will result in disturbance and promote serious disaffection". As a result, he invoked the new defence regulations to request an order "prohibiting the holding of such meetings by Leonard Howell in future".[49] A further report claimed that Howell had stated that no women or children were to attend a third meeting on 11 February, and that "men must come armed with sticks or cutlasses".[50] This sounded ominously like preparations for another Morant Bay–style uprising. Nervous officials were likely to recognize this local parallel, particularly as Rastafarian groups had already been invoking the 1865 uprising's slogans of "colour for colour" and "skin for skin".[51]

The governor banned Howell's third scheduled meeting in Port Morant but did not issue the general prohibition of his Ethiopian Salvation Society's public meetings that the police commissioner had requested. Even this limited action caught someone's eye in England. In late March, a two-sentence paragraph appeared in *Reynold's News*, a Sunday newspaper owned by the Cooperative Party, a Labour Party affiliate: "The Governor of Jamaica has forbidden meetings of the Ethiopian Salvation Society – a body aiming at restoring freedom to Abyssinia. Does Mr Malcolm MacDonald [the secretary of state for the colonies and himself a Labour MP] agree?" Fearing that this item would prompt a question in the House of Commons and wanting information, MacDonald sent a telegram stating that his "attention [had] been drawn to press reports that meetings of the Ethiopian Salvation Society have been banned in Jamaica". For the colony's administrators, this was a heavyweight's intervention, and it prompted a formal dispatch from the governor enclosing notes from Howell's speech (appendix D) and a subsequent transatlantic telephone call.[52] These vindicated Governor Sir Arthur Richards, though official regrets that he had turned to the Wartime Emergency Regulations prompted some caution. This restraint did not last. The following September, after police detectives heard Alexander Bustamante say "there will be bloodshed" in a speech about a dispute between rival dockers' unions, Richards showed no hesitation in locking up Bustamante along with several other Jamaican political activists.[53]

In March 1940, Britain's secretary of state for the colonies had further reasons for caution. The newspaper's linking of Howell's Ethiopian Salvation Society with the liberation of Abyssinia was potentially volatile. Haile Selassie was living in exile in England, but had been offended by Britain's recognition in 1938 of the legality of the Italian occupation of Ethiopia.[54] He could also fear that a British-led liberation would not restore Ethiopian independence but merely exchange his kingdom's clientage from Italy to Britain's empire.[55] In early 1940, the urgency increased for Britain as Mussolini sought to extort further concessions in East Africa in exchange for Italy's continued neutrality. The reinvasion of Ethiopia was already under consideration as a British strategic priority, because the Italian forces in East Africa posed a threat to the Red Sea shipping lanes and hence to the wider British military position in Egypt and the Middle East.[56] In March, a British initiative began to recruit Ethiopian refugees and train them as radio operators for what became known as Mission 101 or "Gideon Force", the reinvasion of Italian-occupied Ethiopia.[57] This was not a time when British officials would want news to reach Selassie of the official gagging of an Ethiopian Salvation Society in a British colony. As the society's leader, Howell apparently enjoyed some political immunity. Writing from Jamaica in early April, Governor Richards commented that "Howell has not attempted to hold any further meetings since that date", but continued, "I propose, if he should do so, to prohibit them also."[58] The colonial government stepped back from a formal confrontation. Howell did so too, despite police fears that his followers were "secretly arranging for other meetings".[59]

Pinnacle, 1940-1941

Instead, Howell was arranging to relocate. On 7 January 1940 – Christmas Day for the Ethiopian Church, which still used the Julian calendar – Howell announced to some five hundred people that "a large estate would soon be at their disposal". On 25 April 1940, 154 acres at Pinnacle, a former mountain pen, were purchased for nine hundred pounds by Albert Chang, a Kingston-based Chinese shopkeeper. Howell subsequently repurchased the land for twelve hundred pounds in the name of the Ethiopian Salvation Society, but only handed over eight hundred pounds.[60] The resulting mortgage would make the property more difficult to seize from the Rastafarians. Living at Pinnacle, the society's members could no longer afford to pay their dues to the society or to buy the Kingston bakery's bread, which left the bakery vulnerable to bankruptcy. Howell's business adviser argued against relocating as "premature" and likely to "spell ruin and end in nothing but disaster", but was overruled.[61]

Undertaking this hegira offered Howell and around seven hundred of his followers a new start. A journalist who interviewed Howell at Pinnacle in November 1940 came away impressed at the community, characterizing it as "the dream of an imaginative man who has a will strong enough to impose it on numerous people", but rather than seeing it as a millenarian cult or a new religion, the reporter offered a secular comparison, considering Pinnacle to be "another case of the inevitable merging of Socialism into tyrannical Communism".[62] One of Howell's followers employed a different frame of reference, recalling him as "a man on him throne like Nebuchadnezzar".[63] In the event, relocating to this mountaintop retreat did not allow Howell to leave either his former contacts in St Thomas or the suspicions of the colonial government and police force behind him.

On 11 June 1941, Detective Corporal R.P. Samuels from the Spanish Town police station travelled to Pinnacle, a trip prompted by information that James Nelson, a bail-jumping gunman from St Thomas, had sought refuge there (appendix E, no. 1).[64] By then, there was no need for the colonial authorities to have any concerns for the well-being of the Ethiopian Salvation Society. It had already been over a month since Haile Selassie had re-entered Addis Ababa in triumph on 5 May 1941, and the last Italian forces had surrendered.[65] The police were not welcomed at Pinnacle. When Samuels and two detective constables drove up to arrest the malefactor, only Samuels was admitted. He was threatened. Howell's companions knocked off the detective's hat while, as Samuels left, Howell said that Nelson would not be handed over. Afterwards, Samuels managed to avoid a further escalation at the gates of Pinnacle when a second constable was invited in but Samuels decided to leave. An impertinent note to the police from the gunman two days later stating that "I can be found at Pinnacle, everyday or anyday" did nothing to cool police tempers, and led the local police sergeant major to conclude that "Howell and his followers are preparing to declare war on the police" (appendix E, no. 2).

The cover letter from the inspector in charge in Spanish Town, forwarding Samuels's report, Nelson's reply and his sergeant major's comments to the commissioner of police, was furious. The inspector's suggestion to repeat the efforts made in St Thomas in January 1937 – when a mob had attacked the yard where Howell and many Rastafarians had gathered, tearing down the fence and buildings, while a squad of police stood by – and proceed to flatten the settlement at Pinnacle was quashed by the solicitor general's response: "In no circumstances can there be any question of 'breaking up the camp.'" Even so, "the attitude adopted by Leonard Howell in thwarting the Police in the execution of their duty" helped provoke the police to move against him.[66] Just over a month later, on 14 July 1941, 115 policemen under the deputy commissioner raided Pinnacle. They sought "the Rastafarian Gang", arresting seventy men while avoiding any significant damage to property, though they did uproot 101 ganja plants from a field close to Howell's house.[67] When the police returned to Pinnacle early in the morning of 26 July to capture Howell, who had evaded their earlier incursion, the detective who "dashed through the door and held Howell in the centre of the room after a struggle" was Corporal Samuels, who was later one of the four witnesses who testified against Howell during his trial.[68]

In the event, the government avoided another public prosecution for sedition. Howell was tried in the low-key setting of the Spanish Town Resident Magistrate's Court, a choice that traded off the magistrate's maximum sentence of two years of hard labour for limited press coverage and the absence of a jury. Allegations that residents from the Pinnacle camp had stolen charcoal, along with several neighbours' complaints of receiving sentences of between 96 and 111 lashes for men and 50 for a woman from a kangaroo court Howell presided over, provided the official justification for the July police raid and this two-year sentence. Charges of "larceny of coal" and assault occasioning actual bodily harm meant that Howell made this appearance in court as a bad neighbour rather than as a prophet of British defeat.[69] Even these accusations were reduced, as his lawyer managed to suppress a further charge of possessing ganja.[70] We have no text of any speeches made by Howell or his lawyer during this trial, though according to witnesses, Howell claimed that "I am Haile Selassie; neither you nor the Government have any lands here" before ordering punishments upon his neighbours.[71] However, the latest wartime version of his message, with its defeatist prophecy, was never expounded in open court to be circulated by Jamaica's newspapers.

Conclusions: Reading Official Files

The official files on Leonard Howell are fascinating. Miguel Lorne's description of Howell as "the most persecuted Rastafarian to date" remains true, despite all the subsequent persecutions of Rastafarians in Jamaica and elsewhere.[72] Even with their gaps and silences, the surviving police reports on Howell's activities between 1933 and 1941 not only offer useful material for discussions considering the question "How Howellite is the present Rastafari?" but also indicate some developments in his teaching during the 1930s, in addition to showing how persistent official surveillance was and its role in contributing to Howell's rejection of the Jamaican state.[73] There are certainly omissions. His *Promised Key* found no place in these files nor in the colonial bureaucrats' discussions, though some of this tract's themes, like the emphasis laid on the attendance of George V's third son, Henry, Duke of Gloucester, at Haile Selassie's coronation in Addis Ababa in 1930 to represent "his father the Anglo-Saxon King", had already provided topics for Howell's contentious sermons in Trinity Ville in mid-April 1933 and, five weeks later, in Port Morant, too.[74] Given the social injustices of Jamaican society, which the prolonged depression of the mid-1920s and 1930s compounded, as well as the narrow opportunities available for the poor African Jamaicans who attended Howell's meetings, his radical critiques of the existing social order and of the existing churches then achieved a far greater appeal than the colony's leaders expected.[75] Here, dreams of a true home in Africa offered considerable satisfaction.[76]

What these hostile notes by the police also demonstrate is that many of the politically explosive elements of Howell's message addressed issues that were already current – and often almost mainstream – in the island's existing public meetings. However, for contemporary audiences, the differences between Howell's exposition and other public speakers' discussions were also apparent. After invoking Haile Selassie as his sovereign, Howell was no longer constrained by the loyalty to Britain expected from imperial subjects and could therefore extend some arguments to their logical conclusion. While addressing a large public meeting in 1935 to protest the Italian invasion of Ethiopia, Amy Jacques Garvey observed of the future: "There must be the clash of arms . . . and after that clash Europe for the Europeans, Africa for the Africans and Asia for Asians. Because after the clash the White race will no longer be dominant. These things go in cycles."[77] Howell's January 1940 speech in St Thomas adopted the same metaphor, but removed the qualification of praise for Britain and

France that Mrs Garvey had included. This was a part of a continuing process of adaptation and reuse in his preaching. Once Marcus Garvey was in England, inhibitions ebbed, too. In 1939, Howell proclaimed from the stage at Liberty Hall that "Marcus Garvey is off the stage of action . . . Ras Tafari is gone up, Marcus Garvey is gone down!" After Garvey's death, it became even easier to invoke him as a precursor.[78]

Finally, the suspicious tradition initiated in these records should also be recognized as a component within the descriptive literature on Rastafarianism. This can expand the typology Jahlani Niaah has proposed for categorizing the ever-increasing publications "documenting the witness of Rastafari" – journalistic accounts, academic expositions and "the testimonial autobiographical from the Movement itself" – by adding a fourth category: hostile reports.[79] The persistence of this negative trend helped to sustain official suspicions, culminating in 1968 in the Jamaican government's expulsion of Walter Rodney as a subversive for engaging with Kingston's Rastafarians.[80] The stereotyping underlying such fearful verdicts is expressed in Ian Fleming's posthumous publication *The Man with the Golden Gun* (1965). The novel's wafer-thin plot device to justify the British Secret Service's James Bond and the CIA's uninvited activities in an independent Jamaica invokes plans of arson against the island's sugar crop, with the aim of raising the price for Cuban sugar, through attacks by "the Rastafaris – that's a beat sect here that grows beards and smokes ganja . . . and believes it owes allegiance to the King of Ethiopia, this King Zog or what-have-you, and that that's their rightful home". As depicted in the novel, they appear an exotic group, who, in exchange for marijuana, will deliver "plenty fires and troubles on the cane lands".[81] This dismissive characterization downgrades the keen interest in Cuba and its revolution among Rastafarians, as observed by Roy Augier, M.G. Smith and Rex Nettleford in 1960. Such interest was also apparent in the crowd of around 150 people, "most of whom were Rastafarians" – though whose placards included one from the Communist Party of Jamaica – who on 6 May 1962 protested at the dockyard gates after the newly elected Premier Bustamante refused to allow the crews from two Russian survey ships which had anchored in Kingston Harbour to come ashore.[82] What also needs to be recognized in considering such dismissals is that the tradition of negative writing about Rastafarianism has nearly as long a past as Leonard Howell's preaching. Occasionally, these critics record useful data. In this instance, the police notes from the 1930s and early 1940s offer us echoes of Howell's original sermons.

Appendix A: Police Report on Leonard Howell, 1933

Detective Office, Central Station, Kingston, 17 June 1933, Detective Inspector R.C. Waters to inspector general, "Re: Leonard Howell".[83]

I beg to report that this man held a meeting at the Coke Chapel Steps on the 14th instant, starting about 8.15 p.m.

The meeting was opened by a man named Richards who introduced Howell to the crowd.

Howell, in a long rambling speech about Ras Tafari, urged the people to recognize him as their King.

He said, "Go down and get Police to lock me up, to stop me. I am telling you at this moment that the Governor of Jamaica cannot lay hands on me, much less an insignificant Jackass."

He then read a Hymn from the Church of England Hymn Book.[84]

He further said, "I am here to inform you that King George's flag is no flag for you. The Ethiopian flag, the green, the yellow and red, which is the robe of the Virgin Mary; that is the Ethiopian flag."[85]

He talked a lot about the Churches, saying they do no good, and then read from a newspaper about the colour question in the U.S.A.

Howell then asked the people to buy photographs of Ras Tafari, which he is offering at 1/- each. These photographs are picture postcards costing 1d. [p. 2] or 1½d. each.

Messrs Harry and Hibbert also made short speeches.[86]

About 200 persons were present. The meeting ended at 11 p.m.

The attendance at this man's meetings is increasing but I am satisfied that his object is to make money by selling these photographs. Some foolish people put them under their pillows and expect miracles to happen.

The type of persons attending these meetings are the poor and ignorant who apparently have nothing else to do.

Appendix B: Police Notes from Leonard Howell's Port Morant Speech, 1933

No 1. Corporal Robert E. Coombs, Notes, 30 May 1933[87]

My dear Ethiopians we commence our meeting tonight and I want to speak to you about the King of Kings the Lord of Lords and Conqueror of the world. Everyone knows & hears about Ras Tafari is the King of Ethiopia.

American Negroes are domiciled. They brought the Black Americans as Baboons and monkeys. They had a piece of lip as thick as a liver. This was the dirty tricks that the white hypocrites brought to you.

Let all those dirty vagabonds go about and tell lies. It will be hell here. I want my share. I have lodged the money in the bank of Nova Scotia. If the white men start any thing we will blast him to hell.

Those dirty vagabonds in Jamaica keep more Police than should be here. Dare them trouble me. The Police live on lies. I caught one Police lying in Kingston. I am here to inform you in Jamaica that I can bring the Gov[ernor] – of Ja[maica] but he can not . . . understand as it is too deep for him. If the Police could do any thing they would do it. The King of England George Stewart make laws to fool the people but I am here to tell you the truth Ethiopians. You have accepted the Doctrine that the King has made but I am here to put foot upon it. If money was the root of all evil why the Government Charge you tax. The Government is not Clean. I am here to get my share. In the bank of Nova Scotia is my name written there. Where do the Parsons get money. The[y] fool the people and speak all kinds of rubbish fooling the people. The Churches should be locked up and the Parsons kicked out. They are thieves and they tell you that after death you will be drinking honey & milk. They are drinking it right now. Those dirty Vagabonds. You think is any God made you. Its your father & mother. You are God and every one of you is God. Any one say that God is up there dropping down Children is a liar. Its hell for you all. Lord have mercy. Ras Tafari is the God. . . . The English people sold You in Ja[maica] in 1780 in Kingston. I will close my meeting by singing the National Anthem. Not to George Stewart that {low-down} Vagabond but to Ras Tafari the King of Kings & Lord of Lords. All the money in the treasury belongs to me. The white men hate you like holy water. God save our Gracious King –

No. 2. Robert E. Coombs (Corporal No 793), states:[88]

I am a Corporal of Police and stationed at Port Morant in the Parish of St Thomas. I had known Leonard Howell for about One month. On the 30th day of May 1933 at about 8.30 pm I was on duty in the village of Port Morant. I received certain certain [sic] instructions in consequence of which I went to a meeting that Howell was keeping on behalf of Ras Tafari the Ethiopian King. This meeting was kept in a booth in the yard where he lives. This premises adjoins the Parochial Road at Chapel Hill {at Port Morant} in St Thomas and the booth is about one Chain away from the road. I was in company of Const[able]s Holmes and Parnell. He began this his meeting by singing hymns then after a few minutes he began to lecture to those present by saying, My dear Ethiopians we had commenced our meeting tonight and I want to speak to you about the King of Kings and Lord of Lords and Conqueror of the World Ras Tafari. He is the Ethiopian King and there is none other except him. Every one knows and hear about Ras Tafari the King . . . of Ethiopia. American Negroes are domiciled. They brought the black Americans as baboons and Monkeys. They had a piece of lip as thick as liver. This was a dirty trick that the white hypocrites brought to You. Let all of those dirty vagabonds go about and tell lies. It will be hell here. I want my share. I have lodged my money in the bank of Nova Scotia and I will help you. If the white men start any thing blast them to hell. Ras Tafari the Ethiopian King will help you and my dear Ethiopians we will all go back to Africa where you wont have to work. You are being oppressed by the Government by paying tax. If the Government was a clean one they would not charge you tax but let us live free. Ras Tafari the Ethiopian King is organizing a scheme to get ships to take the Negroes to Africa where they will be free of every thing. The white dogs are tampering with the people and you should open your eyes and support Ras Tafari and you will succeed. Those dirty vagabonds in Jamaica keep more Police than should be here. They have to bleach at nights in the cold and tell lies to get their pay. They tell lies on their own colour. I caught one in Kingston telling lies already, . . . those ugly black devils. I am here to inform You my dear Ethiopians that I can bring the Governor of Jamaica but he cannot understand me as it is too deep for him. George Stewart of England said he is King and make Laws to fool the people but I am here to tell you Ethiopians you have accepted the doctrine that the King George Stewart has made. I am here to put foot upon it. He is no King, he has sold out the negroes and is laughing at them. The piece of Book they call Bible said Christ was born from a woman. There is no Christ. How can Christ be born from a woman. Ras Tafari is the only Christ. You think is any Christ made you. Its your father and mother. You are God and every one of you is God. Any one who say that God is dropping down children is a liar. The Parsons are a set of liars and thieves, they rob the negroes to bring up their Children. They should be driven out of the Church, and they should be locked up. Ras Tafari is the King of Kings & Lord of Lords. The Parsons speak all kinds of Rubbish and fool the people. My dear Ethiopians in the Bank of Nova Scotia is my name written there. Support Ras Tafari and he will help you. He is the only King. He then said I will close my meeting with ... the singing of the National anthem God save our Gracious {King} but remember we are not singing it to that Vagabond George Stewart of England but to Ras Tafari the King of Kings & Lord of Lords. He concluded by saying the Police at Port Morant cant stop me as I am not doing or saying any thing against the Government, or they would stop me already.

No. 3. 11 June 1933, Charles Alexander Roberts states:

I am a constable stationed at Port Morant in the Parish of Saint Thomas. I know Leonard Howell for about two months. On Tuesday 30th of May 1933 I was in company of Corporal Coombs and Cons[table] Parnell on patrol duty in the village of Port Morant. At about 8.30 p.m. we went to a meeting which Howell was keeping on behalf of Rasta Farie who he says is the Ethiopian King. The meeting was kept in a booth in the yard in which Howell lives. These premises adjoins the Parochial Road at Chapel Hill in Saint Thomas and the booth is built about a chain's distance from the road. A large number of people attended the meeting and Howell was the only person who addressed the people during the course of the meeting, Howell spoke in a loud voice, Corporal Coombs took notes of what he said whilst Const[able] Parnell and myself listened very carefully to what Howell said. Howell started the meeting by singing hymns. I remembered he started his address by saying My dear Ethiopians we had commenced our meeting tonight and I want to speak to you about the King of Kings and Lord of Lords and conqueror of the world Rasta Farie. I also heard him say "let all those dirty vagabonds go about and tell lies it will be hell here I lodge my money in the bank of Nova Scotia and I will help you. If the white men start anything blast them to hell. You are being oppressed by the Government by paying taxes. If the Government was a clean one they would not charge you taxes. Those dirty vagabonds in Jamaica keep more police than should be here. They have to bleach at nights and tell lies to get their pay. George Stewart of England said he is king and make . . . laws to fool the people but I am here to put foot upon it. He is no king he has sold out the people {negroes} and is laughing at them. How can Christ be born from a woman, there is no Christ Rasta Farie is the only king. The parsons are a set of liars and thieves they rob the negroes to bring up their children. They should be driven out of the church. In the bank of Nova Scotia is my name written there." When bringing the meeting to an end Howell said I will close my meeting by singing the national anthem God save our Gracious king, but remember we are not singing it to King George that low down vagabond but to Rasta Farie the King of Kings and Lord of Lords.

No. 4. 11 June 1933, Edward Parnell states:

I am a Constable stationed at Port Morant in the Parish of Saint Thomas. On Tuesday the 30th of May 1933 at about 8.30 pm I was on patrol duty in the Village of Port Morant in company of Corporal Coombs and Constable Holmes. We went to a meeting which was being conducted by Leonard Howell in a booth on a premises which adjoins the Parochial Road at Chapel Hill. This Meeting was being held on behalf of Ras Tafari the Ethiopian King. I have known Howell for the past three months and have heard him conducted several Meetings. He began his Meeting by singing hymns, then after a few Minutes he began to lecture to those present by saying my dear Ethiopians we had commenced our Meeting tonight and I want to speak to you about the King of Kings and Lord of Lords and conqueror of the World Ras Tafari. He is the Ethiopian King and there is none other except him. Every one Knows and heard about Ras Tafari the King of Ethiopia. I have lodged my money in the Bank of Nova Scotia and I will help you. If the white man men start any thing blast them to hell. Ras Tafari the Ethiopian King will help you and My dear Ethiopians we will all go back to Africa where you wont have to work. You are all being oppressed by the Government by paying tax. If the Government was a clean one They would not charge you tax but let us live free. Ras Tafari . . . the Ethiopian King is organizing a scheme to get ships to take Negroes to Africa where they will be free of every thing. The white dogs are tampering with the people and you should open your eyes and support Ras Tafari and you will succeed. Those dirty vagabonds in Jamaica keep more Police than should be here. They have to bleach at night in the cold and tell lies to get their pay, they tell lies on their own colour. I caught one in Kingston telling lies already. George Stewart of England said he is King and make laws to fool the people but I am here to put foot upon it. He is no King, he has sold out the negroes and is laughing at them. How can Christ be born from a woman, there is no Christ Ras Tafari is the only King. The Parsons are a set of liars and thieves the[y] rob the negroes to bring up their children. They should be driven out [of the] Church. In the bank of Nova Scotia is my name written there. Howell said I will close my meeting by singing the National Anthem. God save our gracious King, but remember we are not singing it to King George that low down Vagabond but to Ras Tafari the King of Kings and Lord of Lords.

Appendix C: Flyer by Leonard Howell, 1933

Printed flyer, n.d., originally enclosed in Ronald Robinson, J.P., to Inspector W.C. Adams, 4 September 1933.

ON H.M.S.[89]
King of Kings and Lord of Lords of Ethiopia
BLACK PEOPLE! BLACK PEOPLE!
Arise and shine for the Light is come, and the glory of the Lord is risen upon Thee.

Let all generations of Ethiopia hear the voice of Leonard P. Howell, for in his hands the law is given.

Let not the preachers of Babylon persuade you to turn your back against the Lord God of Ethiopia.

Woe be unto the people of a race who seek not their own foundation. Their wives shall be servants for the wives of other men, and their daughters shall be wives of poor men and of vagabonds, – and there shall be tears because of privation.

I strongly appeal to you to seek and learn of your own foundation – woe be unto a race of people who forsake their own doctrine for another. They shall be slaves to the people thereof.

O people of Ethiopia boast not of the progress of the white race, believing that you are a part of the project you shall be cast over the bridge of death both body and soul.

Generation of Ethiopia, I, Leonard P. Howell, speak unto you, for as the Lord God of Ethiopia liveth, this is a very serious affair and must not be forsaken.

The white men gave the black men the wrong doctrine. They told them to condemn silver and gold, and seek heaven after death.

But now, we the black men have found out their trick. We found that the writers of the story was a cleek [clique]. All their intention was to make themselves strong.

Under the white man's doctrine the black man slights the things in life and seeketh Heaven after death; it has brought us starvation to starve, live in disgrace and die in his honour.

They that refuseth the Ethiopian doctrine now, shall find no other. But slavery and oppression shall overcome them.

Appendix D: Howell's Speech in St Thomas, 7 January 1940

Report of Speech made by Leonard Howell, leader of the Ras Tafari Cult, at a meeting held at Port Morant on 7.1.40.[90]

The meeting commenced at about 1 p.m. It was held at Chapel Hill at Mrs Samms' premises. About 500 people were in attendance.

In the course of his argument Howell said he feared not the eyes of men, or[91] bayonets or guns or bullets.

He said he is the servant of the King of Kings and any man that stands in his way shall be destroyed by his calling upon lightning and thunder.

In 1940 he said (which according to the white man's reckoning will be 1947) Jamaica, which he styles as Jericho,[92] belongs to him. He said, this year is really 1933, but that white men having advanced the time 7 years now is called 1940.

He said in 1947 Europeans will be wiped out and the King of Kings shall come in and rule the world and then all black people shall be liberated from the misery and oppression which they now experience from the hands of white nations.

He said 100 acres of land are available for habitation of all black people in Jamaica also £4000 for construction of their houses and planting vineyards when the time comes in 1947.

At this stage, he tried to arouse superstition in the minds of the people by referring to the ill fate that befell people who tried to obstruct him and his movement. He said one Corporal Brooks of St Catherine who prosecuted him died shortly after. He said Aston Simpson who shot after him twice is now a leper.

He said that to show that the Throne of England is going, the newspapers announced that the Queen of England is now eating out of enamel plate, and a lot of foolishness.[93]

He said he will be leaving Kingston for the John Crow Mountains where he will stay for 13 days.

Collection was taken up.

Sgd [signed] B.A. Palmer. 2. CC. No. 14.

Appendix E: Howell at Pinnacle, June 1941[94]

No. 1. 12 June 1941, Detective Corporal R.P. Samuels to Inspector i/c [in charge] St Catherine.

On the 11th instant I proceeded to "Pinnacle" with two attached warrants for execution on James Nelson who was said to be residing at Pinnacle. I was accompanied by No. 699, 2 CC, V.C. Shaw and No. 796, 2. CC. J. Marston, the driver of the Service Wagon. On arrival I found the gate locked as usual and I asked the gateman if Mr Howell was at home and he said yes. I asked him to allow me in but he said no. I told him that Mr Howell had made a promise that the Police would be admitted in without any trouble. He then informed me that Mr Howell's last word was not to allow any one in without his (Howell's) permission. He told me he would send word to Mr Howell. He then gave three blast on his whistle and a party of about 12 men came to the gate all armed with sticks. I was then informed that Howell said to allow only one to enter. I had a Service Revolver with me and I decided to go leaving Constables Shaw and Marston at the gate. One D. Hay, Howell's Lieut[enant], led the way. I followed and the party of 12 men behind me. I arrived at a large thatched hut, wattled around. I heard Howell's voice, turned round and saw him dressed in a robe. He went in the hut and invited me in. As I was approaching the door way one of his followers told me to take off my hat while I was in the presence of the chief. I told him I know I am to take off my hat in the hut but I don't consider it necessary outside. He grabbed off my hat and threw it in the hut. Howell then asked me what I came for. At the same time another man attempted to search me. I called to Howell and asked him if he knew who I was and he said "Yes" you are Detective Samuels from Spanish Town". I then said, "then why all these things." He told the man to stop and said Government had been giving me lots of trouble. I asked him if he remember giving the Inspector i/c St Catherine a promise that the Police would be given no trouble for admission. He said yes but no whiteman can come here again. I told him this was not necessary and informed him that I have two warrants for the arrest of one James Nelson for Br[each of the] Firearms Law. He said he had no idea who he was but he was not here anymore. He then said "well my friend if it was not you that come up here the matter would be far different and I am asking you not to come back."

He pointed to a room at the back of the hut and said "You would have been dragged in there and all these men would deal with you" pointing to about 150 men. I said goodbye and started for the road. He called me back and told me I have to get a guard. About 12 men then escorted me to the gate. On the way to the gate I was stopped because a messenger was coming. A man then passed us and told us to continue. On reaching the gate Howell came and told me that the man was there but I cant get him unless I send that man. Some one ask if it was the chauffeur and he said no, ["]the big one." Constable Shaw then came out of the wagon to go but I stopped him. I then remember that Constables Shaw and Palmer went to Pinnacle on a previous occasion to arrest one Nathaniel Morgan for larceny of bees. After the case Howell wrote asking for compensation but it was refused. I have been to Pinnacle before but this is the first time I have been treated as such. If any members of the Police should be sent there I would advise strict precaution. I remember while in St Thomas I accompanied Inspector Waters to Howell's camp and help to smash it.[95] When leaving for Spanish Town Howell said to the gateman whenever Det[ective] Samuels comes back blow your whistle and let the guard come down for him but if any other Police come let him in then when he is inside blow your whistle.

No. 2. James Nelson to Sergeant Major, Spanish Town Police Station [Annotated "A"].

>Sea Forth P.O.,
>14 June 1941

>Dear Sir,

>I was informed that the police is out with a warrant for my arrest, wanted for fire arms, my reason why I could not turn up before now, is I was away making preparation with some Fire Arms, and, I can be found at Pinnacle, everyday or anyday, if you should insist, or anxious to intrude on my liberty.
>Hoping to see you soon.

>>I am
>>The same
>>James Nelson

[To] Inspector i/c St Catherine,

"A" respectfully submitted for your information. It would appear as if Howell and his followers are preparing to declare War against the Police.

(sgd.) Chas. [Charles] Malbre. Sgt. Major. 17/6/41 [17 June 1941].

Notes

1. Detective Inspector R.C. Waters to inspector general of police, "re. Leonard Howell", 31 July 1933, quotation in item 7, "Sedition in St Thomas, 1933–34, 1939–40", 1B/5/79/735, Jamaica Archives, Spanish Town (henceforth JA).
2. See, for example, "Political Meetings (Miscellaneous)", a report on the speakers at a street-corner meeting of twenty for a local election in Kingston, made by the acting inspector in charge, Kingston, 4 January 1926, JA 1B/5/79/17, or the bulky file compiled on "Activities of the UNIA, 1926–28", JA 1B/5/79/15.
3. For more on the "incubation" metaphor, see Ajai Mansingh and Laxmi Mansingh, "Hindu Influences on Rastafarianism", in *Caribbean Quarterly Monograph: Rastafari*, rev. ed., ed. Rex Nettleford and Veronica Salter (Kingston: Caribbean Quarterly, 2008), 123.
4. A.D.F. Lidley, acting inspector general of police, to J.D. Lucy-Smith, colonial secretary, 18 July 1937, "Information re. Rastafarian Cult in St Catherine, 1934, 1936–37, 1940–41, 1944", minute 20, 5–6, JA 1B/5/77 – 1934, no. 283.
5. JA 1B/5/79/735. This and most of the other files in the Colonial Secretary's Office series from the 1930s relating to Howell are cited in Robert A. Hill, *Dread History: Leonard P. Howell and Millenarian Visions in the Early Rastafarian Religion* (Chicago: Research Associates School Times Publications and Frontline Distribution International, 2001), an expanded version of his "Leonard P. Howell and Millenarian Visions in Early Rastafarianism", *Epoché: Journal of the History of Religions* 9 (1981): 30–71 (reprinted without references in *Jamaica Journal* 16, no. 1 [1983]: 24–39); locating this monograph in Hill's wider research on Garvey and Howell, David Scott, "The Archaeology of Black Memory: An Interview with Robert A. Hill", *Small Axe* 5 (1999): 80–150. Since Hill explored these collections in the late 1970s, the files have been recatalogued with new reference numbers. This file, like most civil service files of the period, is organized in two sections. Documents were added from the back and were kept in the order of their introduction into the file. There is a second series, "Minutes", at the front of the file, paginated and individually numbered, where officials offered comments on the file's contents as it circulated to different departments.
6. "Leonard Howell Being Tried for Sedition in St Thomas", *Daily Gleaner*, 14 March 1934, 21.
7. G.G. Maragh [Leonard Percival Howell], *The Promised Key* (1935; repr., Kingston: Headstart, n.d.), 18. References are to this edition. The exact date of publication of this pamphlet is not known, Robert Hill suggests 1934 (Scott, "Archaeology", 141). For a further modern transcription, see William David Spencer, "The First Chant: Leonard Howell's *The Promised Key*", in *Chanting Down Babylon: The Rastafari Reader*, ed. Nathaniel Samuel Murrell, William David Spencer and Adrian Anthony

McFarlane (Kingston: Ian Randle, 1998), 361–89; regarding the doctors' high fees, see *Not for Wages Alone: Eyewitness Summaries of the 1938 Labour Rebellion in Jamaica*, ed. Patrick E. Bryan and Karl Watson (Kingston: Social History Project, Department of History, University of the West Indies, 2003), 65–66.

8. Crown solicitor to attorney general, 11 July 1933, item 6, JA 1B/5/79/735.
9. A circular was sent by the inspector general of police to all divisions warning them to keep a strict watch on Howell, 5 June 1933, item 6, JA 1B/5/79/735. For the report compiled by the colonial secretary, marked "Secret", 23 March 1934, item 22; for its destination, see the head of MI5's acknowledgement to the colonial secretary, E. Holt Wilson for Colonel Sir V.G.W. Krell to Sir Arthur Jelf, 16 April 1934, item 23. For more on MI5's imperial role, see Christopher Andrew, *The Defence of the Realm: The Authorized History of MI5* (London: Alan Lane, 2009), 129–30, 137–38.
10. "Labour unrest – St Thomas", attorney general, 15 January 1938, minute 9, item 26, JA 1B/5/77/30; "Leonard Howell Being Tried", 21.
11. For more on cross-fertilization with Indian culture, see Mansingh and Mansingh, "Hindu Influences", 105–33; on the Kumina drumming tradition from St Thomas which developed at Pinnacle, see Kenneth Bilby and Elliott Leib, "Kumina, the Howellite Church and the Emergence of Rastafarian Traditional Music in Jamaica", *Jamaica Journal* 19, no. 3 (1986): 22–28; and on the potential for further influences from the Central African traditions preserved among the descendants of indentured African labourers brought to post-emancipation St Thomas, see Kenneth Bilby, "The Holy Herb: Notes on the Background of Cannabis in Jamaica", in Nettleford and Salter, *Rastafari*, 135–51.
12. Regarding the date of Howell's return to Jamaica and the commencement of his speeches, see Lidley to Lucy-Smith, 18 July 1936; on his prosecution, imprisonment and deportation from the United States on 12 November 1932, see Hill, *Dread History*, 54–55, n. 25; on the other orators at the Coke Chapel steps, see Bryan and Watson, *Not for Wages Alone*, 45, and on speakers on that side of the square, 26, 31, 46, 70, 87–88, 111, 137, 163; on organizing a meeting there, see L.F.C. Mantle, "The Italo-Ethiopian Conflict: 'Things That Affects Us Here'", *Plain Talk* 1, no. 25, 2 November 1935, 11.
13. Later these cards were recalled as a print run of about five thousand photographs, in whose depiction of a bearded black man hopeful purchasers saw "the dead stamp" of a black Christ. On the print run, see M.G. Smith, Roy Augier and Rex Nettleford, *Report on the Rastafari Movement in Kingston, Jamaica* (Kingston: Institute of Social and Economic Research, 1960), reprinted in *Rastafari: The Reports*, ed. Roy Augier and Veronica Salter (Kingston: Caribbean Quarterly, 2010), 7; on the subject's Christ-like appearance, see Barry Chevannes, *Rastafari: Roots and Ideology* (Syracuse, NY: Syracuse University Press, 1994), 114–16.
14. On Garvey's ban, see Hill, *Dread History*, 25, and Scott, "Archaeology", 142–43; on No God Smith, see Bryan and Watson, *Not for Wages Alone*, 31.

15. Recollections of Evon Blake, a former Special Service policeman; see Bryan and Watson, *Not for Wages Alone*, 171–72. On Blake and his politics, see Krista A. Thompson, *An Eye for the Tropics: Tourism, Photography, and Framing the Caribbean Picturesque* (Durham, NC: Duke University Press, 2006), 232–34.
16. "Blatant Swindle Being Carried On in Parish of St Thomas", *Daily Gleaner*, 16 December 1933, 1. A clipping of this article is the earliest item in the file on Howell's seditious activities. JA 1B/5/79/735.
17. In January 1934, the Rastafarians were accused of discouraging people in St Thomas from paying taxes. *Jamaica Times*, 6 January 1934, 2–3, cited in James Carnegie, *Some Aspects of Jamaica's Politics 1918–1938* (Kingston: Institute of Jamaica, 1973), 26.
18. George Eaton Simpson, "The Ras Tafari Movement in Jamaica: A Study of Race and Class Conflict", *Social Forces* 34, no. 2 (1955): 168; George Eaton Simpson, "Personal Reflections on Rastafari in West Kingston in the Early 1950s", in Murrell, Spencer and McFarlane, *Chanting Down Babylon*, 223.
19. See, for example, Hans Sloane, *A Voyage to the Islands Madera, Barbados, Nieves, St Christophers and Jamaica*, 2 vols. (London: B.M. for the author, 1707 and 1725), 1:xlviii. Frequent suicides were attributed to this belief. For more on its continuing currency through to emancipation, see Vincent Brown, *The Reaper's Garden: Death and Power in the World of Atlantic Slavery* (Cambridge, MA: Harvard University Press, 2008), 132–34.
20. Chevannes, *Rastafari*, 33–42, 87–91, 94–95.
21. "Repatriates – Number of for 1930–34", 14 November 1935, JA 1B/5/77 – 1935, no. 291. Return, enclosed in item 5, colonial secretary to E.V. Lockett, Unemployment Commission.
22. Verene Shepherd, *Transients to Settlers: The Experience of Indians in Jamaica, 1845–1950* (Leeds: Peepal Tree, 1993), 101–3; "Return Coolie Ship, 1935", JA 1B/5/77 – 1934, no. 274.
23. "Reparations to Africa", vol. 1, JA 1B/5/77 – 1933, no. 394, includes an extensive correspondence between Gilbert McKenzie, an ex–West India Regiment soldier, and the governor from early 1933, in which McKenzie and 212 other veterans requested repatriation and, rather than being put off by the governor's claim that there was no money to fund their passages or by interrogations at the local police station, replied elaborating their claims (items 1–28). Quotations from item 1. Gilbert McKenzie to Governor Ransford Slater, 12 March 1933; McKenzie et al. to governor, 20 March 1933, item 4; McKenzie et al. to colonial secretary, 29 May 1933, item 23. The interrogations, same to same, 1 May 1933, item 16. They also sent a petition directly to Britain's secretary of state for the colonies (item 40A, 18 June 1935, copy enclosed in item 30, 26 July 1935, secretary of state to Governor Denham; also item 36, 8 November 1935, secretary of state to McKenzie et al.). The policy also remained

under discussion in the United States, where Mississippi's Senator Theodore G. Bilbo proposed a Black Repatriation Bill, which received the endorsement of the UNIA's Eighth International Convention in 1938; see Robert L. Fleegler, "Theodore G. Bilbo and the Decline of Public Racism, 1938–1947", *Journal of Mississippi History* 68, no. 1 (2006): 1–27; and Rupert Lewis, *Marcus Garvey: Anti-Colonial Champion* (Trenton, NJ: Africa World Press, 1988), 91.

24. This was the assistant attorney general's phrase at Howell's trial. "Leonard Howell Being Tried", 21.
25. Telegram from police of Trinity Ville to inspector, Morant Bay, 17 November 1933, JA 1B/5/79/735.
26. Statement of Madalin Kildare, 19 April 1933, item 6, JA 1B/5/79/735; see also statements by District Constable Thomas Kelly, John A.A. Ross and Corporal Leonard Moulton Thomas.
27. Ronald Robinson, J.P., to Inspector W.C. Adams, 4 September 1933, JA 1B/5/79/735.
28. E.B. Smith, Port Morant Station, to Adams, 15 September 1933, JA 1B/5/79/735.
29. Elder W.E. Barclay (Church of God, Port Morant), to Adams, 31 October 1933, JA 1B/5/79/735; Smith to Adams, 15 October 1934.
30. "Centenary Celebration of the Emancipation of the Negroes by the Universal Negro Improvement Association, Kingston", 19 February 1934, item 37; Marcus Garvey to governor of British Somaliland, 19 April 1934, item 37; telegram from governor of Northern Rhodesia to secretary of state for the colonies (copy), 20 February 1934, item 21A; Marcus Garvey to governor of British Guyana (copy), and associated correspondence, JA 1B/5/77/159 – 1934, no. 159; Lewis, *Marcus Garvey*, 91.
31. *Daily Gleaner*, 15 August 1934, 10.
32. "Leonard Howell Being Tried", 21. The next day, a slightly different version was cited: "Leonard Howell seeks me and he finds me / Fills my heart with glee: / That's why I am happy all day, / For I know what Leonard Howell is doing for my soul". "Leonard Howell, on Trial Says Ras Tafari Is Messiah Returned to Earth", *Daily Gleaner*, 15 March 1934, 20. On the transferral of the police's notes, see Henry Clarke, crown solicitor, to colonial secretary, 2 January 1934, minute 3, no. 8, JA 1B/5/9/735.
33. "Leonard Howell Being Tried", 21. Hinds (d. 1950) was a former Bedwardite and Garveyite who later established his King of Kings Mission in Kingston, which was organized along the lines of a Revival band. Although in 1936, Howell was named its president general, Hinds sustained the group during Howell's incarcerations and after his moves to St Thomas and Pinnacle. It continued under Hinds's direction into the early 1940s. See Chevannes, *Rastafari*, 126–42; on Howell as president general, see Hill, *Dread History*, 37, fig. 4.
34. On the war, see George L. Steer, *Caesar in Abyssinia* (Boston: Little, Brown, 1937), and Anthony Mockler, *Haile Selassie's War* (1983; repr. Oxford: Signal, 2003), 44–173. On the readiness of some in Britain to accept the Italians' rationales for their inva-

sion, alongside solid black opposition, see David Whittall, "Colonial Fascism", *History Today* 60, no. 10 (2010): 42–48; on the united responses in the West Indies, see Robert G. Weisbord, "British West Indian Reaction to the Italian-Ethiopian War: An Episode in Pan-Africanism", *Caribbean Studies* 10, no. 1 (1970): 34–41; for a discussion of the speeches and protests in Kingston against the Italian invasion, see Rupert Lewis, "Marcus Garvey and the Early Rastafarians: Continuity and Discontinuity", in Murrell, Spencer and McFarlane, *Chanting Down Babylon*, 150–51. For a counter-argument that downgrades the invasion's impact on popular Ethiopianism in Jamaica, see Ken Post, "The Bible as Ideology: Ethiopianism in Jamaica, 1930–38", in *African Perspectives: Papers in the History, Politics and Economics of Africa Presented to Thomas Hodgkin*, ed. Christopher Allen and R.W. Johnson (Cambridge: Cambridge University Press, 1970), 185–207.

35. On Jamaicans requesting information on enlisting and quoting the *Gleaner*, see "Ethiopian-Italian War – Joining up of West Indians to fight for Ethiopia", items 10, 6 and 5, letters from Timothy Heath, Wilfred Grizzle and Alan Woodly, all October 1935, JA 1B/3/77 – 1935, no. 232; on the government lawyer's naysaying, ibid., minute 2, 21 October 1935. In 1937, the civil war in Spain prompted further official invocations of Britain's 1870 Foreign Enlistment Act; see "Spanish Civil War: Non-intervention of British Subjects", JA 1B/5/77 – 1937, no. 239. This European war did not generate such passions in Jamaica.

36. On the public meetings and a throng of petitions to the king and the British government in 1935 and 1936, see "Abyssinian/Italian Dispute – Protests against action of Italy", JA 1B/5/77 – 1935, no. 290; for a discussion of a meeting of four hundred people in Spanish Town addressed by St William Grant, the Kingston UNIA leader, see R. DePass, "Mass Meeting Spanish Town", *Plain Talk* 1, no. 22, 12 October 1935, 7. On violence towards Roman Catholic nuns and clergy, see Lewis, *Marcus Garvey*, 172. An effort by Alexander Bustamante to calm such passions suggests how this prejudice developed; see "The Pope and Ethiopia", 30 September 1935, reprinted in *Bustamante and His Letters*, ed. Frank Hill (Kingston: Kingston Publishers, 1976), 68.

37. Lidley to Lucy-Smith, 18 July 1936, minute 20, items 5–6, JA 1B/5/77 – 1934, no. 283.

38. Inspector general of police to colonial secretary, 11 November 1938, minutes 7–8, JA 1B/5/79/735, no. 28.

39. Smith, Augier and Nettleford, *Rastafari Movement*, 5–7. This account is based on two weeks' intense fieldwork in 1960. The chronology for when specific groups were established can be imprecise. As both a snapshot from 1960 and an overview, it remains invaluable.

40. General secretary, Kingston, and St Andrew Civic League to Colonial Office, London (against "Rasta-farian Cult"), 23 January 1937, item 25, and "in Caution" to Sir John Maffery, 7 April 1936, item 18B, JA 1B/5/77 – 1934, no. 283.

41. Lidley to Lucy-Smith, 18 July 1936, minute 20, items 5–6, JA 1B/5/79/735, also same to same, 8 July 1936, item 18, JA 1B/5/77 – 1934, no, 283.
42. Krell to colonial secretary, 14 September 1938, item 26, JA 1B/5/79/735. On Padmore's activities in Britain, see Jerome Teelucksingh, "The Immortal Batsman: George Padmore the Revolutionary, Writer and Activist", in *George Padmore: Pan-African Revolutionary*, ed. Fitzroy Baptiste and Rupert Lewis (Kingston: Ian Randle, 2009), 1–20.
43. Hélène Lee, *The First Rasta: Leonard Howell and the Rise of Rastafarianism* (Chicago: Lawrence Hill, 2003), 117; "Serge Island St Thomas Strike", *Plain Talk* 4, no. 1, 8 January 1937, 1–2. Compounding the problems of assessing what was at stake, the estate belonged to the parish's elected member of the legislative council, Rudolf Ehrenstein; see "Hon. Ehrenstein Answered", *Plain Talk* 4, no. 2, 15 January 1938, 1.
44. See James Robertson, "'The First of August, 1838, Never to Be Forgotten through All Generations': Recalling Emancipation in Spanish Town", *Jamaica Journal* 31, nos. 1–2 (2008): 44–52.
45. Commissioner Owen Wright to colonial secretary, 15 July 1939, minute 9, no. 37, JA 1B/5/79/735.
46. Alexander Bustamante to colonial secretary, 6 July 1934, item 34, JA 1B/5/79/735. On the mutual ambivalence of Kingston's Rastafari and Bustamante, see Chevannes, *Rastafari*, 147–51.
47. On the incorporation of the Ethiopian Salvation Society, see R.A. Leevy, "The Laird of Pinnacle", *New Negro Voice* 2, no. 28, 10 April 1943, 4; on the January date, see "Rules and Constitution of the 'Ethiopian Salvation Society, Friendly and Benevolent Society, Kingston, Jamaica'" (copy), 11 January 1939, item 57A, JA 1B/5/77 – 1934, no. 283; on dating the celebration, see Hill, *Dread History*, 59–60, n. 50; the incorporation of Howell's society occurred four months after the foundation of the first Jamaican chapter of the New York-based Ethiopian World Federation in August 1938, Charles Reavis Price, "'Cleave to the Black': Expressions of Ethiopianism in Jamaica", *New West Indian Guide* 77, nos. 1–2 (2003): 31–64, at 58–59; on the bakery, see Leevy, "The Laird of Pinnacle, Chapter II", *New Negro Voice* 2, no. 29, 17 April 1943, 4.
48. Wright to colonial secretary, 15 January 1940, item 35, JA 1B/5/79/735.
49. Ibid.; also attorney general to colonial secretary, 5 February 1940, minute 10, no. 42, and same to same, 15 February 1940, item 52.
50. Wright to colonial secretary, 29 January 1940, item 41, JA 1B/5/79/735.
51. Example, Altamont Reid, Philip Walker and R.N. White, Officers of Ethiopian King of Kings Salvation to Governor Edward Denham, [n.d.] June–July 1937, item 26, JA 1B/5/77 – 1934, no. 283.
52. "Ethiopian Salvation Society", CO 137/840/6, the National Archives, London (henceforth TNA); clipping from *Reynolds News*, 24 March 1940, annotated "I would like to

know more about the forbidding of meetings of the Ethiopian Salvation Society", 27 March 1940, item 1; on the fear of a parliamentary question, see minutes, 29 March 1940; on the transatlantic telephone call, see minutes, 10 April 1940. I am grateful to Christer Petley for copying this file for me. The minister's telegram, which has been removed from the London file, is secretary of state to governor, 29 March 1940, item 60, JA 1B/5/79/735 (two further copies are in 1B/5/76/68, "In-bound Telegrams, Secret and Confidential, 2 January 1940–27 August 1940").

53. Agreeing that Governor Richards made the right call, but commenting that "it is a pity he had to use the Emergency Regulations", Sir George Gates, 6 May 1940, minute 3, TNA, CO 137/840/6; regarding detectives at Bustamante's speech, see Philip Sherlock, *Norman Manley: A Biography* (London: Macmillan, 1980), 110; on the subsequent arrests, see Richard Hart, *Towards Decolonization: Political, Labour and Economic Developments in Jamaica, 1938–1945* (Kingston: University of the West Indies Press, 1999), 82–93. News of these arrests also spread widely, including mentions in both Britain's Communist *Daily Worker* and the English-language broadcasts from Nazi Berlin by "Lord Haw-Haw"; see Sherlock, *Norman Manley*, 108.

54. Britain's recognition of the Italians' de jure claim is noted in Haile Selassie, *My Life and Ethiopia's Progress, 1892–1937*, vol. 2, *Addis Ababa, 1966 E.C.*, ed. Harold G. Marcus, Ezekiel Gebissa and Tibebe Eshete (East Lansing: Michigan State University Press, 1994), 93; this British concession is further discussed in Alberto Sbacchi, *Legacy of Bitterness: Ethiopia and Fascist Italy, 1935–1941* (Lawrenceville, NJ: Red Sea Press, 1997), 287–300.

55. On Selassie's ambivalence about Britain's motives, which led him to open negotiations with the Americans in 1941, see Harold G. Marcus, *Ethiopia, Great Britain, and the United States, 1941–1974: The Politics of Empire* (Berkeley: University of California Press, 1983), 8–23; and more generally, Theodore M. Vestal, *The Lion of Judah in the New World: Emperor Haile Selassie of Ethiopia and the Shaping of Americans' Attitudes towards Africa* (Santa Barbara, CA: Praeger, 2011); besides, implicitly, the preface to G.L. Steer, *Sealed and Delivered: A Book on the Abyssinian Campaign* (London: Hodder, 1942), 2–3.

56. From the German seizure of Czechoslovakia in March 1939 to 10 June 1940 and his declaration of war, Mussolini sought to extort concessions from Britain in the Red Sea and the Suez Canal in exchange for Italy's continued neutrality; see Sbacchi, *Legacy of Bitterness*, 306–8. Given the Italian army's shortages of equipment, blackmail was a safer tactic; see Emanuele Sica, "June 1940: The Italian Army and the Battle of the Alps", *Canadian Journal of History* 47, no. 2 (2012): 356–78. On Ethiopia's wider strategic importance for Britain at this juncture, see Michael Carver, "Wavell and the War in the Middle East, 1940–1941", in *Adventures with Britannia: Personalities, Politics and Culture in Britain*, ed. Wm. Roger Louis (Austin: University of Texas Press, 1995), 217–33.

57. The initial project was proposed in late 1938, forwarded by the Sudan Defence Force to the Foreign Office in February 1939, while the first potential Ethiopian radio operators were recruited in March 1940. Mockler, in *Haile Selassie's War*, 196–97, 199–200, 203, citing Italian source Sbacchi, *Legacy of Bitterness*, dates this policy to summer 1939. Selassie had sent his own agent to Ethiopia in 1939, who returned to England in March 1940 with letters from local chieftains promising their support; see Steer, *Sealed and Delivered*, 8–9. On Selassie's use of these letters to help obtain formal British support for his claims in June 1940, see Steer, *Sealed and Delivered*, 18–20.
58. Richards to MacDonald, 9 April 1940, item 4, TNA CO 137/840/6; draft dispatch to secretary of state for the colonies, April 1940 item 63A, JA 1B/5/79/735. The original wording of the governor's concluding sentence had been both wordier and firmer: "I consider that if he should do so, such meetings should also be prohibited."
59. Wright to colonial secretary, 13 February 1940, minutes 13–14, no. 50, JA 1B/5/79/735.
60. Lee, *First Rasta*, 127–28; noting that Mr Chang had put the property up for sale on 10 March 1944, Wright to colonial secretary, 25 March 1944, minute 66, JA 1B/5/77, 1934, no. 283; describing the thoroughly confused tenural legacy of these procedures, D.A. Dunkley, "Occupy Pinnacle and the Rastafari's Struggle for Land in Jamaica", *Jamaica Journal* 35, nos. 1–2 (2014): 36–43.
61. R.A. Leevy, "The Laird of Pinnacle: Chapter III", *New Negro Voice* 2, no. 30, 24 April 1943, 4.
62. John Carradine, "The Ras Tafarites Retreat to Mountain Fastnesses of St Catherine", *Daily Gleaner* (magazine section), 23 November 1940, 26.
63. Chevannes, *Rastafari*, 124.
64. He may be the James Nelson of Duckenfield in St Thomas, fined fifty pounds for ganja possession in 1938. *Daily Gleaner*, 1 September 1938, 10.
65. Showing the wider circulation of the news, see "Emperor Beheads Stone Roman Eagle at Palace and Thanks Britain", *New York Times*, 11 May 1941, 16; "Selassie to Ease British Army Task: Intends to Release Troops Engaged in Ethiopia and Lend Aid Elsewhere", *New York Times*, 13 May 1941, 3; "Duke of Aosta Surrenders, Many Prisoners", *New York Times*, 22 May 1941, 5.
66. L.P.R. Browning, inspector in charge of St Catherine, to Commissioner Owen Wright, 18 June 1941 [unnumbered item], JA 1B/5/77 – 1934, no. 283. Nelson's note, dated 14 June 1941 and directed to "Sergeant Major, Spanish Town Police Station", and Sergeant Major Charles Malabre's cover note, 17 June 1943, were both copied as appendices to Browning's letter. For the St Thomas incident, see Lee, *First Rasta*, 111–14; the solicitor general's response, 24 June 1941, Memoranda, 5, JA 1B/5/77 – 1934, no. 283; cover note to colonial secretary, 18 June 1941.
67. Wright to colonial secretary, discussing Howell's arrest, 17 July 1941, Memoranda, JA 1B/5/77 – 1934, no. 283; Michael Hoenisch, "Symbolic Politics: Perceptions of the Early Rastafari Movement", *Massachusetts Review* 29, no. 3 (1988): 432–49.

68. "Cult Leader Held by Police in His Home", *Daily Gleaner*, 26 July 1941, 1; "'Ras Tafarian' Head Convicted at Spanish Town", *Daily Gleaner*, 25 August 1941, 16.
69. "Robbed, Tried, Found Guilty, Flogged by Ras Tafarians", *Daily Gleaner*, 9 July 1941, 1; "Police Raid 'Pinnacle', Ras Tafarian Den, Seize Seventy, But Miss Chief", *Daily Gleaner*, 15 July 1941, 1, 14; "Camera Record of Police Raid on Ras Tafaris at 'Pinnacle'", *Daily Gleaner*, 16 July 1941, 16; "No Trace Yet Found of Howell, Chief of 'Pinnacle'", *Daily Gleaner*, 17 July 1941, 1; "Three Freed in Pinnacle Camp Cases", *Daily Gleaner*, 23 July 1941, 9; "Cult Leader Held by Police in His Home", *Daily Gleaner*, 26 July 1941, 1; "Howell before R.M. Court in Spanish Town", *Daily Gleaner*, 29 July 1941, 14; "Charges against Howell to Be Heard Saturday", *Daily Gleaner*, 4 August 1941, 10; "'Ras Tafarian' Head Convicted at Spanish Town", *Daily Gleaner*, 25 August 1941, 16. For further recollections of the raid, Howell's initial evasion of capture and his sentence, see Lee, *First Rasta*, 145–50, 157–59.
70. The surprising absence of charges for growing ganja was the result of a protest made by Howell's lawyer, Frank A. Pixley, at a preliminary hearing, that the publication on 16 July in the *Daily Gleaner* of a photograph of a policeman holding a clump of marijuana plants was prejudicial. This contrasts with the way in which a later generation of Rastafarians describe how "Brother Howell was arrested and sent to prison for cultivating ganja", a retelling that places ganja-growing at the centre of both the Rastafarian movement and its clashes with the police. See Douglas R.A. Mack, *From Babylon to Rastafari: Origin and History of the Rastafarian Movement* (Chicago: Research Associates School Times Publications, 1999), 60. The claim is repeated in Yasus Afari, *Overstanding Rastafari: "Jamaica's Gift to the World"* (Kingston: Senya-Cum, 2007), 48–49.
71. On Howell's claim that he was Selassie, see "Cult Followers Sent to Prison", *Daily Gleaner*, 31 July 1941, 16; this was repeated in "Chieftain of Camp Pinnacle before Court", *Daily Gleaner*, 19 August 1941, 6.
72. Lorne, introduction to Howell, *Promised Key*, x.
73. Spencer, "First Chant", 362.
74. Howell, *Promised Key*, 1; statement by Jane Empty, 19 April 1933, JA 1B/5/79/735. Smith, Augier and Nettleford, in *Rastafari Movement*, 21, report remarkable elaborations on these stories, whereby the Duke of Gloucester was transformed into his eldest brother, the Duke of Windsor, the future Edward VIII. The duke's return from Ethiopia in 1930 then caused the death of George V (who actually died in 1936), while Edward VIII's abdication would allow him to succeed his niece, Elizabeth II, to "rule as the last king of Babylon" and witness Britain/Babylon's apocalyptic defeat.
75. Erna Brodber, in *The Second Generation of Freemen in Jamaica, 1907–1944* (Gainesville: University Press of Florida, 2004), explores both the social claustrophobia of this period and the appeal, within these narrow options, of "shifting", either physically by relocating or intellectually by changing congregations.

76. The Rastafarians remain the primary group maintaining this campaign. For other groups, the increased popular access to Jamaican politics achieved after 1938, along with independence in 1962, have placed building a better society on the island as a higher priority. However, while in the 1930s millenarian themes predominated, since the 1960s, when Rastafarian delegates visited Africa, their campaigns have emphasized practical issues, like British reparations to fund would-be migrants' passages. These seem nearer to the hopes of the British West India Regiment veterans who applied to the governor for passage in 1933, than to Howell's hopeful auditors in 1934. See Werner Zips, "'Repatriation is a Must!' The Rastafari Struggle to Utterly Downstroy Slavery", in *Rastafari: A Universal Philosophy in the Third Millennium*, ed. Werner Zips (Kingston: Ian Randle, 2006), 149–60. This is not to deny that millenarian themes remain, shaping popular Rastafarian images of an Africa where the hills are green with ganja; see L. Alan Eyre, "Biblical Symbolism and the Role of Fantasy Geography among the Rastafarians of Jamaica", *Journal of Geography* 84, no. 4 (1985): 144–48.
77. Amy Jacques Garvey, "My Husband's Back to Africa Idea Was Right", *Plain Talk* 1, no. 24, 19 October 1935, 5.
78. Leevy, "Laird of Pinnacle", 4; on some of the modern Rastafarian myths that invoke Garvey, see Barry Chevannes, "Garvey Myths among the Jamaican People", in *Garvey: His Work and Impact*, ed. Rupert Lewis and Patrick Bryan (Trenton, NJ: Africa World Press, 1991), 123–31.
79. Jahlani Niaah, "Sensitive Scholarship: A Review of Rastafari Literatures", in Nettleford and Salter, *Rastafari*, 74–75.
80. Rupert Lewis, *Walter Rodney's Intellectual and Political Thought* (Kingston: University of the West Indies Press, 1998), 99–101; on wider fears, see Terry Lacey, *Violence and Politics in Jamaica, 1960–70: Internal Security in a Developing Country* (Manchester: Manchester University Press, 1977), 81–85.
81. Ian Fleming, *The Man with the Golden Gun* (New York: New American Library, 1965), 100. Fleming's copy editors missed the substitution of King Zog (1895–1961), the exiled king of Albania, for the Emperor Haile Selassie.
82. Smith, Augier and Nettleford, *Rastafari Movement*, 36, 3; regarding the demonstration, see "Visit of Russian Ships to Jamaica", TNA FCO 141/5406/67.
83. Item 2, JA 1B/5/79/735.
84. Howell's use of the Anglican *Hymns Ancient and Modern* was feasible enough, as not only were his father and grandfather both Anglicans, but his father was an Anglican lay preacher; see Lee, *First Rasta*, 11, 13. However, this practice contrasts with George Simpson's experience in 1953, when the singing at Rastafarian meetings in Kingston combined original songs with "modified Sankey and Methodist hymns"; see Simpson, "Personal Recollections", 222. Ira D. Sankey (1840–1908)

was an influential American gospel singer whose hymns were widely adopted by evangelical congregations.
85. This claim for the colours of the Virgin's robe differed from the western European artistic tradition, where painters use blue. Michael Baxandall, *Painting and Experience in Fifteenth-Century Italy: A Primer in the Social History of Pictorial Style* (Oxford: Oxford University Press, 1972), 82–83.
86. For notes on Joseph Nathaniel Hibbert as an early preacher of Haile Selassie who joined Howell and subsequently founded the Ethiopian Coptic Church, see Smith, Augier and Nettleford, *Rastafari Movement*, 5–7.
87. Item 7, JA 1B/5/79/735.
88. Item 7, JA 1B/5/79/735. Quotation marks were added in a different ink alongside each direct quote from Howell's speech.
89. Commenting that "O.H.M.S." was a generally recognized abbreviation on official mail for "On His Majesty's Service", Lee suggests that Howell's application of it here with reference to Haile Selassie was a further expression of disloyalty. *First Rasta*, 69.
90. Item 35A, JA 1B/5/79/735; a further copy, item 4, TNA CO 137/840/6. Enclosure is the copy sent to the secretary of state for the colonies.
91. Typed as "of" in the National Archives copy.
92. On the TNA CO 137 copy, an administrator's footnote appeared in ink: "Considered sufficient I suppose, as a place to go to."
93. I have not located the origin of this "enamel plate" story, but given the context of the early months of the war, the incident that Howell referred to was drawn from a period when the British royal family exerted themselves to share their subjects' wartime experiences, which could lead to occasions where the palace's gold plates might well be replaced by enamel at a royal visit to a barracks or hospital.
94. Copy enclosed in Inspector L.P.R. Browning to Commissioner Owen Wright, 18 June 1941, JA 1B/5/77 – 1934, no. 283.
95. Reginald Charles Waters, born in England, 1886, served as a sergeant in Canada's North West Mounted Police, was a lieutenant and then captain with the Jamaica Contingent of volunteers during the First World War, serving between 1915 and 1919, and was appointed an inspector of police on his return. In 1937, he was based at Morant Bay. L.A. Thoywell-Henry, ed., *Who's Who and Why in Jamaica, 1939–40* (Kingston: Who's Who [Jamaica], 1940), 191.

4

LEONARD P. HOWELL'S LEADERSHIP OF THE RASTAFARI MOVEMENT AND HIS "MISSING YEARS"

D.A. DUNKLEY

A **symposium held** at the University of the West Indies, Mona, in June 2011 highlighted the need to reassess the "disappearance" or "missing years" of Leonard Percival Howell.[1] Members of the audience, such as the well-known Jamaican Rastafarian and dub poet Mutabaruka, used those terms in reference to Howell's activities after the police had raided his community of Pinnacle a second time in 1954 and went back a third time in 1958 to clear the community of its remaining residents. No one in the audience offered any explanation as to Howell's alleged "disappearance". All seemed to agree that this is the best term to use when referring to Howell during the post-raids period.

Howell was one of the founding leaders of the Rastafari movement in Jamaica, and to some he was the actual "First Rasta".[2] The claim that he disappeared after either 1958 or 1960, that his leadership of the Rastafari stopped, and that almost no one heard about him or interacted with him again until the announcement of his death in 1981, is not valid. This essay will show that a viable point of departure is to view Howell's conduct in the post-raids period as a new approach taken to continue the work he had been doing in previous years. For this work, Howell was persecuted by the colonial government, which saw his influence as a destabilizing force, and by local nationalists, who viewed him as a serious contender for the loyalties of the majority of Jamaicans, who were of African descent. This persecution warranted a new strategy by Howell in order to continue his resistance to colonial ideology and the undermining of the potential of black Jamaicans, who had already been displaced by traumatic enslavement and the continuation of British colonial rule.

The Political Context

Highlighting the context of the beginning of the Rastafari movement under Howell's leadership is important in order to understand the challenges faced by Howell and the early Rastafari as the movement evolved, as Rastafarians believed, in fulfilment of biblical prophecy. Howell returned to Jamaica in 1932, two years after the coronation of Ethiopian emperor Haile Selassie I in Addis Ababa. The coronation inspired Africans all over the world into believing that their condition was about to improve significantly, since it was established that Haile Selassie I was the descendant of the wise and celebrated kings Solomon and David, who were the saviours of their people. Howell was one of the first to preach the divinity of the emperor in Jamaica, the notion that his coronation was the realization of prophecy and that the emperor was the "eschatological figure" or "eschatological person designated *the Messiah*".[3] Howell participated in renewing the optimism of black Jamaicans with his promise of liberation from oppressive British colonialism and white supremacy. African Jamaicans naturally linked their poverty to colonial rule and to their enslavement by the British up to 1834.[4]

Howell returned to a Jamaica undergoing change caused by "the spread to Jamaica of the general feeling of unrest and even rebellion in the British West Indies", mainly among the working class.[5] The problems of low wages and exploitative working conditions had continued into the twentieth century. Labourers were being organized by middle-class agitators, such as Alexander Bustamante and Norman Manley, who then made the transition into political leadership and formed political parties that relied on the organized labour movement for support. Jamaica's acquisition of universal adult suffrage in 1944 led to a general election in that year, and the two main parties which contested that election were Bustamante's Jamaica Labour Party (JLP) and Manley's People's National Party (PNP). The victory went to the JLP, which would lead Jamaica until the third general elections in 1955, when Manley emerged victorious. Manley, winning the general elections again in 1959, would continue to lead the partially democratic government until April 1962, just prior to independence.[6] However, it was Bustamante who earned the distinction of being the leader of the Jamaican government at the moment that the nation-state was formed, with the acquisition of independence from Britain on 6 August 1962. Among the nationalists, Bustamante was also, importantly, the most aggressive of the self-appointed opponents of Howell during the late colonial period.

The Other Nationalism

Much to his disadvantage, Howell offered a different kind of nationalism to the one that was offered by the political and labour leaders, namely Bustamante and Manley. Howell appealed for identification with Africa, while Bustamante and Manley were offering a Jamaican creole nationalism. Howell, in effect, made himself an opponent of the labour nationalists, even though he appealed not to the working class but to the peasantry, who subsisted and earned their living through small farming. It seems Howell knew he could not contend with Bustamante and Manley for leadership of the working class. What Howell had to his benefit was that the peasantry had been without significant leadership since 1921, when Alexander Bedward, who was the preacher of a church in the African-based Native Baptist tradition in St Andrew, just north of the island's capital of Kingston, was sent to the mental asylum by the colonial government.[7] Bedward was kept there until his death in 1930.

Marcus Garvey, who had also inspired the peasantry, returned to Jamaica in 1927, his reputation somewhat damaged by his conviction for mail fraud in the United States and his deportation to Jamaica in exchange for early release. Though his movement remained strong in the United States and Jamaica, Garvey faced difficulty pursuing his political aspirations in Jamaica.[8] Even with many of Bedward's peasant followers joining the Garvey movement after Bedward's confinement, Garvey was unable to win a seat in the 1930 Jamaican elections. His People's Political Party, formed in 1929, "had mass support and fielded three candidates" for those elections, but none won a seat. This was mainly due to the fact that most of his supporters were disenfranchised. But an unintended consequence of this defeat was that the peasantry in many parts of the island, though inspired by Garvey, were still virtually leaderless. They also needed a leader who was speaking directly and exclusively about their need for land on which to build homes and cultivate. Garvey took on a multiplicity of issues almost all at once, and increasingly confined his speeches to Kingston and St Andrew, especially in the years after the purchase of Edelweiss Park, in Cross Roads, Kingston, in 1929, which "became a centre for spiritual upliftment, self-improvement, political indoctrination and purposeful recreation".[9]

Since a great proportion of the peasantry could not read, Garvey's newspapers *Blackman* and *New Jamaican* and his *Black Man* magazine could only reach them through the minority who were functionally literate. Howellites have also reported that there was tension between Howell and Garvey after the former's return to Jamaica in 1932. Accordingly, Sister Hodesh, a Howellite and a director of the L.P. Howell Foundation in Kingston, has stated that formerly, "the Howell clan and Marcus were very close", and "Mr Howell dined with Marcus every Thursday on [Howell's] return to Jamaica" in 1932, but a rift developed after Garvey reputedly called Howell's "Rastafari movement a clan", meaning a cult, and "the first time Gong [Howell] got locked up in JA was the result of the Garveyites".[10] Documented verification of this has not been forthcoming. However, it is still apparent that some amount of animosity existed between Garvey and Howell over the Rastafari movement, which would have insulted Garvey's traditional Christian beliefs. Though Garvey initially saw the coronation of Emperor Haile Selassie I as a great event in the struggle for African nationalism, unification and uplift, unlike the Rastafari, he did not view the emperor as a Messiah in the biblical sense; further, we have Garvey's discontinuation of his support for the emperor in 1937, a stance never taken by the Rastafari, as one piece of evidence of his disagreement with Rastafari beliefs. Garvey had criticized the emperor "as a great coward" for choosing exile in London following the Italian invasion of Ethiopia in 1935, an invasion which Garvey said "he brought upon them because of his political ignorance and his racial disloyalty".[11]

The leadership vacuum with respect to the peasantry was filled by Howell. He accomplished this with a powerful message of black liberation that was similar to Bedward's message, one that relied on biblical prophecy. Howell had the benefit of an event that had occurred in recent memory, the grand coronation of Ras Tafari (Haile Selassie I) as emperor of Ethiopia in 1930, an event that his followers knew about and saw as a great sign of black improvement in the future. The coronation and its grandness appeared only to validate Howell's message that the emperor's ascension was indeed the promised return of the Messiah, and that he had returned to enable the redemption of African people around the world.

Howell seems to have underestimated the impact of his decision to preach the divinity of Emperor Haile Selassie I on the colonial government. As early as 1933, he was placed under police surveillance in Kingston, which continued even after he migrated most of his preaching to the rural parish of St Thomas, in the eastern section of the island.[12] In time, the police built up what they considered a valid case against Howell and his lieutenant, Robert Hinds. Both were charged with "sedition" and then tried and convicted in the courthouse in Morant Bay, the capital of St Thomas, in March 1934.[13] Sedition, though a lesser offence than treason, was nonetheless viewed by the colonial authorities as a serious crime, warranting court action. Sedition, in the case against Howell, meant talking against the government in Jamaica and Britain, and against the Queen of England, for which Howell received two years at hard labour, while Hinds was given the shorter sentence of one year at hard labour because of the view that he was acting under orders from Howell. Without a doubt, the target was Howell, and the reason was that he had been offering blacks an alternative to British rule, one that was based on the religious notion of a black Messiah who was "King of Kings and Lord of Lords of Ethiopia", sent to redeem "all who believe in the power of the true and living God".[14]

One of the main reasons for the counteraction from the colonial authorities was that Howell had made himself appear as an unstoppable force during these years. He was in prison when his book, *The Promised Key*, was published. Appearing in 1935, the book gave the impression of a war declaration against colonialism and white rule. This small but powerful book became very popular. Its circulation was enhanced by its heavy reliance on other works, such as Robert Athlyi Rogers's *Holy Piby: The Blackman's Bible* and Fitz Balintine Pettersburgh's *Royal Parchment Scroll of Black Supremacy*, both published in the 1920s. In spite of its grammatical errors and apparent plagiarism,[15] Howell's book was seen as significant and troublesome, and he was eventually sent to the mental asylum in Kingston in 1938.[16] Howell had brazenly made inflammatory statements in the book, such as labelling the Roman Catholic pope as "Satan the devil". He referred to preachers in Jamaica as false prophets. He objected to locally made religious systems such as Revivalism and the folk practice known as Obeah. He called the latter witchcraft and advised adherents that they would be barred forever from the "balm yard" of Rastafari, where there was redemption and liberation. Most importantly, Howell mentioned "white supremacy", which in his view would be replaced by "Black Supremacy", a provocative idea that drove more fear into the authorities receiving regular updates on Howell's activities from the colonial police force.[17]

Howell had an alternative nationalism steeped in the tradition of Ethiopianism. Louis Moyston has argued that Howell was exposed to this movement in the United States, as well as to Garveyism, which was also deeply influenced by Ethiopianism in the Caribbean, Central America and the United States.[18] Referring specifically to Jamaica, Robert Hill states that "there had been in existence in Jamaica, prior to the coronation event in Ethiopia in 1930, a considerable tradition of 'Ethiopianism'", and "the 1930s in Jamaica witnessed the full flowering of Ethiopianism as a broad-based popular movement".[19] Influenced by this focus on Ethiopia, Howell challenged creole nationalism and the means through which it was infiltrating the popular consciousness of the Jamaican masses: the trade union movement. In his 1935 book, Howell argued that countries such as Jamaica "are at this junction of our history scattered"; however, "all our local bands throughout the globe are bent towards King Alpha's Royal Repository. The Royal Authority is to admit all Bands, Mission Camps, Denominations into the supreme Royal Repository." In other words, while the ideal was the physical return to Africa of its entire people, who had been forcibly removed by slavery and colonialism, there was still hope of salvation and liberation for those who desired to stay outside of the African continent. This was possible, however, only through those groups accepting the "Royal Authority" of the emperor of Ethiopia, wherever they might be in their "sectional groups", which were "scattered over the globe".[20]

When Howell advised that the trade unions were not to be trusted and suggested that they should not aid in the construction of the future identity of Jamaica as a liberated nation, Bustamante, naturally, reacted aggressively. Bustamante wrote in 1939 to the colonial secretary of Jamaica, C.C. Woolley, warning that Howell was "a danger to the peace of the Community" and should be seen as "the greatest danger that exists in this country today". Bustamante added that "the only right and proper place for this man is the Asylum", which "the police can confirm"[21] (see figure 4.1). Later, Howell was also attacked by opponents of Bustamante who themselves were also creole nationalists. R.A. Leevy, a writer for the leftist newspaper *Public Opinion*, which was tied to

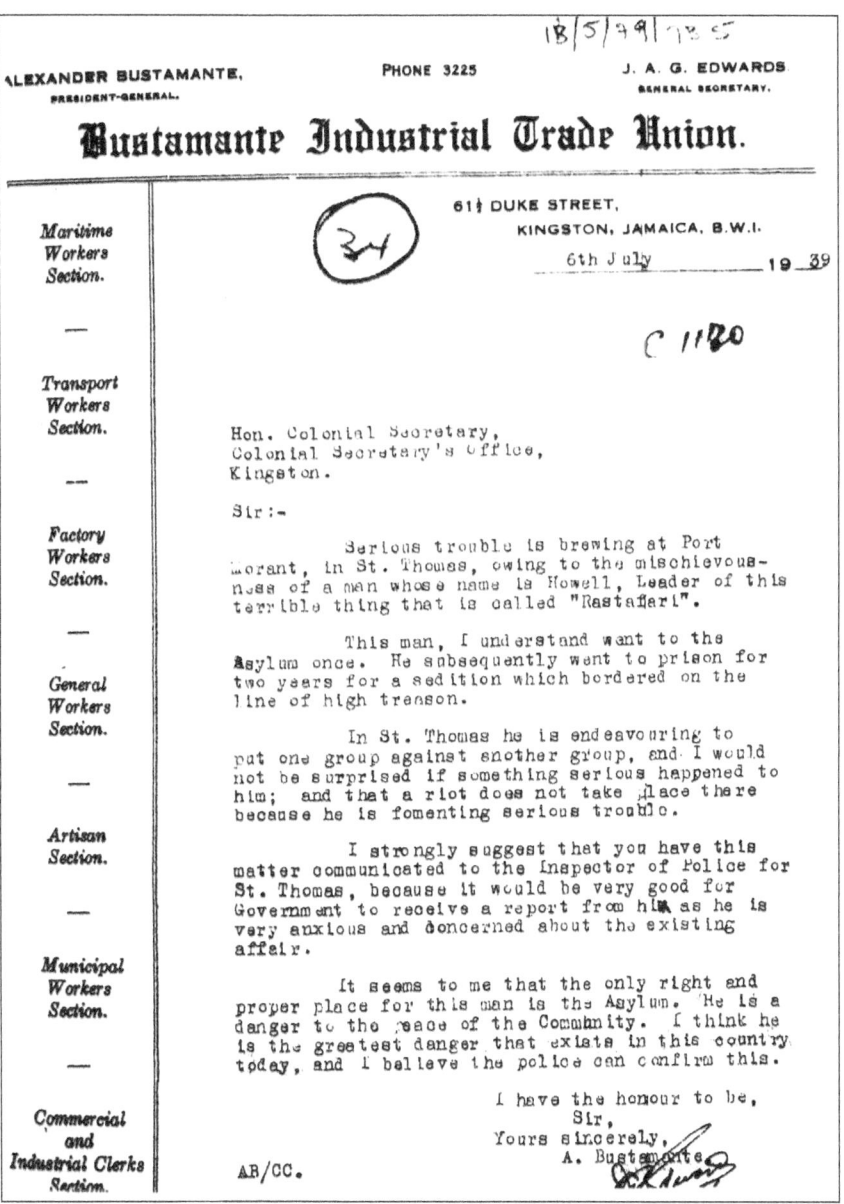

Figure 4.1. Letter from Alexander Bustamante about Leonard Howell, Kingston, 6 July 1939. Courtesy of the Jamaica Archives, Spanish Town.

Manley's PNP, wrote a four-part article on Howell and the Rastafari movement that was published in 1943. Leevy made it clear to Howell in the interview used in the article that most Jamaicans were not followers of Rastafari and would never regard Emperor Haile Selassie I as the Messiah.[22]

Howell's Leadership

The leadership Howell gave to the peasantry was charismatic and authoritarian. According to O. Nigel Bolland, early labour leaders in the Caribbean, such as Bustamante, were the same kind of "charismatic authoritarian" leaders.[23] Also worrying to a labour leader such as Bustamante would have been the fact that Howell appeared when there was conflict between Bustamante and other labour leaders. Richard Lachmann has described this kind of environment of conflict among the leading social groups as one which makes collective action by the masses more feasible, or one where "opportunities and alliances which can justify the risks of collective activism" suddenly appear.[24] Race was also important. Howell was clearly black and therefore had a connection with the Jamaican majority that neither Bustamante nor Manley had. Bustamante, nonetheless, tried to position himself as an advocate of all poor people in Jamaica, which was noticeable during his campaign speeches for the 1944 election.[25] Manley avoided race as much as he could, advocating instead the political ideology of Fabian socialism to achieve an egalitarian and just society in which all Jamaicans, despite race, ethnicity and class, could anticipate improvement.[26]

Howell used mysticism in his teaching, which enhanced his leadership, and which none of the labour nationalists incorporated or perhaps could have incorporated into their leadership. Howell did not, for example, declare himself as the author of *The Promised Key* but instead used the pseudonym G.G. Maragh. This can be seen as hidden resistance, an effort to mask his identity from the colonial authorities. However, it was also a form of mysticism because of the Hindu connection. When "G.G. Maragh" was expanded, it became "Gangunguru" or "Gong" Maragh, names which Howellites used for their leader after 1935.[27] Howell had been born in the parish of Clarendon in 1898.[28] This was where most of Jamaica's thirty-seven thousand Indians had arrived in the period between 1845 and 1916, when the indentured labour system which brought them to the island was stopped.[29] Other aspects of Hindu culture were adopted by Howell, such as the smoking of ganja (marijuana) as a sacrament, which in Hinduism is referred to as a type of *sadhana* that gives the ability to communicate better with God, with the high from smoking called *prasad*, or a blessing.[30]

With the establishment of the Ethiopian Salvation Society (ESS) in 1937, Howell showed that he was the kind of leader who fulfilled his promises. One objective of the organization was the use of collective savings to better its members. The constitution of the ESS also proposed to assist with "the propagation of the Christian religion and the message of salvation", and dedicated the organization to "the inculcation of the principles of Self-help and *good citizenship*" (my emphasis).[31] With these, the ESS was shielded from the suspicion that it was promoting sedition. Howell had learned how to circumvent some of the attempts to suppress his activities. The ESS used the image of the "Christian Black", which, as Horace Russell has recounted, was developed mainly during the first half of the nineteenth century to create "an image or stereotype for the British public who had to be convinced that emancipation was necessary".[32] In Howell's hands, this same image became a way to capitalize on a stereotype to protect an organization that was working towards black improvement inside a hostile colonial environment.

Not long after the formation of the ESS, however, the colonial government parted with the view that the Rastafari movement had diminished because of Howell's imprisonment and therefore "need not be seriously regarded".[33] Howell's subsequent confinement in the asylum in 1938 could be viewed as one of the results of this renewal of his suppression. Clearly, interest in his leadership increased after 1937, and even his letters overseas were monitored. In 1939, one of these was intercepted in London, and a copy sent back to the colonial secretary in Jamaica. It uncovered Howell's connection with the International African Services Bureau in London, to which he had sent a donation of five pounds to help with its work. The letter was also addressed to the known Marxist and pan-Africanist George Padmore, a fellow West Indian born in Trinidad but living in London at the time.[34] Significantly, the letter showed that Howell was no longer to be seen as a threat only to Jamaica. He was reaching across the Atlantic, capitalizing on and helping to develop the international network of pan-Africanists. Howell's view of the future of the Rastafari movement was a global view of the liberation of black people, of course a view that none of Jamaica's creole nationalists could link to their cause. The resentment created by Howell's organization and internalization effort was seen in 1940, when the Jamaican governor yielded to pressure from the colonial secretary and the labour leadership, and banned a further meeting of the ESS that was to take place in Morant Bay, St Thomas.[35]

In many ways, the community known as Pinnacle marked the highest point of Howell's leadership during the colonial period, and therefore was seen as the greatest threat to the stability of the Jamaican society. It was famously situated about five miles from Sligoville, in the hills of St Catherine. The selection of a location near to Sligoville was symbolic, because Sligoville had been the first free village established to house ex-slaves in Jamaica, and the land had been paid for by the ex-slaves themselves. Situated where it was, Pinnacle was also strategically isolated and protected from intrusion without detection. Its residents could see as far as sections of the Kingston waterfront on a clear day. Howell leased the property, but the arrangement was to buy it over time. According to Howell's secretary, Gertrude Campbell, Howellites have claimed that he did complete the payments to the Chinese businessman Albert Chang, and might have even paid for the land up to "two time" [sic].[36] The cost was twelve hundred pounds for somewhere between 200 and 600 acres of land. There is still uncertainty as to the exact size, but every estimate places it above 150 acres.[37]

Pinnacle was by no means a "marginal" accomplishment; neither was it marginal in terms of the subsequent development of the Rastafari movement.[38] Howell had sold, at one shilling each, about five thousand copies of his picture postcards of Emperor Haile Selassie I, sales which were enhanced by their marketing as "passports to Ethiopia".[39] The money from these sales would have made a contribution to the lease or purchase arrangement regarding Pinnacle, in which case the property was the result of black entrepreneurship and financial management. Contribution would have also come from sales of his 1935 book, *The Promised Key*, and the funds of the ESS, making Pinnacle the materialization of the aims of the organization to promote self-help and salvation among Jamaica's African descendants. Wherever the money came from, Pinnacle remained the first real proof of Rastafari self-reliance and was evidence of Howell's capacity to lead the movement in the direction of that goal.

Suppression and Its Failures

One of the reasons Howell's suppression was intensified after the establishment of the community at Pinnacle was the success of this community. Pinnacle indicated confirmation of what Hill has dubbed the "dual nature" of Howell's leadership.[40] In this sense, Howell was altogether a spiritual or prophetic or mystical leader and one who took up the task of providing political directorship and business management for his following. Simply put, Howell traversed religious and secular realms in terms of his role as a leader. Some seven hundred people were drawn to Pinnacle the same year it started.[41] Its populace "rapidly expanded to embrace hundreds".[42] They were attracted by the symbolic spiritual and material improvement, the opportunity to worship together while also working individually or as families for subsistence and to earn a living. They cultivated a range of food crops, burned coal, operated a bakery, made crafts and household articles, and raised livestock, all for their own consumption and for selling to neighbouring villagers.

Pinnacle, therefore, represented black entrepreneurship and empowerment through strong leadership and organization, or as Michael Hoenisch has explained, "A 'microphysics' of power was developed which organized the members of the commune under black control."[43] Obviously, all this was a challenge to colonial domination and a working alternative to the middle-class leadership by Jamaica's creole nationalists. Howell further enhanced the intellectual side of his leadership with the creation of a newspaper, *The People's Voice*, which doubled as a mouthpiece for Rastafari doctrine.[44] In this, Howell was navigating landscape previously cornered by Manley, the intellectual alternative to Bustamante. Howell had assumed the respective intellectual and populist capacities of his two adversaries for leadership of the Jamaican people.

The first attempt to suppress Pinnacle was an effort to label the community a "communist" experiment in 1941.[45] Within the context of Britain's war against Nazi Germany and fascist Italy (the Second World War), the possibility of communism in Jamaica awakened the fear of a totalitarian takeover to replace the individualism of the colonial social and economic order. Unfounded and inaccurate, this fear was nonetheless fuelled by the prospect of an alien ideology taking root in Jamaica and aggravated by the reports of Howell's autocratic trials, whippings and expulsions of people from Pinnacle he deemed as "undesirables".[46] The first raid on Pinnacle, on 14 July 1941, took place within this context, and the contingent of 115 police, "half of them armed",[47] signalled the seriousness of the decision to suppress the community. The raid was able to materialize because of an allegation that Howell was harbouring at Pinnacle a man named James Nelson, who later disclosed in a note to police that he "was informed that the police is out with a warrant for my arrest, wanted for fire arms, my reason why I could not turn up before now, is I was away making preparation with some Fire Arms, and, I can be found at Pinnacle, everyday or anyday, if you should insist, or anxious to intrude on my liberty".[48] Two warrants were secured ahead of the raid, but neither of these was executed. Neither Nelson nor Howell was found. Howell, however, was captured on the night of 25 July when the police returned for another search. Nelson was still not found and was never mentioned again. Howell was charged with "four counts" of assault, along with seventy other males from the community who had been arrested on 14 July. The evidence used to make these arrests was collected from residents of the surrounding communities, who were brought to Pinnacle by the police on the day of the raid "to identify the assailants", though only twenty-eight convictions were made based on this evidence. Howell was sentenced to two more years at hard labour.[49]

The suspicious way in which the evidence was collected against Howell and his people in 1941 is another part of the story of their suppression that deserves its own attention in another article. Important here are the events in the aftermath of that raid, including the subsequent actions by the police. In 1945, the *Daily Gleaner*, the island's biggest newspaper, published an article informing the public that Howell and his people had been ejected by the police from Pinnacle. The celebratory tone of this article, entitled "Jamaica's Great Rastafari Kingdom Comes to an End", was a clear indication that the newspaper shared the colonial powers' anxiety about Pinnacle and their eagerness to see the community and its leader undermined.[50] The 1941 convictions had only temporarily succeeded in removing Howell and also only some of his followers from the community. Following this, an attempt was made in 1944 to sell Pinnacle, and three prospective buyers expressed their interest in purchasing the property.[51] Uncertainty regarding the ownership of Pinnacle was probably the reason the sale either did not take place or was not effective in permanently removing Howell and his people from the property. They were still there in 1954 and 1958, when the second and third police incursions took place.

The raid in 1954 was arguably the biggest, resulting in the convictions of 140 men and women from Pinnacle, including Howell. Howell was, however, acquitted after he appealed. His followers received sentences ranging from six months to two years at hard labour. Among them were old women and teenagers. The strategy had changed to undermining Howell by imprisoning his followers. However, Pinnacle survived, and even after the raid and ejection in 1958, coordinated again by the police, with help from "concerned" civilians, it did not succeed in ending the community or Howell's presence there. Additionally, after the 1941 incursion, it was ganja cultivation and possession that were used to justify the subsequent police actions against Pinnacle. However, ganja had been illegal in Britain since 1924. With the failure of the 1941 raid to permanently destroy Pinnacle, ganja cultivation and possession were identified – especially after 1948, when the Dangerous Drugs Law of Jamaica was amended to make the "possession, cultivation and use" of ganja into "punishable offence[s]"[52] – as the only other prosecutable charges that could validate the return of the police to the community. In other words, ganja cultivation and possession were never the motive for any of the raids, merely the means identified to authenticate or legitimize the actions of the police, and the measures seen as potentially effective in ending Howell's leadership of the community.

The Matter of Howell's Disappearance

When the police did a survey of the Rastafari in Jamaica following the 1958 raid, they discovered exactly what the government was now eager to hear. The number of Rastas in the island had declined to a mere 1,640.[53] However, what the police strategically did not emphasize was that the movement had spread to ten of the island's fourteen parishes. Numerically smaller, the Rastafari were, however, in a better position to spread their influence even further over the coming years. Indicating this potential were the attempts by various political parties to solicit the assistance of the Rastafari in their own efforts to win popular support. These parties, namely the People's Freedom Movement and the Progressive Independence Party, felt that the Rastafari were still influential and that there was a good possibility that this influence would continue and even grow.[54]

All of this suggested that the momentum Howell had created in helping to build the Rastafari movement had not diminished, nor were the results of his hard work erased by the attempts made to suppress him. Pinnacle became a legend to many of the new Rasta communities that began appearing in the 1950s and afterwards. Hélène Lee has correctly observed that each of these communities was "in effect a miniature Pinnacle".[55] The connection was probably due to the mysticism surrounding Howell, which he himself had cultivated. As his long-time secretary Gertrude Campbell commented years later, Howell was simply "not a man what's easy to know".[56]

Even after the 1958 raid and his subsequent confinement again for about a year in the mental asylum in 1960, Howell did not abandon Pinnacle. He was still living there as well as at South Camp Road, Kingston, where he also had a house.[57] Dividing his time between the two places made it harder for the police to monitor his activities. Howell's adoption of this strategy showed that he had reached a clearer understanding of the operations of the state police and of how he could possibly avoid further harassment by the force. It was also necessary to embark on a new strategy because his name had been mentioned at the trial of fellow Rastafari leader Claudius Henry, who was tried for and found guilty of treason in 1960. The judge, summing up this trial, had expressed the view that "a man called Leonard Howell", in his own time, had "assumed exactly the same role as Henry now assumes – a self-appointed prophet to lead the people of Jamaica back to Africa".[58] In other words, Howell's influence was still very present, even if only at the inspirational level, and the authorities were well aware of this, despite the fact that in 1960, the year of Henry's trial, Howell himself was under confinement in the asylum in Kingston.

So while it is true that Howell had "receded into the background",[59] it is certainly not accurate to also state that he was overcome by a "deep sense of isolation and weariness", as Lee proposes.[60] If he had been weary, then his presence and activities at Pinnacle would have ceased in 1960, after the year in the asylum. Not only was this not the case, but Howell was also still engaged in the cultivation of ganja at Pinnacle, alongside providing leadership for the (albeit smaller) number of adherents who had remained living at the community. As late as 1978, for example, Howell was convicted for the "possession of 15 pounds of ganja" and "fined $1,200" after being invaded by "gunmen" looking for marijuana.[61] The next year, the *Daily Gleaner* again reported that "gunmen" had invaded Pinnacle and found Howell there with some of his people, and demanded that they hand over any ganja that they had. Howell refused, and the gunmen searched and left the property without further trouble.[62] It is quite likely that a number of such invasions took place in the 1970s, especially as the economy plummeted and hardship increased after 1974, when Michael Manley announced that his government would adopt democratic socialism.[63] More certainly, there were a number of police raids on Pinnacle for the purpose of ganja eradication during the 1960s and 1970s.[64]

These events were making Howell more visible than he wanted to be. They kept his name in the media, even though Howell's approach had changed to remaining (rather than receding) in the background. In other words, he was not allowed to disappear or to remain missing, even if this was his intention. In 1971, and again in 1973, he was involved in cases at the Home Circuit Court, Kingston, as the defendant, possibly over the dispute with regards to his ownership of Pinnacle.[65] Barry Chevannes also noted that "a core of Howell's following did remain" close to Pinnacle, mostly "out in Tredegar Park", St Catherine; they had "scattered" or were "dispersed", but they remained as Rastafari adherents and still regarded Howell as their spiritual and temporal leader.[66] The *Daily Gleaner* reported in May 1979 that "several families live on the property [Pinnacle] where a wide variety of agricultural products are grown, donkeys reared and coal burnt".[67] Chevannes further stated that Howell carefully chose the people who were allowed to gain access to him and added that he himself, despite being a known Rastafari scholar who was teaching at the University of the West Indies, was not allowed to interview Howell. Chevannes noted, however, that Howell was not completely cut off from the outside world, and conjectured that had he been persistent in his efforts to meet with Howell, "maybe [he] would have got through".[68]

Other considerations would have been weighing heavily on Howell's mind during those first two decades of Jamaica's post-independence period. While the country became independent of British rule in 1962, the government for the first ten years was a JLP government. Bustamante, Howell's main nationalist rival, was the first prime minister of independent Jamaica and remained in that office until his retirement from politics in 1967. Coming out of the Henry affair in 1960, the government of independent Jamaica was still reluctant to grant the Rastafari the same accommodations as the Christian groups with longer associations with the country. Panic quickly overcame the government when, in 1963, two Rastas in the parish of St James committed arson in reaction to their persecution by another civilian. The government dispatched the police and army to round up all of the Rastafarians in western Jamaica. Today, the memory of what is referred to as the Coral Gardens Massacre understandably resurrects resentment for the JLP among the Rastafari community. One of the persons who were present can only remember that "dem bruk up a lot of batons on innocent Rastas at the time".[69] And despite having enabled the visit of Emperor Haile Selassie I to Jamaica in 1966, that same year the JLP government broke up Rasta communities in western Kingston, forcing many to the rural town of Bull Bay, in order to create the low-income housing community known as Tivoli Gardens. Tivoli would subsequently become a major stronghold of the JLP, one of Jamaica's notorious garrison communities that was eventually overrun by violent gangs involved in gunrunning and the illegal drug trade.

In many ways, the banning of Walter Rodney from Jamaica in 1968 was linked to the Rastafarians. Rodney, a historian of Guyanese birth who taught at the University of the West Indies, had included the Rastafari among the communities and groups with which he interacted and discussed black consciousness.[70] It was feared that Rodney was promoting a black nationalist and Marxist revolution in Jamaica, hence the declaration by the JLP government that he was a "persona non grata".[71] This indicated that as late as the end of the 1960s, there was still a great deal of anxiety about ideologically motivated groups such as the Rastafari and their potential to participate in anti-government activities. It was the kind of situation that Leonard Howell knew well, having been a prime target of government suppression during the colonial period. Norman Manley's decision to commission a study of the Rastafari, which was done in Kingston by three academics from the University of the West Indies in 1960, offered Howell only a modicum of hopefulness that the anxiety regarding the Rastafari in general was abating.[72] Similarly, the two missions that went to Africa in 1961 and 1962, though both were inspired by the Rastafari's longstanding interest in physical repatriation to the continent, involved only marginal input from the Rastafari brethren and were monopolized by the government.[73]

It seemed, as would become more evident during the 1970s when Norman Manley's son Michael was the prime minister, that even though there was interest in Africa and the African contribution to Jamaica, the Rastafari were sidelined in these developments. Michael Manley's cultural policy, for example, was formulated to promote the political ideology of democratic socialism, which was more aligned to Europe than Africa, and with input mainly from academics, such as his cultural adviser Rex Nettleford,[74] whose interests tended more towards developing the creole identity of Jamaica, rather than fully reorientating Jamaican culture as an African culture in accordance with Afrocentric messages, such as those of Howell and the Rastafari movement as a whole.[75] Sensing that the government was making political use of Africa without taking any serious decision to accommodate the Rastafari doctrine in these and previous developments, Howell decided not to make an appearance at the airport when Emperor

Haile Selassie I arrived as a guest of the government of Jamaica in 1966. Instead, according to the Howellites, Howell sent a contingent of his people and was therefore present in spirit to honour the emperor, without showing any accordance with the direction that had been taken by the Jamaican government.[76]

In 1981, when Howell died, he had witnessed the unsuccessful attempts of Rastafari leaders to gain entry into mainstream politics, and also their betrayal by the political establishment. The most famous case of the former was that of Ras Samuel Brown, who established his own party, the Suffering People's Party (also known as the Black Man's Party), and vied for political office in the 1961 general elections, but received insufficient votes.[77] During the 1960s and 1970s, Rastafari's music, reggae, was used by the two main political parties to enhance their campaigns among the poor communities across the island. However, when these same musicians turned their lyrics towards criticizing government policies, the parties that had once supported their music used their position as the government to declare those songs inappropriate for airplay. There was, for example, the infamous banning by the JLP of the song "Everything Crash", written by the Rastafari group the Ethiopians. And in the 1970s, reggae artiste Max Romeo, after releasing the song "No, Joshua, No" criticizing Michael Manley, "voluntarily" left Jamaica and went to California.[78] Even while it seemed that Rastafari had been gaining greater acceptance in mainstream Jamaican society, these betrayals showed that the headway made was only short-lived, confirming to elders like Leonard Howell that independent Jamaica had not produced the kind of society from which the Rastafari could expect greater tolerance and perhaps even acceptance.

Conclusion

From this analysis, it should be clear that Leonard Howell did not disappear after 1960. It is inaccurate to refer to this period of his life as the "missing years". Howell divided his time between his roles as leader of Pinnacle and as Rastafari foundational leader even after the third of three major infiltrations at Pinnacle in 1958, and following his confinement in the mental asylum in 1960. He decided to become less visible because of the suppression he had faced during the late colonial period. Yet he remained accessible to the people he considered important or to whom he felt that he mattered the most. Not surprisingly, this was a select group of his followers, assistants and family members.

It is apparent that Howell also felt he had done enough to establish a foundation for the Rastafari movement in Jamaica, one on which it could base its future growth, or at least some parts of that development, in the coming years. Based on the assertiveness of his anti-colonial ideas, the path taken towards independence for Jamaica was a disappointment for Howell. The Rastafari doctrine enunciated by Howell had called for the complete removal of imperial Britain from the Jamaican future, but instead, Jamaica's creole nationalists had opted to maintain links with the former colonizer on the political, social and economic levels. The very system of government, for instance, under which the fledgling nation-state had chosen to govern its people, was the British Westminster system. Only one of the two main political parties, the PNP, seemed willing and even eager to embark on any serious effort establishing stable and binding links with Africa and especially Ethiopia. The other, the JLP, used mainly symbolic gestures to give the impression that they were not opposed to the Rastafari, such as hosting the emperor of Ethiopia during his visit in 1966. One must remember that this was the same government that only three years earlier had turned the police on the Rastafari in western Jamaica. Both parties, especially in the 1970s, manipulated the cultural influence of the Rastafari in order to gain political power.

It was hardly likely that Howell, a foundational leader of the Rastafari, could have become invisible while so much interest existed in the Rastafari, and the fact that much of this interest had a negative impact on the movement made it important for Howell himself to continue his work, but in a different way. He had experienced first-hand the consequences of putting himself out in public. He was, arguably, one of the most persecuted people in the late colonial period. Uncertainties and anxieties about the Rastafari continued during the post-colonial period. These factors understandably necessitated Howell's revision of his approach, but not his "disappearance". Those who had access to him also knew this. His secretary Gertrude Campbell said it best, so it is worth repeating: Howell was "not a man what's easy to know".

Acknowledgements

I wish to thank *Caribbean Quarterly*, its editor and editorial board, for allowing me to republish this chapter, with very minor changes, which was first published as follows: D.A. Dunkley, "Leonard P. Howell's Leadership of the Rastafari Movement and

His 'Missing Years'", *Caribbean Quarterly* 58, no. 4 (2012): 1–24. I wish to also thank Raymond Ramcharitar and Jahlani Niaah for their helpful comments on various drafts of the original essay prior to its publication in *Caribbean Quarterly*. It goes without saying that any errors that might still remain are mine.

Notes

1. Leonard Howell Symposium, hosted by the Faculty of Social Sciences and the Rastafari Studies Unit, University of the West Indies, Mona, in collaboration with the Leonard Howell Foundation, held at the University of the West Indies, Mona, Jamaica, 17–18 June 2011.
2. Hélène Lee, *The First Rasta: Leonard Howell and the Rise of Rastafarianism* (Chicago: Lawrence Hill Books, 2003).
3. The Rastafari movement qualifies as a messianic religion, which views Ethiopian emperor Haile Selassie I as the returned Messiah. For further reading on messianism, see James H. Charlesworth, "Messianology in the Biblical Pseudepigrapha", in *Qumran-Messianism: Studies on the Messianic Expectations in the Dead Sea Scrolls*, ed. James H. Charlesworth, Hermann Lichtenberger and Gerbern S. Oegema (Tübingen: Mohr Siebeck, 1998), 121.
4. Howell's message of hope was to be found in his book *The Promised Key*, written under the pseudonym G.G. Maragh (1935; repr., Kingston: Headstart, n.d.).
5. Robert J. Alexander, *A History of Organized Labor in the English-Speaking West Indies* (Westport, CT: Praeger, 2004), 30.
6. For a good reconstruction of Jamaica's electoral history, see Trevor Munroe and Arnold Bertram, *Adult Suffrage and Political Administrations in Jamaica, 1944–2002: A Compendium and Commentary* (Kingston: Ian Randle, 2006).
7. Veront M. Satchell, "Colonial Injustice: The Crown v. the Bedwardites, 27 April 1921", in *The African-Caribbean Worldview and the Making of Caribbean Society*, ed. Horace Levy (Kingston: University of the West Indies Press, 2009), 46–48.
8. "American Series Introduction", The Marcus Garvey and UNIA Papers Project, UCLA African Studies Center, http://www.international.ucla.edu/africa/mgpp/intro01.asp (accessed 27 November 2011).
9. Philip Sherlock and Hazel Bennett, *The Story of the Jamaican People* (Kingston: Ian Randle, 1993), 308–9. For Garvey's growing focus on the working class after 1929, when he was elected to the Kingston and St Andrew Corporation Council, see Sherlock and Bennett, *Story of the Jamaican People*, 310, and Tony Martin, "Marcus Garvey, the Caribbean, and the Struggle for Black Jamaican Nationhood", in *Caribbean Freedom: Economy and Society from Emancipation to the Present*, ed. Hilary Beckles and Verene Shepherd (Kingston: Ian Randle, 1996), 364–68.

10. Email from Sister Hodesh, Leonard P. Howell Foundation, 26 Banana Walk, Kingston 8, Jamaica, 30 November 2012.
11. See Marcus Garvey, "The Failure of Haile Selassie as Emperor", editorial, *Black Man*, March–April 1937.
12. The following report indicated that police surveillance on Howell had continued after his migration to St Thomas: acting inspector general to private secretary, Colonial Secretary's Office, 18 July 1936, "Rastafari Followers Information, No. 387/36 (Pinnacle Papers)", JA 1B/5/77/283, Colonial Secretary's Office (henceforth CSO) 5073/34.
13. "Leonard Howell Being Tried for Sedition in Saint Thomas", *Daily Gleaner*, 14 March 1934, 21.
14. Howell, *Promised Key*, 2.
15. Robert Hill is the one who makes the point that Howell "plagiarized extensively" other works published in the 1920s; see Hill, "Leonard P. Howell and Millenarian Visions in Early Rastafari Religion in Jamaica", *Jamaica Journal* 16, no. 1 (February 1983): 27.
16. References to Howell's confinement in the asylum in 1938 are numerous. It was mentioned by Alexander Bustamante, who wrote complaining about Howell to the colonial secretary of Jamaica in 1939; see Bustamante to the colonial secretary, 6 July 1939, CSO 1B/5/79/735.
17. Howell, *Promised Key*, 4, 12–14.
18. Louis Moyston, address at the Leonard Howell Symposium.
19. Hill, "Leonard P. Howell", 26, 27.
20. Howell, *Promised Key*, 7, 8.
21. Bustamante to the colonial secretary, 6 July 1939.
22. R.A. Leevy, "Ras Tafarianism", *Public Opinion*, 13 February, 20 February, 27 February and 13 March 1943.
23. O. Nigel Bolland, *The Politics of Labour in the British Caribbean: The Social Origins of Authoritarianism and Democracy in the Labour Movement* (Kingston: Ian Randle, 2001), 517.
24. Richard Lachmann, "Agents of Revolution: Elite Conflicts and Mass Mobilisation from the Medici to Yeltsin", in *Theorising Revolutions*, ed. John Foran (London: Routledge, 1997), 74.
25. Munroe and Bertram, *Adult Suffrage*, 121.
26. Darrell E. Levi states that Norman Manley was "an intellectual Fabian socialist" and founded his political party, the PNP, as "nominally socialist"; see Levi, *Michael Manley: The Making of a Leader* (Kingston: Heinemann Caribbean, 1989), 52.
27. Hill, "Leonard P. Howell", 35.
28. Ibid., 24.
29. Verene Shepherd, "Emancipation through Servitude: Aspects of the Condition

of Indian Women in Jamaica, 1845–1945", in *Caribbean Freedom*, ed. Beckles and Shepherd, 245.
30. See Ajai Mansingh and Laxmi Mansingh, "Hindu Influences on Rastafarianism", in *Caribbean Quarterly Monograph: Rastafari*, rev. ed., ed. Rex Nettleford and Veronica Salter (Kingston: Caribbean Quarterly, 2008), 105–33.
31. "Rules and Constitution of the Ethiopian Salvation Society, Friendly and Benevolent Society, Kingston, Jamaica, 11 January 1939", CSO 5073/34, 57A, 18, 1. This copy of the constitution of the ESS was supplied by the acting attorney general, Jamaica, on 18 February 1939.
32. Horace Russell, "The Emergence of the Christian Black: The Making of a Stereotype", *Jamaica Journal* 16, no. 1 (February 1983): 51.
33. Acting inspector general to private secretary, Colonial Secretary's Office, 18 July 1936, CSO 5073/34.
34. L.P. Howell, president, ESS, to George Padmore, 12 March 1939, CSO 1B/5/79/735, C74U.
35. Acting Inspector General Sidley to the colonial secretary, 1939, CSO 1130; "Governor Puts Ban on 'Rastafari' Meeting", *Daily Gleaner*, 9 February 1940.
36. Gertrude Campbell, interviewed by Jahlani Niaah and Ishmahil Blagrove for the documentary *Roaring Lion: The Rise of Rastafari* (Kingston: Frontline Productions, Rice N Peas Films, 2002; Brampton, ON: Knowledge Bookstore, 2002), 6.
37. Lee, *First Rasta*, 127; John Carradine, "The Ras Tafarites Retreat to Mountain Fastnesses of St Catherine", *Daily Gleaner*, 23 November 1940; Louis E.A. Moyston, "Sligoville Heritage", letter to the editor, *Gleaner*, 28 February 2007.
38. According to Frank Jan van Dijk, "Pinnacle was perhaps far more marginal to Rastafari than generally assumed"; see van Dijk, "Sociological Means: Colonial Reactions to the Radicalization of Rastafari in Jamaica, 1956–1959", *New West Indian Guide* 69, nos. 1–2 (1995): 75.
39. Nathaniel Samuel Murrell, "Introduction: The Rastafari Phenomenon", in *Chanting Down Babylon: The Rastafari Reader*, ed. Nathaniel Samuel Murrell, William David Spencer and Adrian Anthony McFarlane (Kingston: Ian Randle, 1998), 7.
40. Hill, "Leonard P. Howell", 35.
41. Carradine, "Ras Tafarites Retreat".
42. Yasus Afari, *Overstanding Rastafari: "Jamaica's Gift to the World"* (Kingston: Senya-Cum, 2007), 48.
43. Michael Hoenisch, "Symbolic Politics: Perceptions of the Early Rastafari Movement", *Massachusetts Review* 29, no. 3 (Fall 1988): 446.
44. Barry Chevannes, *Rastafari: Roots and Ideology* (Syracuse, NY: Syracuse University Press, 1994), 122.
45. Carradine, "Ras Tafarites Retreat".
46. Ibid.

47. Attorney general to the colonial secretary, 2 July 1941, minutes, CSO 5073/34.
48. James Nelson to the sergeant major, Spanish Town Police Station, 14 June 1941, CSO 5073/34 (copy).
49. Commissioner Owen Wright to the colonial secretary, 17 July 1944, minute 5, CSO 5073/34.
50. "Jamaica's Great Rastafari Kingdom Comes to an End", *Sunday Gleaner*, 14 October 1945.
51. Commissioner Owen Wright to the colonial secretary, 25 March 1944, minute 17, CSO 5073/34.
52. Suzette A. Haughton, *Drugged Out: Globalisation and Jamaica's Resilience to Drug Trafficking* (Lanham, MD: University Press of America, 2011), 48.
53. "The Rastafarite Cult", Headquarters, Jamaica Constabulary, Kingston, 13 January 1959, Public Record Office, London, appendix 1, CO 1031/2767.
54. Ibid., appendix 1 and 2.
55. Lee, *First Rasta*, 218.
56. Campbell, interview, 2.
57. Lee, *First Rasta*, 217. I disagree with Lee's assertion that "in November 1958, Howell no longer resided at Pinnacle, having settled at South Camp Road, Kingston". A newspaper report shows that he was at Pinnacle even during the 1970s. See "Gunmen Terrorise Rastas Demanding 'the Weed'", *Daily Gleaner*, 23 May 1979.
58. "Judge's Summing Up at the Treason Felony Trial", *Daily Gleaner*, 31 October 1960.
59. Jérémie Kroubo Dagnini, "Remembering Rasta Pioneers: An Interview with Barry Chevannes", *Journal of Pan African Studies* 3, no. 4 (December 2009): 23.
60. Lee, *First Rasta*, 218.
61. *Daily Gleaner*, "Gunmen Terrorise Rastas".
62. Ibid.
63. Levi, *Michael Manley*, 151.
64. *Daily Gleaner*, "Gunmen Terrorise Rastas".
65. "Home Circuit Trial List", *Daily Gleaner*, 20 March 1971; "Home Circuit Trial List", *Daily Gleaner*, 26 August 1973. In fact, the struggle over the ownership of Pinnacle has continued to the present day.
66. Dagnini, "Remembering Rasta Pioneers", 23.
67. *Daily Gleaner*, "Gunmen Terrorise Rastas".
68. Dagnini, "Remembering Rasta Pioneers", 23.
69. Adrian Frater, "Rastas Remember Massacre – 1963 Coral Gardens Riot Brings Back Bitter Memories", *Gleaner*, 17 April 2003.
70. Rupert Lewis, *Walter Rodney's Intellectual and Political Thought* (Kingston: University of the West Indies Press, 1998), 97–99.
71. Colin A. Palmer, "Identity, Race and Black Power in Independent Jamaica", in *The*

Modern Caribbean, ed. Franklin W. Knight and Colin A. Palmer (Chapel Hill: University of North Carolina Press), 117.

72. I refer here to the famous Rastafari study conducted by M.G. Smith, Roy Augier and Rex Nettleford in 1960, only the second major attempt by academics to study the movement. The first was conducted by George E. Simpson, an American anthropologist, in 1954. See M.G. Smith, Roy Augier and Rex Nettleford, *Report on the Rastafari Movement in Kingston, Jamaica* (Kingston: Institute of Social and Economic Research, 1960), reprinted in *Rastafari: The Reports*, ed. Roy Augier and Veronica Salter (Kingston: Caribbean Quarterly, 2010); and George E. Simpson, "The Rastafari Movement in Jamaica: A Study of Race and Class Conflict", *Social Forces* 34, no. 2 (December 1955): 167–70.

73. The first "Mission to Africa" in 1961 was made up of ten persons, and among them were only three Rastafari brethren: Mortimer Planno, Douglas Mack and Filmore Alvaranga. The second, "The Jamaica Technical Mission to Africa" in 1962, was comprised of Aston Foreman, Don Mills, Wesley Miller and Rex Nettleford, and included no Rastafari brethren. See Augier and Salter, *Rastafari: The Reports*.

74. For Nettleford's ideas of Jamaica's creole identity, see Rex M. Nettleford, *Mirror Mirror: Identity, Race and Protest in Jamaica* (1970; repr., Kingston: LMH Publishing, 1998), especially the chapter entitled "The Melody of Europe, the Rhythm of Africa", 171–211.

75. For work on Michael Manley's cultural policy within the context of the ideology of democratic socialism, see D.A. Dunkley, "Hegemony in Post-Independence Jamaica", *Caribbean Quarterly* 57, no. 2 (June 2011): 12–17.

76. Interviews by the author with Gerald Lloyd Downer (b. 1934), Alphanso Gallimore (b. 1946) and Florence Stewart (b. 1939), Tredegar Park, St Catherine, Jamaica, 24 April 2011.

77. Rupert Lewis, *Walter Rodney: 1968 Revisited* (1994; repr., Kingston: Canoe Press, University of the West Indies, 1998), 22n33. See also "Rastafari", *International Encyclopaedia of the Social Sciences* (2008), http://www.encyclopedia.com/doc/1G2-3045302184.html.

78. Eldon V. Birthwright, "Reggae as a Rastafari Poetic of Disenchantment", in *Readings in Caribbean History and Culture: Breaking Ground*, ed. D.A. Dunkley (Lanham, MD: Lexington Books, 2011), 266, 267.

5

LEONARD HOWELL'S PHILOSOPHY OF RASTAFARI MANHOOD

JAHLANI A.H. NIAAH

Instead of saying Civilization hereafter we all shall say Black Supremacy."[1] This is Leonard Howell's initial articulation of Rastafari as a philosophy of transformative manhood. Now acclaimed as Rastafari foundation patriarch, Leonard P. Howell helped to establish an indelible aesthetic, perhaps even the template for Rastafari as an Ethiopian-centred spirituality. This image of Rastafari does not sufficiently capture the spirit of Leonard Howell that is still preserved within the movement: the father or provider, wise counsellor, doctor-philosopher, healer-scientist and community developer – all memorialized in songs and oral accounts rendered by those of his followers who currently reverence his legacy. There are now stories that have consistently recounted Howell's mysterious behaviour and supernatural powers; indeed, his celebrants often transfigure him into His Imperial Majesty Emperor Haile Selassie I. This essay seeks to reconstruct an image of the character of this man by way of analysing his teachings and the myths and memories accounted of him among the Howellites and others of his followers.

J.E. Chamberlin locates Rastafari as the only genuine "myth" to have emerged from the African American slave experience.[2] From the ashes of Africa, kept alive in the hearts of blacks and the mud of slavery, some would rise up to reconstruct a vision for their civilization. They would question themselves about their conditions, they would study the corpus of social understanding given to them, and they would read the signs of the time and come up with their own stories, theories, solutions, and indeed their own mythology. Slavery may have been the essential crucible from which this hope for humankind emerged. Who would have imagined a character arising in Jamaica in the twentieth century with a most compelling narrative about the return of Christ to earth in this time, a character immediately troubling the sensibilities of official and colonial authorities, ultimately requiring state intervention to break the tides awakening the African masses who heard his message?

This character was audacious, one actualizing the teachings of the Bible in this time through the announcement of a transition of contemporary political powers, a character who taught his audiences that the Pope was "Satan the devil" and published this interpretation.[3] Indeed, this character spoke of the earth as being under one ruler, one "rightful ruler", and claimed that the time had now come for the rule of "Black Supremacy".[4] This character was Leonard Howell, born in 1898 in the hills of Clarendon, Jamaica, but a transnational figure who spent much of his young adult years abroad in the United States, where he worked as a seaman, travelled and subsequently became a businessman and one of Marcus Garvey's listeners in New York City. Before his return to Jamaica in 1932, two events occurred which seem to have affected his consciousness. These were the dismantling of Garvey's Universal Negro Improvement Association (UNIA) and the coronation of Haile Selassie I as emperor of Ethiopia.[5] These two events impacted grassroots expressions of "radical blackness"[6] – that is, black supremacy. The break up of the UNIA created a void which was to be filled by the Nation of Islam and what came to be known as the Rastafari movement. To this extent, Howell and the Rastafari movement in general add to the (modern) Ethiopianist trajectory through the cogitations resulting in Rastafari*anism*, which I am arguing to be New World African mythology, to initiate a transformative manhood.[7] This idea of a *new human*[8] is radical and counter-hegemonic, premised on principles of concert, equity and global responsibilities, sentiments consistently expressed within the speeches of the Ethiopian emperor, and famously echoed by Rastafari's cardinal messenger and reggae king Bob Marley in his song "War".[9] Within this trajectory, Rastafari vocalizes all of man's aspirations, and black supremacy reflects a *new ("another") standard*. In this way, the movement immediately grants itself a transnational connecting mythological sphere, especially for those who have lost the knowledge of how civilizations are built. Its appeal is seen as a critical moment of encounter[10] for engaging with the "self" and "society", offering a platform for pedagogies of transformation,[11] with particular appeal to the African male especially by way of active or visible membership.[12]

Leonard Howell resurrects the idea of an African empire among a population crippled by a history of physical and mental slavery. Howell becomes one of the most articulate and outstanding teachers of Africa, translating this into popular mass consciousness, making him a key political leader in the 1930s, 1940s and 1950s. This chapter brings together these accounts about Howell: stories of his trials, promises, teachings and instructions, stories preserved among his followers today. The analysis of the research provided here is motivated by the understanding that the lore surrounding Howell is perhaps the most cogent reproduction of his persona that remains and, if subject to systematic analysis, can offer more insights into this exemplary leader at the genesis of the movement of Rastafari. Within this context, I will endeavour to highlight a critical contribution to the sociopolitical leadership of twentieth-century Jamaica in the language and aesthetic of the masses of the people. In this light, Howell might be seen as having left a manifesto for national transformation through black supremacist alternative psycho-social praxes.[13] This, I am arguing, is his template and core ideational legacy which still stands as the blueprint for Rastafari practice today.

Restated, Howell's example of manhood may be used as a reference point for analysing in particular existing Rastafari humanity and masculinity. I will approach this task by placing Howell's contribution into two broad categories: Teachings or Instructions, and Myths. In the former, I will look at the teachings transmitted especially through his court testimony and his book, *The Promised Key*, with particular attention to his pedagogy for social transformation. This is mindful of the state of the African Caribbean male, who had been historically "kept down",[14] marginalized and alienated from the performance of manhood, as he was characterized as a "subform" within white patriarchy.[15] Hilary Beckles has pointed out that the notion of black fatherhood as a specific aspect of masculinity is non-existent within the historical archives of the slave plantations, as attention was focused on black motherhood.[16] Terms such as *quashee* were used to ideologically characterize black men as "docile but irresponsible, loyal but lazy, humble but chronically given to lying and stealing . . . infantile".[17] Howell, like Garvey, his contemporary, was tasked with the construction of a new African man,[18] or a new human, capable of managing the big affairs of communal, national and international proportions. This is a project that has interestingly been philosophically explored by Sylvia Wynter, who, in her "After Man Towards the Human" thesis, articulates the need to deconstruct the given notions of "man" and "human", as these have only been reflections of white supremacy in which all non-Europeans are interpreted as defective human beings.[19]

The irony was that there was a type of deficit that the non-European had suffered at the hands of "civilized" humans, who, in their efforts to advance Europe, had robbed non-Europeans of their human dignity. Howell was seeking to eliminate this deficit through knowledge of Africa and leadership which was connected to this continental homeland of the majority of Jamaicans. The consequent assessment, therefore, is that Howell was part of the inauguration of a counter-hegemonic tradition of African American male leadership steeped within an Ethiopianist teacher-preacher[20] aesthetic.

A Picture of HIM: The Gong Sounds the African Redemption

Just as it took locks and keys to capture and subjugate Africans who found themselves ensnared in the Caribbean for centuries in slavery, Howell, known as "the Gong" or Gangunguru Maragh and the teacher of enlightenment and wisdom, fashioned a legendary tool, *The Promised Key*, to begin a dialogue about attaining ultimate freedom through unlocking the mind, thus bringing forth the African's redemption. This tool, furnished to Howell through Emperor Haile Selassie's accession to the Ethiopian throne, has over the years come to represent the embodiment of a worldview held by Rastafari to demonstrate the assertion of the notion of a new *livity*, meaning an enlightened way of life.

Howell, at the very outset, establishes the core way of being for Rastafari as an integrated philosophy of self-empowerment, enunciated in the lyrics of this song:

Once they painted Christ white
But he's a Negro
And he no more shall be white
Jesus Christ is an E-thi-op-ian Negro
Born and grown up in Africa

The white man told we
That he came from heaven
But that "heaven" was
King David's Royal Throne
He's the Father of ev-ry nation
Who the white world must obey...

Ras Tafari is our King
He is our mighty King
We are marching onto vic-to-ry
...with the King of Kings.[21]

How does one teach liberation and self-empowerment? Howell's answer was through meditating on the newly crowned emperor, or at least this seems to have been his methodology when he produced pictures of the emperor, selling them to his audiences and instructing them to adore him and honour his laws. Howell set out on a mission of redemption of the word, correcting the falsehoods that had been given the people about their past and the African continent, embarking on a new message of truth. Songs such as the one quoted above illustrate Howell's ideas and teachings to his followers.

Howell was one of the first leaders to emerge claiming a sense of entitlement directly related to the coronation of the Ethiopian emperor Haile Selassie I. For such leaders, this momentous occasion signalled the emancipation of the Africans who were in bondage and the appointment of alternative governance over these newly liberated peoples. This is a point in time when there were no predetermined spheres of hegemonic influence, and thus Howell potentially produced a cleavage within the society in favour of the new sovereign of Ethiopia, who, he advised, ruled by divine prophecy and, according to the song, was an "E-thi-op-ian Negro" who was "Jesus Christ".[22] Michelle Ann Stephens picks up on this point when she seeks to position the politics of the interwar years for African American intellectuals and argues,

> Both the war and these immediate post-war events compelled many Black intellectuals to view domestic racial relations and race politics in the United States from a more global perspective. Their lens tended to be much wider than that of the imperial powers, as seen in the starting premise of Du Bois's 1925 essay that the war had left behind more than simply a new Europe of nation-states.[23]

Hence, some black intellectuals were also paying attention to the Russian

Revolution, which produced a different internationalist vision than that of the League of Nations. Likewise, some black intellectuals were looking for a new world order through biblical exegesis. For Howell, Ethiopia was this new, prophetic and rightful inheritor of the new society.

Howell immediately took on the task of being an enabler of the emperor's new order, establishing his Ethiopian Salvation Society and indicating that he was the ambassador of the emperor in Jamaica. In this context, Howell opens a door towards mobilizing and centralizing Africa as a political force among the consciousness of the hitherto undirected African masses as to a way forward to a more progressive community. Given the overarching dominant Christian narrative that had been fed to the enslaved over the previous one hundred years, Howell used these familiar stories to deconstruct the falsehoods about Africans, their station in life and the so-called backward continent of Africa that had been planted among the enslaved population to keep them as illegitimate people from nowhere of significance, or as subhumans subject to white supremacy. This context of the African representation subsequently has been theorized within Rastafari as *his-story*, the voice and interpretation of those who fall outside of the Euro-publication of documentation and interpretation. Howell established that Africans could hold claim over the stories of the Bible by declaring the following: "We were told that we were Gentiles, but thanks to God we had awakened from our sleep by the coming of the Messiah, to a fuller understanding to know that we were the Jews."[24] The awakening of the people had begun. Furthermore, Howell asserted that from the time of King Nebuchadnezzar, the Ethiopians, the rightful Jews, were given over to worshipping the god of idolatry set up by that king.

The significant first key that Howell brought to the people was a knowledge of Africa that had been hidden from them previously:

Ethiopian Story was hidden in the dark
Ethiopian Story was hidden in the dark
Nobody ever tell it to we
Ethiopian story was hidden in the dark...
It's only Leonard, it's only Leonard, it's only Leonard tell it to we
It's only Leonard, it's only Leonard, it's only Leonard tell it to we.[25]

He began his teachings with information about the land, people and sovereignty of Ethiopia. He contextualized Ethiopia as an unchanged land populated by primitive Christian people who were being ruled by a king directly related to the line of the biblical King David, but who had greater glory than even Solomon. Howell came to articulate the coming of a new civilization that was based on and founded in the power and glory of the Supreme Black King. Howell preached that the Emperor Haile Selassie I was the measure of civilization and asked his audience to adore this emperor as supreme God over all of mankind: "His body filleth all in all." Through this new emperor, Howell charged his audience "forward to the King of Kings", to "rebuild our character", to learn the worth of "manhood" and "womanhood" and to learn social order "so that virtue will gain victory over our bodies".[26]

Howell now fashioned a clear message that it was through Ethiopia that these truths had been preserved and were now unfolding for the world to see through the new emperor. Howell indicated that Ethiopia had been the crowned head for the ever-living God since heaven and earth were built. He identified Ethiopia as a land with a perfect language, the one uncorrupted language on earth, possessing a glory extending forever, long before and after this world. This idea of a pure language in Ethiopia has been further interpreted by teachers after Howell as having been predicted by the biblical prophet Zephaniah, when he spoke of the people acquiring "a pure language that they may call upon the name of the Lord, to serve him with one consent".[27] Howell presented Ethiopia as an unchanged land with unmatched people, who had fashioned a hybrid culture which was now re-emerging to succeed the Anglo-Saxon hegemonic forces that had kept Africans in bondage. Howell also represented Ethiopia as a woman: "that rich national woman that has charmed the men of nations to lie with her".[28] In his description, the country was a rich treasure sought after by the Western slavers who went into her, robbed her land and money, and took her seed to be slaves.

Remnants: The Ethiopian/Jamaican Axis

Howell not only argued for Ethiopia's centrality within the new emergence of black supremacy, but he also included Jamaica as a key space for "the triumphant lot"[29] of faithful subjects of Ethiopia to be preserved, now seemingly manifest through the Rastafari claim to Ethiopian identities: "Mount Africa, the world's capital, the new Bible land, the triumphant lot is for King Alpha own lot until this day. Slave Traders called the world's capital, Jamaica[,] British West Indies."[30]

Jamaica within this context was a part of a new Bible land, a New World capital, Mount Africa. Howell saw Jamaica's role as being linked to a preservation of Ethiopia in the Caribbean, thus explaining the prophetic acclaim for and cleavage unto the emperor by those to whom he, Howell, ministered.

So compelling was the character of Emperor Haile Selassie that it seems to have illuminated the darkness of African redemption for not only Howell but also for three other Jamaican teacher-leaders of his generation: Joseph Nathaniel Hibbert, Henry Archibald Dunkley and Robert Hinds. These four individuals are responsible for the rooting of this new tradition of sagacity, but one anchored in a scholarly Ethiopian framework. These individuals were not only preaching an African doctrine but were reading the continent differently, as a space of redemption and hope through the new emperor. They positioned Africa as a fulfilment of deliverance in their longings for freedom. It is not difficult to imagine the climate within the Jamaican landscape a hundred years after the British act that had emancipated the slaves, a population devoid of a conscious framework from which to minister to and lead the majority of the people.

W.F. Elkin contextualizes the 1890s to 1920s in Jamaica as a fervent atmosphere of depression and social disruption among the masses, leaving room for those who displayed innovative leadership to emerge. Key persons among these were street preachers, healers and herbal doctors. Both Garvey and Howell had emerged as pan-African leaders, but Howell was to distinguish himself as educated but street-smart, having grassroots appeal; perhaps this was because in addition to his Ethiopian orientation, he catered to the cultural interest in preachers and healers. This religious and mystical element was essential for any successful mobilization of the masses and is a clear aspect of the combined religious and political approach taken by many leaders from the late eighteenth century, as demonstrated by Native Baptist–inspired resistance leaders such as George Liele, Samuel Sharpe, Paul Bogle and Alexander Bedward. Howell's fledgling movement picked up on this religio-political trajectory.[31]

Within traditions such as Revivalism, Howell would perhaps have been considered somewhat a "warner" prophet; however, I wish to argue that, especially due to the fact that it was clear that Howell was a learned and well-travelled man,[32] he could not be dismissed as an ignorant Revivalist, as was the tendency. He combined the uneducated spiritualist tradition with that of the *Negro* intellectual, a complement which had real political implications.[33] This was where he began to provoke the status quo, as Garvey did, but Howell seems to have been more intent on a localized case versus a global one, more focused on community development than on immediately seeking to engage a larger (explicitly political) platform. Garvey, unlike Howell, was also critical of the emperor, calling him a "toothless lion" when he went to live in Bath, England, during the Italian occupation.[34] This is in direct contrast to what Jake Homiak describes as Howell's high regard for the emperor, which placed him uncritically within the centre of African hope and a new worldview.[35] Howell's ability to bring political understanding of the times, the shifting global hegemony and the emergence of the Ethiopian emperor, also separated his message, as he had historical and scriptural texts that he could reference and teach, while demonstrating how these texts were currently manifested by Emperor Haile Selassie I. Within the two years of his local ministry, Howell had captivated thousands from the ranks of the poor and had become a concern to the authorities, and soon came attempts to stem his growing impact. Howell was taken out of circulation through imprisonment on charges for sedition. Subsequently, the strategies to discredit Howell centred on marking him as a deviant lunatic. To this extent, the two major strategies for control of the *other* "defective humans" from the official society were charges of madness and criminality.[36]

Howell further separated himself from his three cohorts, Hibbert, Hinds and Dunkley, by having a liturgical text, *The Promised Key*, attributable to him by 1935. A knowledge of the use and application of this text within the developing Rastafari movement is critical for understanding how the core cosmological orientation of the movement became widely anchored, especially orally, into what we could now refer to as a Rastafari aesthetic. Howell offered leadership in the Freirian sense, in which he engaged in a dialogue with his constituents to raise their understanding of the political conditions in which they existed. He did this through an interpretation of a longer history, dating from the commencement of King Nebuchadnezzar's reign in 606 BCE, citing the current times as marking the end of more than twenty-five hundred years of white domination.[37] But he also became something of a poignant vernacular orator, similar in sentiment to Bedward, who one generation previously had caused the colonial government to confront him and his followers when they were mobilized to demonstrate in the streets of Kingston.[38] Howell declared in 1935, "Now we are disgusted with them [white colonial authority], we wash our hands of them for life."[39]

These ideas, when written down and animated at the street meetings, were perceived as inflammatory, but more critically they reflected a type of audacity of thinking and preaching against the official system. This is demonstrative of Howell's highly engaging and charismatic approach.[40] His arguments were date-specific in delivering word of the prophetic times in which his audiences found themselves. He explained the reality and significance of the Great War as proof of the return of Jesus Christ on earth to reign as a righteous king and to set up righteous laws. Further, Howell later indicated, referring to his followers, "I told them that on November 9, 1918, a man was seen at the river Jordan, and He was Christ Himself."[41] Within Howell's analysis, the emergence of the Christ is one of tumultuous unsettlement for the seat of European power and deception. Notwithstanding this, Ras Tafari still emerges as prince regent and king from 1916 to 1930, when he was eventually crowned emperor. Consequently, the Great War and the one to follow were products of Europe's refusal to accept that their time had come to bring their dominance to an end. Howell taught the people, "Just as what the people are, that is the state of your government. Do not follow the court house and the doctors [as] they will fake you to death."[42]

His book, in this sense, is more of an Afro-Caribbean manifesto for mobilization and *conscientization* of an Ethiopian remnant.[43] Howell, like Garvey, seemed clear about the nature of the people and the resultant state of their minds and their need to evolve as a liberated society. The message had been structured to bring some amelioration to the illiterate masses of Africans, who were in need of teaching about *virtue* as a means to achieve victory over their lives. Howell, by virtue of his greater means, business reputation and experience, was to become the trainer for all the other leaders of this faith who were to subsequently emerge.

Howell identified the afflictions hindering African transformation: there was need to overcome white bondage and black hypocrisy. He thus recommended fasting, baptism under water, regular attendance at the balm yard and seasonal love feasts every three to six months. But the key ritual for transformation was fasting, which Howell advocated as the way to remove devils from the homes of those in distress.[44] He further provided a face for the congregation to meditate their victory through, as he challenged them to believe in the power of King Rastafari, the living God. This is where Howell brought a new tradition, as he recognized that King Rastafari had ordained a new priesthood after his own name and order.[45] It is this new priesthood that is of particular significance to the idea of Rastafari manhood, and this, I argue, was a profound alternative developed by Howell for African Jamaicans. As a result of this, Rastafari, through this trajectory established by Howell, provides a system for regaining humanity, manhood and specifically fatherhood for a society in which the African man, the male presence, and more specifically the father, had been seriously annihilated.

Reconstructing an Ethiopian Patriarchy

Tekla Mekfet has identified repatriation as also meaning a return to *the way of the father*, with the Ethiopian emperor emerging as the grand hope – in reality, the new light for Africans everywhere. African patriarchy was an alien image for the Jamaican society, as all they had experienced within colonialism was the worst representation of white-hegemonic patriarchy. Howell therefore set himself the task of teaching his flock of a new father and mother within the principle of the Alpha and Omega, who had come to reclaim them. What specifically did Howell teach of the emperor? I would like to engage with what Robert Hill describes as "millenarian inversion", contextualized within the ideology of a renewal and popularization of Ethiopianism, to argue for what I think Howell construed as being an alternative leadership for African Jamaicans, one based on previously unknown or unrepresented history. Howell engaged the binaries of colonial existence and thus placed the comparison as evidence before his audiences in the context of what they had experienced hitherto. Hence, he argued, a righteous and prophetic redeemer had appeared; deliverance was coming; HIM had freed all now, broken every chain; turn attention and sing for the new King the national anthem; all shall bow down and all shall serve HIM; HIM was to be the unifier of African religion, responsible for the construction of a new society.[46]

The leadership of the formerly enslaved population of Africans became an imperative at the turn of the century. Among the bids to represent and lead these people, Garvey's system is the best documented and arguably the most successful. But Howell became the application and the embodiment of Garveyism, manifesting himself at an opportune moment as a new type of patriarch, eventually described as Rastafari. This is what Hill describes as a type of religious revivalism, evolving through cultural "conversion" towards the establishment of a black religious and political nationalism.[47] Howell became the medium for projecting an understanding of the Ethiopian emperor upon the society, an illiterate and disconnected lot or a remnant of the African continent, now almost left like a fallow field, untended and seemingly worthless. Howell therefore had to awaken these people to self-worth, promoting an understanding of their identity and how their futures were related to the ultimate patriarch, His Imperial Majesty Emperor Haile Selassie I, returned to redeem the oppressed from the bondage of the British king, George Stewart.

But Howell also employed a political usage of photography, a multimedia technique, which he used to make a concrete impression of black liberation and black supremacy. Photography had been incorporated from the mid-1800s onwards by Ethiopian sovereigns to transmit important political messages visually, without the need for words.[48] This seems to have emerged as a continuation of an age-old Ethiopian practice of illustrative sacred art, which usually adorned their places of worship depicting familiar biblical stories, perhaps as a way of engaging the non-literate congregants with the visual text of the Christian faith. This practice also had a place in the Jamaican context, as this population was also mostly illiterate and would better relate to the visual medium. Many had never imagined an African sovereign, indeed royalty, much less seeing one so regally depicted, with jewels upon his crown. But even more compelling than Howell's usage of the medium of photography was its usage by the very same emperor.

The Ethiopian royal court, under the leadership of the new emperor, employed an engagement with visual representations of itself that was without precedent.[49] This was strategically used to convey meaning to the emperor's subjects about his character and reign. Howell picked up on this tradition of visual representation, as Garvey did, bringing into being a counter-hegemonic visual exemplar. There was a very urgent need to visually create the black man of big affairs. Here you had your very own passport to power; the Christ returned and he resembles you. Within Rastafari, this was perhaps one of Howell's most enduring contributions: the idea of the faithful holding the image of the emperor dearly on their persons (as buttons, rings and pendants) and in portraits in their personal spaces. And within this tradition was therefore the further development of assemblages to depict the emperor and his life journey.[50] It is also noticeable how over time many of the Rastafari brethren have come to fashion themselves to resemble the emperor through their countenance and bearded visages.

It was on the matter of the circulation of the emperor's image that the colonial authority sought to discredit Howell as a common swindler of the people, because he introduced this photo on his platforms as a part of convincing the people of the truth about which he spoke. It is reported that when asked by the court about his sale of the image, Howell defended the value of images and thus the need to sell them to transmit that value to the people.[51] Howell was faced with the challenge of how to portray a modern yet ancient and progressive African king. This issue was resolved by the emperor himself, as his life circumstances dictated and became a part of the dialogue being conducted with the emergent African community of intellectuals at the start of the twentieth century. The question of how to invest him convincingly with the mystic of inspiration and power became important visually. Images of the emperor's coronation were abundantly circulated in the press, and after the Italo-Ethiopian War of 1935–41, his aura was further magnified by images that depicted him on the battlefield at the helm of the empire's defence.[52]

Howell was a thinker, a practitioner, a businessman, who led his congregation like a shepherd and served as a social activist engineering his community of African freedom and empowerment. Though he had taken to public platforms early in his career, he was prepared to abandon this route and liberate the people by way of example through his commune at Pinnacle, near to Sligoville in the parish of St Catherine. Rather than engaging with being censored by way of threats of arrest and prison or institutionalization, Howell chose to practise his black supremacy doctrine. His strategy shifted after he had disseminated the word through street meetings, the newspaper transcript of his testimony in court and eventually his book regarding the emergence of the African redeemer. The new strategy seemed to be one of retreat. It was, however, with this retreat that the establishment of a Rastafari movement and community of adherents mushroomed within the Jamaican landscape. Howell had moved into another phase of his work by establishing a livity or praxis.

Howell raised hopes among the poor about their station in life. Not only did he teach of the emperor as a great king but he also understood himself as a king, with a kingdom over which he presided. In Trinity Ville, St Thomas, he is said to have lived in a house of seven furnished rooms. This story, told by Sister Gertrude, Howell's secretary, was her way of establishing the fact that Howell's sense of self and of his place in society was unparalleled by other African Jamaicans at this time. He had a bakery as well as an office on Church Street, Kingston. But most critical was his retreat (or expansion) into the countryside, where he was able to establish the most ambitious collective settlement of Rastafari hitherto, from which he presided over the *new* governance of the people. Pinnacle represented the implementation of an alternative society for the Africans. This seems to have created fear among the official society of an independent African community that "drowned" out European connections. Howell is reputed to have barred white persons from entering Pinnacle.[53]

Attempts to undermine the control Howell had at Pinnacle ranged from claims of unsanitary conditions and disease to, eventually, arguments surrounding the cultivation of ganja, all to present compelling justification for officially locking down his enterprise.[54] The old Great House set upon the peak of the property would serve as a symbol of the highest potential held within the Howell vision. According to one informant, "it served to symbolize Rasta Big House upon the Hill", as well as being Howell's perch for protective watch over his flock; he occupied residences adjacent to the ruins, a location from which he could survey all the lands and parishes surrounding him. Pinnacle became likened unto a "Howell District", with Howell literally being the *big-man* about the place, and some say with influence and impact over thousands of people and acres of land in the surrounding hills of St Catherine.

Howell brought organization and administration to a peasant people, and this caused them to turn around their lives, resulting in lucrative enterprises. A part of this organization was his collective settlement at Pinnacle, akin to a people's cooperative, in the tradition of Stony Gut almost a century before. He provided the administration for returning the scattered people to traditional African methodologies of shared labour within the "day-fi-day", "work-fi-work" traditions[55] and of communal living, and they were able to develop the reputation of a food basket. Many of them now began to see Howell as a type of demigod. They had known no black man who previously delivered this evidence of hope, who led like a capable patriarch meeting their every need, and who was a father who brought them much salvation. In addition to establishing an economy, Howell initiated celebrations and rituals which drew from the drumming folk traditions of Kumina and Burru as well as the philosophies of Ethiopianism, Hinduism and Islam, unveiling alternatives to white supremacy and Eurocentrism that had previously been condemned and suppressed.[56] Howell, in this regard, became the learned citizen of the world who was synthesizing a developmental paradigm that was restorative to a crippled African population. He convincingly positioned himself as the harbinger of not only a message of redemption but also a practice, a livity that was redemptive for the people.

Through him, many were moved to turn away from the city and cleave to his hilly retreat to develop themselves through industry and hard work, but with certain reward. Sister Gertrude suggests that so enticing was life at the camp that young children who were abandoned found refuge there, as did those who were not abandoned but saw the light brought by Howell. It was within the Pinnacle encampment that the seeds of Rastafari as a community of self-sufficiency and sustainability were first sown. Accounts from informants indicate that Howell was able to cleverly harvest water through the construction of elaborate catchment systems, allowing for not only the cultivation of crops but also the herding of animals. Individuals participated in both collective and individual agricultural enterprises, and most importantly, they were encouraged to develop crop cycles that provided them with ready food (peas and beans, cassava, vegetables), alongside recycling enterprises to manufacture common household furnishings and personal items, such as brooms, mats, lanterns, graters, sandals and baskets. Pinnacle became a thriving district, at whose gates a bountiful market is said to have flourished.[57] One informant has argued that "Dada Howell use to sey him is no 'boss man' because him don't have no payroll".[58] Persons were therefore encouraged to be fruitful and to work hard to sustain themselves.

Howell was perceived as a god, and was considered to have secret powers and to have performed miracles.[59] In one account, he is said to have healed a blind congregant.[60] Indeed, Howell did have a philosophy of man-God, and thus it is likely that he did offer this image of himself. Sister Gertrude and others from her circle related how he had the capacity to appear and disappear at will, even making himself invisible. She relates that "Mr Howell", as she insisted he should always be called, was

> a man ... but not a man ... know every language ... a funny man. When you see him, you have fi stand up, take off you cap and bow to him, and a Blackman you know. Him say Blackman arise and shine because the light has come. And the light is Jesus, the light of the world is Jesus and him come with the light ... so the light a shine fi all a we ya, cause we Black. But him come fi Black and White you know, a no one nation God come for you know, him come for the world. To who receive Him.[61]

At the same time that Howell's message was being received favourably and being seen as the fulfilment of Christian prophesy, educated Jamaicans were ridiculing this message. For many, especially within the educated elite, nothing *civilized* could come out of the African continent, but on the other hand, the illiterate peasants lapped up Howell's teachings, reflecting the polarization of the society. Commenting on the emperor's title "Light of the World", an editorial in the *Daily Gleaner* put this question about the emperor to learned Jamaicans: "What has Abyssinia done to enlighten any of us, and how shall we be illuminated by the actions or dicta of this particular gentleman?"[62] There was an antagonistic audience waiting to accept a characterization of lunacy for individuals such as Howell who preached the divinity of the emperor. The social polarization surrounding the phenomenon of Howell was directly facilitated by the authorities. Their hope was that neither Howell nor his message would be perceived as credible. Michael Hoenisch underscores this by pointing out how the authorities sought to control access to Howell through the courts for fear that he would be seen as a hero, while at the same time filtering out through the press sensational reports about Howell as a threat, especially to the middle and upper classes.[63] Justice C.M. MacGregor, in sentencing Howell, is reported to have lamented not being able to sentence him to a flogging of eighteen lashes[64] in an attempt to belittle his stature; he was after all not only invested with property but also a highly entitled man, one who told his audiences that they were children of King Alpha and Queen Omega of Ethiopia.[65] This fabrication of the black self, which he sought to imbue in his followers, was perceived as audacious and problematical.

Howell also created photographic representations of himself, including the now-classic images of him surrounded by books, reflecting his scholarly pursuits, and a less well-known photo of him and his wife, to depict his force of character in the context of his family. Howell represented himself to the people; he was leading as a modern Jamaican king, and they were willingly committed to being his subjects. But he was a king who fundamentally inverted the narrative of the absent father from the slave legacy and represented the return of the father as patriarch, present with authority and dignity.[66] Howell was also well-travelled,[67] and it is commonly suggested that he was present at the coronation ceremony for the emperor. His recounting of the event was transmitted from the perspective of a witness. It is very easy to understand how Howell became an enigmatic and mystical figure within the collective of the early Rastafari. He was of superior learning, well-studied in the Bible as well as the more esoteric texts related to the Books of Moses, the works of de Laurence, the Koran and Kabalistic knowledge sources.

Hibbert, one of the cohort of leaders emerging at the time of Howell, recounted one of the predictions made by the latter that "gigantic men would be coming from Europe". He understood Howell to mean men of great intellect who were coming "to tell us our emancipation".[68] The *Daily Gleaner* also reported the testimony of one Charles Fairweather, who relayed what could be read as a prophecy by Howell of the emperor's visit to Jamaica thirty years later. He indicated that Howell had said that Christ would return to the earth as the Messiah in the flesh, and that "they would be able to see Him, touch Him and eat with H.I.M.".[69] Only an extraordinary prophet, as Howell was considered to be, could have anticipated the emperor's visit to the Africans in the Caribbean in 1966, a visit which ignited the imagination of those who were present. The representation of the Rastafari movement by the time of the visit had grown beyond the parameters dictated by Howell; the faithful had splintered into multiple streams with various interpretations and expressions. More importantly, the visit cemented the example of international diplomacy, underscoring the need for travel within the emergent Rastafari. From as early as 1924, while still prince regent, Ras Tafari departed from the convention which dictated that the sovereign send emissaries, and left the Ethiopian highlands to engage the outside world. These visits became a major aspect of Ethiopian diplomatic advancement but also captivated the impressionable onlookers and media that made Haile Selassie's reign an indelible part of the twentieth-century imagination. It was through such visits abroad that the emperor was first able to make his mark on the African diaspora observing him, as early as his tour of Jerusalem in 1924, which was subsequently reported by Howell as evidence of the future emperor's manifestation of being the Christ.[70] In 1924, Oxford University used a visit by the future emperor to the United Kingdom to bestow him with his first of many honorary doctorate degrees.[71] Indeed, on the occasion of his visit to the United States and Canada in 1954, the emperor received six such degrees. In 1966, when he arrived in Jamaica as Howell had promised, having advised that "they would eat with H.I.M. and drink with H.I.M", the University of the West Indies bestowed on the emperor a Doctor of Laws degree. The important point is that it could be said that the emperor was very "degreed" and lettered, and likewise, Howellites ascribed such qualities to their leader, Leonard Howell.

The Bearded Brotherhood: A Cogent Philosophy of Transformation

Perhaps it was due to the photograph of the emperor circulated by Howell, but the fraternity of Rastafari which emerged in and around Jamaica became known as the "bearded men". An alternative cosmology had become available to the masses; a father figure had re-emerged.[72] The Quashee, what Sylvia Wynter describes as being "less than man" or a "defective human", was being directed to have virtue and victory over his life, and this could happen by looking through the lens of Ethiopia and particularly this new emperor, who inspired members of the African diaspora to seek knowledge of the world, to employ themselves in industry, rituals and righteous living, and to have a sense of community and belonging. Howell gave them pride and belonging as he taught them that "All ye warriors of the King of Kings lift high King Alpha's Royal Banner, from victory to victory King Alpha shall lead His army till every enemy is vanquished".[73]

There is more than a suggestion in the historical record that there was concern about the potential for an outbreak of race war in Jamaica, especially towards the end of the 1930s, when colonial conditions resulted in unrest in most islands of the Caribbean region. Howell's message resonated like a match to a keg of explosives. As a result, he became a target of the official society[74] and was keenly monitored while he was abroad and when he returned to Jamaica in 1932. Howell seemed to have transcended the limits of the relatively harmless teacher-preacher typology of leaders, and also had a field marshal's command and seriousness of purpose. He was deliberately issuing a call to action and was convinced of victory over the enemy. It is likely that the mobilization for the Ethiopian patriarchs during the Italo-Ethiopian War and for citizens throughout the history of Ethiopia's defence against the West has drawn on similar words of inspiration. The Battle of Adwa, led by Emperor Menelik II against the nineteenth-century ambitions of Italy over Ethiopia's territory, used similar cries for action.[75]

The signal of overthrow had come. Howell taught his congregants that King Alpha and Queen Omega, their parents, had overthrown their old, white, European colonial mother country; that is, "Black Supremacy [had] taken charge of white supremacy".[76] This articulated a counter-hegemonic action, deliberately engaged to demonstrate to the Africans that they were the rightful inheritors of the *civilized* world. Howell declared, regarding the black man's sacrificial contribution to the Anglo-Saxon, that "we have given our blood, souls, bodies and spirits.... We have given him access to the tree of life, we gave him the Garden of Eden, we gave him Egypt, we gave them Daniel and the body of the Black Virgin, the mother of Jesus and they took Joseph also. We gave ourselves to be slaves for hundreds of years."[77] Howell signalled a conclusion of the miseries and legacies of slavery, and captured the attention of the entire society at the time.

Conclusion: The Audacity of Leonard Howell

There is a mythologizing tendency among the folk ideologue that provides for the acknowledgement of the spirit of a character rather than of that specific character. That is, there is a great appreciation for the word, which immediately transcends the messenger, as it does at the same time acknowledge that messenger. To this extent, Howell and HIM are one within certain aspects of the Howellite community. This is no different from how when President William V. Tubman visited Jamaica in 1954, many read this as the spirit of Garvey returned,[78] or, in a more extended assessment, how Garvey is seen as the reincarnation of biblical figures, such as John the Baptist and the famous patriarch, Moses of the Old Testament. Similarly, the same obtains for the Bobo Shanti and their characterization of Prince Edward Emmanuel as the black Christ.

In a real sense, this was one of the objectives of Howell, as he sought to show his congregation that they were the very same people, with the same capacities, as the great ones of whom they had heard, who walked the earth at the time of the Bible stories. Howell came with a sense of entitlement. For those who had been part of the control and suppression of the African, Howell seemed audacious, but his audacity would have been unremarkable if not for the fact that he did not have a receptive audience. Even his enemies were listening keenly; indeed, law enforcement took notes at his first meeting in St Thomas.

Howell was placed in an elevated position upon the landscape of the Jamaican African. He had constructed from his life experiences, travels and readings an alternative to the static existence of the leaderless masses. He literally provided food for many individuals and a system of thought that empowered and sustained them. He offered a figure of respect, a father for the fatherless. He gave a blueprint towards the genuine construction of a new society. From the mould set by Howell, the core foundation of Rastafari was framed, and one might say an aesthetic was created. Howell was something of the Rastafari totality: philanthropist, herbalist and philosopher, a doctor of divinity, farmer, spiritual leader, justice and counsellor. He represented the benevolent Ethiopian patriarch and was mindful of the needs of his people, who had long suffered. He brought the hope of a new generation, one which was inspired by the magnificence of the new Ethiopian emperor. From his legacy emerged a compelling alternative African diaspora masculinity, one with a new cry for a new human excellence, so that instead of saying civilization, hereafter all shall say Haile Selassie I, the Light of the World.

Notes

1. G.G. Maragh [Leonard Percival Howell], *The Promised Key* (1935; repr., Kingston: Headstart, n.d.), 18.
2. J.E. Chamberlin, "A Map of the World", *Index on Censorship* 4 (1999): 110–11.
3. Howell, *Promised Key*, 4.
4. Ibid., 5.
5. See William David Spencer, *Dread Jesus* (London: Society for Promoting Christian Knowledge, 1999), 3–10, for accounts of these two events and how they created a void, and how Howell was a part of filling this void, as well as for a discussion of the Ethiopianistic Christology.
6. I have chosen this turn of phrase, "radical blackness", versus "black radical", which is more popularly used to emphasize the black supremacist ideology and practices within the former that are not so apparent in the latter. See Anthony Bogues, *Black Heretics, Black Prophets: Radical Political Intellectuals* (New York: Routledge, 2003).
7. See Jalani Niaah, "Rasta Teacher: Towards the Establishment of a New Faculty of Interpretation" (PhD thesis, University of the West Indies, 2005).
8. Sylvia Wynter is perhaps the only contemporary intellectual who seems to be theorizing in this direction, and her ideas are still considered radical, even for this time. See *After Man, Towards the Human: Critical Essays on Sylvia Wynter*, ed. Anthony Bogues (Kingston: Ian Randle, 2006).
9. Mortimo Planno theorizes Bob Marley as "Rastafari Bishop", drawing on the analogy of chess. See Mortimo Planno, "Bob Marley, Christ and Rastafari: The New Faculty of Interpretation" (Radio Education Unit, Library of the Spoken Word, University of the West Indies, Mona, Jamaica, 1997).
10. See Christopher Charles's essay in this volume, which addresses the issue of becoming black through nigrescence theory.
11. See Niaah, "Rasta Teacher".
12. Notwithstanding the consistent references to King Alpha and Queen Omega, and the strong participation of women in the early years, within a generation of its emergence, Rastafari was numerically male-dominated.
13. It is here recognized that Howell may have been exposed to various sources of inspiration from which he drew in formulating his teachings and message. These could have included such texts as Robert Alexander Young's 1829 book *Ethiopian Manifesto*, which in a spirited way depicted the ultimate liberation of Africans to come through divine intervention. There is rife within the United States at this time a discussion about black empowerment/black empire and various artistic and political engagements of the subject. For discussion of the United States/Harlem context, see M.A. Stephens, *Black Empire: The Masculine Global Imaginary of Caribbean Intellectuals in the United States, 1914–1962* (Durham, NC: Duke University Press,

2005); Winston James, *Holding Aloft the Banner of Ethiopia: Caribbean Radicalism in Early Twentieth-Century America* (London: Verso, 1998); and Spencer, *Dread Jesus*.

14. Hilary Beckles points out that 70 per cent of the slaves in Jamaica at the start of the nineteenth century were males. Given Jamaica's reputation for rebellion, the regard for and treatment of black males was especially targeted at emasculating and keeping in check this repressed labour force. See Hilary Beckles, "Black Masculinity in Caribbean Slavery", in *Interrogating Caribbean Masculinities: Theoretical and Empirical Analyses*, ed. Rhoda E. Reddock (Kingston: University of the West Indies Press, 2004), 225–43, for a discussion of Caribbean masculinity historically. Demographically, the Rastafari movement is considered as male-dominated, with some 85 per cent of its membership in Jamaica being male.
15. Sylvia Wynter would argue that the idea of "man" was a category reserved for European males, and all else became "the other", a subcategory of the Euro-normative interpretation. See Bogues, *After Man*, for more details. Also see Beckles, "Black Masculinity", 230.
16. Beckles, "Black Masculinity", 230.
17. Ibid., 231.
18. I am not in any way suggesting that Howell set out to construct a manhood focused on males; instead, I am saying that his new human potential was of particular appeal to a fractured male – constructed through a painstaking historical process.
19. Bogues, *After Man*, 59–61.
20. I am here referring to the leadership categories identified by Carole Yawney in describing how the dominant modes of discourse operate (iterative versus generative or preacher versus teacher), noticeable within Rastafari oratorical practice. See Carole Yawney, "Don't Vex Then Pray: The Methodology of Initiation Fifteen Years Later" (paper presented at the Qualitative Research Conference, University of Waterloo, Ontario, 15–17 May 1985).
21. Howell chant copied from J.P. Homiak, "Pinnacle Redux: Remembering Leonard Percival Howell", *Reggae Festival Guide* (2009): 62–71.
22. The dominant hegemonic categories became established after the Second World War, when the world was divided into the east-west spheres of ideological control. When local self-government was awarded, the Jamaican premier, Bustamante, thought it important to declare that Jamaica was solidly within the Western camp, or was not seeking to overturn the society away from its Westminster principles and political attitudes. Within this global sphere, Africa was invisible or excluded by those in authority over global affairs due to racism and neocolonial ambition.
23. Stephens, *Black Empire*, 36.
24. Quoted from "Leonard Howell, on Trial Says Ras Tafari Is Messiah Returned to Earth", *Daily Gleaner*, 15 March 1934.

25. Howell chant cited in Homiak, "Pinnacle Redux".
26. Howell, *Promised Key*, 5.
27. *The King James Bible*, Zephaniah 3:9–10. Such was the teaching of Mortimo Planno; see Niaah, "Rasta Teacher", 97–98.
28. Howell, *Promised Key*, 8.
29. This "lot" was perhaps not dissimilar to the Beta Israel group (Ethiopian Jews known commonly as the Falashas), who were engaged in an unprecedented repatriation exercise back to Israel in the 1980s and 1990s.
30. Howell, *Promised Key*, 17.
31. See Barry Chevannes, "Jamaican Lower Class Religion: Struggle against Oppression" (MSc thesis, University of the West Indies, 1971).
32. Stephens, *Black Empire*. In dealing with the "travelling black subject", Stephens picks up on the way travelling educated the black intellectual about blackness – and most importantly allowed them to negotiate alternative forms of identifications (see 59–62). Hence, Howell could declare in court that he was not going to swear on the Bible, and that he was "Mohammedan". See "Leonard Howell, on Trial".
33. Niaah, "Rasta Teacher", 102.
34. There are countless debates within Rastafari about the position of Marcus Garvey on the emperor and the Rastafari movement. Notwithstanding this, Marcus Garvey is still the most central prophet invoked within Rastafari.
35. Details related to this were provided by email dialogue between J.P. Homiak and Niaah on 22 April 2012.
36. It is this that Planno refers to as "polite violence", a feature of colonial control after emancipation. In putting the situation crudely, Planno argues that it was either the "mad-house" or "bad-house" for the African rebel leaders. See Niaah, "Rasta Teacher".
37. "Leonard Howell, on Trial".
38. See Chevannes, "Jamaican Lower Class Religion", for a discussion of the counter-colonial stance taken by Bedward.
39. See Howell, *Promised Key*, 26.
40. See Chevannes, "Jamaican Lower Class Religion", for a discussion of this "gift" of charisma among lower-class Jamaican religious leaders.
41. "Leonard Howell, on Trial".
42. Howell, *Promised Key*, 18.
43. See Paulo Friere, *Pedagogy of the Oppressed* (New York: Continuum, 2003), for a discussion of "conscientization" as a strategy for meaningful transformation.
44. Howell, *Promised Key*, 15–16.
45. Ibid., 12.
46. Ibid.
47. Robert Hill, *Dread History: Leonard Howell and Millenarian Visions in the Early*

Rastafari Religion (Kingston: Research Association School Times Publications and Frontline Distribution International, 2001), 44–46.

48. For an engagement of the strategic usage of photography by the Ethiopian nobility from the earliest inception of this medium, see Richard Pankhurst, "The Political Image: The Impact of the Camera in an Ancient Independent African State", in *Anthropology and Photography, 1860–1920*, ed. Elizabeth Edwards (New Haven, CT: Yale University Press, 1992), 234–41.

49. It has been argued that at one time HIM Emperor Haile Selassie I was reputedly the most photographed man in the world. See Girma Yohannes Iyassu Menelik, *Rastafarians: A Movement Tied with a [sic] Social and Psychological Conflicts* (Munich: GRIN, 2009).

50. This is what scholar J.P. Homiak describes as the "vernacular archives", which he has noted as a part of the Rastafari modality of pedagogy.

51. It is reported that he sold about five thousand such photos. See M.G. Smith, Roy Augier and Rex Nettleford, *Report on the Rastafari Movement in Kingston, Jamaica* (1960; repr., Kingston: Department of Extra-Mural Studies, University of the West Indies, 1988), 7.

52. See Niaah, "Rasta Teacher".

53. See the report "Dearth, Disease and Death" in the *Daily Gleaner*, 22 December 1940, which makes reference to conditions at Pinnacle. The idea was to destabilize this attempt by Howell at collective survival, to "nip it in the bud", so to speak. See also Michael Hoenisch, "Symbolic Politics: Perceptions of the Early Rastafari Movement", *Massachusetts Review* 29, no. 3 (1988): 432–49. Hoenisch explores inter alia the symbolism of "Howell" and "Pinnacle" representing for the official society their greatest and protracted fears of black independence.

54. These sentiments, ironically, were similar to the propaganda generated by the Italians about the emperor's reign. This is to allude to the challenge that serious leadership of Africans presents to white supremacy. Haile Selassie was understood to be a leader with tremendous ambition for his empire's development. Similarly, when Pinnacle as an enterprise started to thrive, the official response was that this was as a result of a thriving ganja trade. Mortimo Planno, a contemporary witness who visited the camp as a young adult, supports the idea that ganja was cultivated at Pinnacle, but further suggests that this was for export. In support of the British war efforts, Jamaican ganja was exported seemingly under cover of "tobacco" to the United Kingdom. See Niaah, "Rasta Teacher".

55. This is in reference to a West African field labour practice referred to by various names in different parts of the island; it is also called "morning sport".

56. The various threads of influences that were drawn on by Howell have still not been properly investigated in their own right. One such example is the statement in his court testimony in which he declares that he is Mohammedan or of the non-Christian

Islamic faith; further, he is described as being dressed in a rosette of gold, black and green – not the colours of the Ethiopian flag, red, green and gold. Could this be linked to a possible association with the African National Congress? These are questions yet to be answered.

57. This is supported by the account of social worker John Maxwell in July 2003 at the opening ceremony of the Rastafari Global Reasoning, held at the University of the West Indies. Maxwell indicated that as a child, he witnessed such scenes when passing by Pinnacle's gates in the late 1940s.
58. This is a statement made by a Howellite while providing a testimony of the experience of living at Pinnacle, at a symposium entitled "The Foundational Contribution of Leonard P. Howell, Rastafari Patriarch", at the University of the West Indies, Neville Hall Lecture Theatre, May 2011.
59. Hill, *Dread History*, 39–40.
60. Homiak provided this information in email correspondence on 22 April 2012.
61. *Roaring Lion: The Rise of Rastafari*, Frontline Productions, Rice N Peas Films, 2002.
62. *Daily Gleaner*, editorial, 6 November 1930.
63. Hoenisch, "Symbolic Politics", 432–33.
64. Ibid., 434.
65. Howell, *Promised Key*, 22.
66. See Niaah, "Rasta Teacher".
67. See Barry Chevannes, *Betwixt and Between: Exploration of a Caribbean Mindscape* (Kingston: Ian Randle, 2006).
68. "Chief Justice Denounces Leonard Howell as a Fraud", *Daily Gleaner*, 17 March 1934, 19.
69. Ibid.
70. See "Leonard Howell, on Trial".
71. See Niaah, "Rasta Teacher", and Haile Selassie I, *Academic Honours of His Imperial Majesty Haile Sellassie I, Emperor of Ethiopia: A Commemorative Volume, 1924–1963* (Addis Ababa: University Office of Public Relations, 1964).
72. This is interpreted by individuals such as Mortimo Planno in his biography "The Earth Most Strangest Man: The Rastafarian" (unpublished, available at http://www.cifas.us/sites/g/files/g536796/f/201304/TheEarthMostStrangestMan_Original.pdf), as a fulfilment of the prophecy of Malachi of the day when the Fathers' hearts are returned to the children. See Niaah, "Rasta Teacher", for further discussion.
73. Howell, *Promised Key*, 6.
74. See D.A. Dunkley's essay in this volume.
75. See Abebe Hailemelekot, *The Victory of Adowa and What We Owe to Our Heroes: The First Victory of Africa over Colonialists* (Addis Ababa: Abebe Hailemelekot, 1998).
76. Howell, *Promised Key*, 18.

77. Ibid., 25–26.
78. Barry Chevannes, *Rastafari: Roots and Ideology* (Syracuse, NY: Syracuse University Press, 1994), 101.

6

THE PROCESS OF BECOMING BLACK
Leonard Howell and the Manifestation of Rastafari

CHRISTOPHER A.D. CHARLES

This chapter is dedicated to all "man and man" who have been abused and killed by the security forces and civilians in Jamaica.

This chapter deals with the process of how a person who is born physically black becomes also psychologically black. The foregoing separates physical blackness from mental blackness, which may surprise some people. This separation explains why some black people are grounded in their racial consciousness, because unlike others, they were converted to psychological blackness through racial socialization. Rastafari in Jamaica is a classic exemplar of black racial socialization through religious conversion. This conversion leads to the development of moral blackness. Racial identity is the strong regard people attach to their race, thereby making it an important part of their sense of self.[1] This chapter uses nigrescence theory, or the process of becoming black, to explain the black religious conversion of Leonard Percival Howell, the first Rasta man.[2] The chapter starts with an outline of nigrescence, its application to Rastas and non-Rastas and the theory's connection to the tradition of radical blackness in Jamaica. Next is the application of the theory to explain Howell's process of becoming black, in which he developed a positive black racial identity.

The Stages of Black Identity Development

Nigrescence or black identity development across the life course involves the pre-encounter stage, the encounter stage, the immersion-emersion stage and the stage of internalization (table 6.1). This theory explains linear identity development, which assumes that the stages are sequentially fixed, at least for the first conversion experience of nigrescence, because a person who goes through these stages can recycle through some or all of the stages. This process of becoming black starts at adolescence and beyond.[3]

Stage 1

The attitude of a person in the pre-encounter stage ranges from low salience towards race, which is expressed as a pro-establishment assimilation identity, to a neutral position, to an anti-black stance. With the anti-black stance, there is the identity path of miseducation, where the person holds negative stereotypes about blacks, and there is also the self-hate identity path, where the person internalizes the negative stereotypes about blacks such as they are inferior and less intelligent compared to whites and so on. Such a person has a non-Afrocentric identity, and his or her attitude towards blacks is akin to that of white racists. This individual views race as an imposed social stigma that he or she has to occasionally deal with. This person was socialized to embrace Eurocentric values, so he or she was miseducated about black people, their history, culture and achievements. Therefore, this individual becomes anxious when he or she has to engage blackness because of Eurocentric racial stereotyping. Such an individual tends to blame the victims of white racism, because the victims did not try hard enough to make whites accept them. Persons in this stage of blackness tend to become members of organizations that place low importance on blackness.[4]

Stage 2

In the encounter stage, which does not have an identity path, the person experiences some life event(s) that triggers the process towards black identity conversion. Some exemplars of transforming events are the encounter with a black leader or social movement, the presence of an influential Afrocentric friend or relative, and the experience of colourism or racism. The individual moves

Table 6.1. Nigrescence Theory

Racial Salience	Black Identity Development			
	Pre-encounter Stage 1	Encounter Stage 2	Immersion-Emersion Stage 3	Internalization Stage 4
High	[Self-hate −] (internalizes the negatives about blacks) [Miseducation −] (holds negative stereotype of blacks)	***	[Anti-white +] (rejects everything white) [Intense black involvement+] (romanticizes blackness)	[Afrocentric +] (focus on black empowerment) [Bicultural +] (accepts blackness & another cultural orientation) [Multicultural +] (accepts blackness and other cultural orientations)
Moderate				
Low	[Assimilation +] (support the dominant group)			

***= there is no identity orientation in this stage because the individual is dealing with life events (racism, Afrocentric relative/friend and a black leader and/or social movement) that triggered a reexamination of his or her existing identity   [ ] = identity orientation   ( ) = core of identity orientation
+= positive racial salience   −= negative racial salience

away from the irrelevant pre-encounter identity, which no longer meets his or her psychological needs, to a more psychologically relevant identity. The internal change commences when the potential convert personalizes the triggering encounter event. He or she tends to have some insight into the new identity path, but response to the encounter may cause confusion, depression, worry and so on. These responses are informed by the person's new belief system: he or she feels that the old pre-encounter identity was dysfunctional because it was not sufficiently black. The person experiences a range of temporary emotions, such as rage, angst and remorse. These emotions serve as the catalyst of racial socialization towards Afrocentricity and the receding of the old pre-encounter identity.[5]

Stage 3

The immersion-emersion stage is the "vortex of psychological nigrescence" in which the construction of the new identity and the destruction of the old one are simultaneous.[6] The person is more knowledgeable about the old identity compared to the new one. The rejection of the old self requires the convert's commitment to change, buttressed by the fact that he or she now believes the norms and values of the rejected self were inadequate. The rejected self is linked to negative images and feelings during the dismantling process. The person with an intense black involvement identity tends to create overvalued, idealistic, exploratory and unsophisticated images of the new self because of a lack of knowledge and experience with this self. There is also the anti-white identity path, where the person rejects everything white.[7]

The convert will experience anxiety because he or she has no internal roadmap about how to create the right kind of black person. The irony of this stage is that the person with the most dramatic and spectacular displays of blackness is usually the least comfortable with his or her new identity. The symbols of the emerging identity become very attractive to the convert, so he or she sees the world in uncompromising "either/or" categories. This person, more often than not, is confrontational with people who place little or no importance on blackness. The convert also feels that he or she is blacker than others. Moreover, feelings of goodness and superiority are placed on all things black, unlike all things white, which are deemed bad and inferior. The individual tends to have a preoccupation with whites and their culture. There is psychological instability in this stage, which may make the emerging identity dormant, fixed or recede.[8]

Stage 4

In the internalization stage, the convert internalizes the new identity after a resolution of the problems and crises of the transitional stage. The black identity convert has now achieved inner peace, because he or she is comfortable with the new identity. The convert's black ideology determines the level of importance he or she gives to blackness and the identity path taken. The convert with an Afrocentric identity emphasizes black empowerment, while the convert with a bicultural identity path accepts a black identity and another cultural identity. Blackness and other cultural orientations are internalized by the convert, who embraces a multicultural identity.[9]

Black Identity in Jamaica

Religion is central to the black experience, but its expression in black identity development has not received much scholarly attention. However, the nigrescence theory has been applied to black identity development among the early Rastafarians in Jamaica, where religion was central to their black identity. The encounters some members of the Afro-Jamaican masses had with colonial oppression in the 1930s triggered their socialization towards a black anti-systemic identity, one with positive meaning for its adherents. Becoming Rasta is a way of life that is achieved through black racial socialization and spiritual awakening. The core of this identity, which is achieved through the process of becoming black, is the deification of the Ethiopian Emperor Haile Selassie I as the black Christ, a rejection of the values of the oppressive Babylonian West, a demand for repatriation to Africa and a perpetual quest for knowledge of the black self. This positive affirmation of the black self is a subversion of the colonial and neocolonial stereotypes of blacks.[10]

Nigrescence has also been used to explain the miseducated identity of black skin-bleachers in Jamaica at the pre-encounter stage of blackness. The Afrocentric critics of the skin-bleachers can be placed in the internalization stage of black identity development, because they believe in black empowerment.[11] This chapter focuses on how the first Rastafarian, Leonard Howell, became psychologically black through religious conversion.

The doctrine of Rastafari added religious awakening to a tradition of radical blackness which opposed white supremacy in Jamaica. This tradition is the forerunner to the manifestation received by Howell. The tradition of radical blackness is heterogeneous and provides a racial domain of moral resistance within which to construct a positive black identity. The captive Africans who were taken to Jamaica by the Spaniards after their arrival in 1494, and subsequently by the British after 1655, resisted through rebellions and the establishment of Maroon communities. Captive Africans on the plantations retained forms of African cosmology, values, dress, child-rearing and relationship practices, music, rituals, and health and dietary habits, despite the slave laws, which required them to give up the African self by attending church and becoming tractable. The resistance of the Maroons and the captive Africans to the "superior" white values, norms and worldview of the British colonial oppressors are the genesis of the resistance to white supremacy in Jamaica by people with a positive black racial identity.[12]

Three Jamaican-born Africans, Paul Bogle, Alexander Bedward and Marcus Garvey, are classic exemplars of the resistance, started by the captive Africans, to white supremacy in post-slavery colonial Jamaica through the assertion of a positive black identity. In 1865, the colonial governor refused to hear the grievances of a group of petitioners led by Bogle. The group was subsequently accused of disrupting a trial in Morant Bay, and the police who went to search for them destroyed their village. The angry villagers, led by Bogle, who shouted "Cleave to the black", went to the courthouse and were attacked by the colonial militia. In the ensuing violence, the courthouse was set ablaze, and fifteen white officials and three planters were killed. The leaders of the rebellion were captured and executed without fair trials, because the violent assertion of the black self for justice was a threat to colonial hegemony and oppression.[13]

The assertion of blackness by Alexander Bedward of the Native Free Baptist Church was also deemed a threat to the establishment. Members of the church journeyed from all over Jamaica to "dip" (baptize) in the "healing stream" of the Mona River. The colonial authorities became alarmed when Bedward told his followers in 1895 that the whites were thieves, that they should remember the Morant Bay Rebellion of 1865 and that they should knock down the white wall of oppression. Bedward had several confrontations with the police in 1921 and was subsequently arrested, convicted and placed in the lunatic asylum, where he died in 1930.[14]

The most successful pan-African leader, Marcus Garvey, established the Universal Negro Improvement Association (UNIA) in Jamaica in 1914. The UNIA had millions of members worldwide. Garvey preached black racial pride and economic empowerment. He declared that Africa was for the Africans on the continent and in the diaspora. The message of Garvey facilitated the creation of positive black identities among his followers. Marcus Garvey was rejected by the colonial establishment, but his ideas persisted.[15] Rastafarianism is the lineal pedagogy of radical blackness started by the captive Africans and continued by radical blacks such as Bogle, Bedward and Garvey, among others. These radical blacks had a high regard for their race and challenged white supremacy. Howell drew on this black radical tradition with the manifestation of Rastafari in Jamaica and his conversion to religious blackness. Cultural resources of blackness that were stigmatized by whites, but were worked and reworked by blacks over the centuries, became a new collective identity with positive meanings.[16]

Leonard Howell's Conversion to Blackness

Howell's conversion to blackness must be seen within the context of overlapping linear stages of nigrescence, but the stages are discretely outlined below, so as to better organize the data (table 6.2).

Pre-encounter Stage

The first stage dates from Howell's birth on 16 June 1898 and moves through his childhood and adolescence, when he left Jamaica at age eighteen in 1916, and his early adulthood, when he fought in the First World War for the British. Howell witnessed a murder in 1915 and was sent away by his father, who did not want his son to testify in the case. The identity of Howell at this stage in his development was miseducation, in which he held stereotypes of blacks and negative salience towards the black race. This assessment is based on the fact that schools in colonial Jamaica during Howell's childhood were operated by the church. The British government did not think that educating the descendants of Africans in Jamaica was a worthwhile endeavour. The young Howell went to a church-operated school. These schools taught a Eurocentric curriculum. The children were taught about the history, culture and achievements of Britain and about white heroes like Isaac Newton, Oliver Cromwell and Lord Nelson, among others. However, African history, culture and achievements, colonialism, slavery and African heroes were not a part of the curriculum.[17]

Table 6.2. Black Identity Development of Leonard Howell, 1898–1981

Critical Life Events	Stage of Nigrescence	Identity Orientation	Black Identity Behavioral Expression
• Born 16 June 1898 • Early childhood to adolescence • Left Jamaica in 1912 at age 14	Pre-encounter	Miseducation	Howell was influenced by Eurocentric colonial institutions such as the Anglican Church, which he attended with his lay preacher father, as well as the school in the community. He was miseducated about blackness and held negative stereotypes of blacks.
• Travelled to Africa and then the United States • Lived in Harlem in 1924 • Joined the UNIA in the United States • Selassie's coronation in 1930	Encounter	No identity orientation at this stage	The Harlem Renaissance was the encounter which triggered the process of change to blackness in Howell, who joined the UNIA. Selassie's coronation triggered the incorporation of spirituality into the emerging black identity using the Christian theology.
• Returned to Jamaica in 1932 • Started preaching in 1933 about Ras Tafari and selling his pictures • Associated with the UNIA up to 1934 • *The Promised Key* published in 1935	Immersion-Emersion	Anti-white and intense black involvement	Howell preached to the black masses that the black king of Ethiopia, Rastafari, was the living God, and sold his picture. He said the white Christian clergy were thieves and the queen of England was a harlot. Howell was very supportive of black organizations and their leaders locally and overseas.
• Arrested, tried and convicted in 1934 • Preached in prison in 1935 • Released from prison in 1936 • Post-imprisonment preaching/use of Hindu cosmology as Gangunguru Maragh • Arrested in 1937 and sent to the psychiatric hospital in 1938 • Bought Pinnacle in 1939 for £1200 • Pinnacle encampment began in 1940 • Security forces destroyed Pinnacle in 1954 • Left Pinnacle in 1958 • Sent to Bellevue in 1960 • Became a recluse on release • Died in 1981 at the Sheraton Hotel	Internalization	Afrocentric	Howell internalized the revelation of Rastafari and achieved inner peace, so he did not resist his arrests and conviction, imprisonment and placement in the asylum. Howell was willing to go to prison and the asylum for his beliefs, to which he remained committed, continuing to preach about Rastafari in prison. This deep commitment was seen in his post-incarceration preaching and his use of Hindu cosmology to spread his message. Howell's Afrocentric identity led him to the ideology of economic empowerment based on collective self-help and black self-reliance. This ideology led to the establishment of Pinnacle, the communal model of collective black self-reliance. This successful model of Rastafari was viewed as a threat by the colonial establishment and was violently destroyed. Howell remained steadfast in his belief in Rastafari after his final release from the asylum in 1960, up to his death in 1981

Moreover, Charles Howell, the father of Leonard Howell, was an Anglican lay preacher who took his son to church several times a week. The church preached a Eurocentric version of Christianity, with a white Jesus. This version of Christianity taught black Jamaican children about a white God who was anathema to the children's black physicality as well as to their history and culture. Given Leonard Howell's Eurocentric socialization, it is not surprising that he supported the British and fought in the "mother" country's army in the First World War. Howell held positive stereotypes of the British. The three key institutions that socialized him – his family, the Anglican Church and the church-run school – created a Eurocentric worldview for the young Howell.[18]

The miseducation identity is the most plausible identity for Howell at this stage of his life, based on the limited existing evidence discussed above. The self-hate identity is not plausible because Howell appears to have been a well-adjusted and self-confident boy who was able to leave his home and country at a young age and survive overseas on his own. Equally implausible is the pro-system assimilation identity, because Howell's black physicality, his peasant or working-class background and his low level of education made it impossible for him to assimilate into colonial Jamaica, with its rigid racial and skin-colour hierarchy.

Encounter Stage

In this second stage of Howell's black identity development, the available evidence does not point to a single life event but rather to a series of events that are plausible triggers in the process of change from the pre-encounter identity that became irrelevant to Howell's psychological needs to a more relevant identity (table 6.2). Future research on Howell may uncover a single triggering event, such as his experience of white racism as a black immigrant in the United States. Howell travelled the world, including Africa, and ended up in Harlem in 1924, during the Harlem Renaissance. During this period, black intellectuals and creative artists, including the Jamaicans Claude McKay, a poet and novelist, and pan-African leader Garvey and his UNIA, were generating classics and transforming ideas and works. Ethiopianism, black creativity and intellectual fervour during this time seem to have been the triggers for Howell's insight that his pre-encounter identity was not black enough and so had to be dismantled. The powerful social movement of the UNIA, of which he became a member in the United States, also influenced Howell's encounter with blackness. Another important triggering event was the coronation of His Imperial Majesty Emperor Haile Selassie I of Ethiopia in 1930. Ras Tafari, as he was previously known, at his coronation was given the title of King of Kings, Lord of Lords and the Conquering Lion of the Tribe of Judah. The coronation triggered the manifestation that Ras Tafari (which in Jamaica became Rastafari) was the living God. This manifestation was based on biblical interpretations of the coronation, so Howell incorporated the religiosity of Rastafari into his emerging black identity.[19]

Immersion-Emersion Stage

Howell returned to Jamaica in 1932, at age thirty-four, with the manifestation of Rastafari.[20] According to his sister, Avinel, Howell developed a conflict with the family when he returned to Jamaica and left the family home. His sister did not reveal the cause of the conflict, but it is possible that this was over Howell's belief in the divinity of Emperor Haile Selassie I.[21] Howell's immersion into blackness was evident in 1933, in his street sermons in Kingston about Rastafari, guided by his childhood Christian teachings and some ideas from the UNIA. Howell's doctrine, and his behaviour, reflected a fusion of the anti-white and intense black involvement identity orientations of nigrescence, because he found the emerging Rastafari identity attractive. Howell challenged the white supremacy of colonialism by preaching the divinity of Rastafari, the black God, the King of Kings and Lord of Lords. This God, the Lion of Judah, would break the chains of white oppression. Howell rejected everything white by preaching black supremacy. The Howellites were also told that a ship would come to Jamaica to take them to Ethiopia. Howell mobilized and inspired blacks who listened to his sermons. The Rasta preacher was very involved in the lives of his followers and the black masses in general, whom he repeatedly told that they were free. He sometimes ended his meetings by asking his congregants to sing the national anthem, "God Save the King", and belligerently told them that their king was Rastafari of Ethiopia. Howell's doctrine subverted the white racist colonial ideology, because he made blackness morally superior to whiteness, after the manifestation of Rastafari. Howell documented his message in *The Promised Key*, which was published by a Ghanaian publisher in 1935.[22]

Black symbols are very important during the immersion-emersion process. In Howell's new worldview, blacks needed a new representation of the Messiah that they could relate to. Howell sold to the people photographs of Haile Selassie I, whom he declared was the Prince of Peace, the eternal Messiah, who had returned. Howell connected with other black groups like the Afro-Athlican Constructive Gaathly and the UNIA, and visited Garvey. He also became close to Joseph Nathaniel Hibbert, Henry Archibald Dunkley and the former Bedwardite Robert Hinds. The connection with local black social movements and other Rastafari leaders provided support and validation for Howell's immersion-emersion into blackness. Support for Howell also came from the Trinidadian Marxist George Padmore, with whom Howell corresponded.[23]

However, by 1934, Howell had fallen out with Garvey, because Garvey criticized Emperor Haile Selassie I and Garveyites felt that the fledgling movement led by Howell was a "cult". Howell, at this stage of his process of becoming black, was not afraid of confrontation with the people whom he disagreed with or who ridiculed his ideas. One such confrontation occurred on 14 June 1933. Howell started preaching on the steps of the Coke Methodist Chapel, the favourite speaking spot of Garvey, which infuriated Garvey's supporters. Howell was uncompromising in his stance and might have felt that he was blacker than others. The Garveyites felt that Howell's claim that the Ethiopian flag was their flag, rather than the flag of King George, was seditious. Howellites interrupted UNIA meetings, and in at least one instance, Garveyites chased Howell from a UNIA gathering. Despite the schism between Howell and the UNIA, Howell's message retained many of the tenets of Garvey's ideas. During this stage of blackness, Howell demonized whites by vehemently arguing that the British were oppressors, the Queen of England was a harlot, and the Christian clergy were thieves. Alexander Bedward had said similar things about the whites in Jamaica decades earlier. Howell continued to defend his position in 1934 by verbally confronting any member of the audience, planter or police constable, who challenged his ideas because they had low salience towards blackness.[24]

Howell remained committed to the process of change by fusing the anti-white and intense black involvement identities in his message of Rastafari. This message rejected the old dysfunctional miseducation identity of the pre-encounter stage, and Howell successfully entered the stage of internalization with a positive black racial identity.

Internalization Stage

Howell achieved inner peace by internalizing the manifestation of Rastafari, which gave him a new faculty of interpretation. This inner peace and strong commitment to his faith were evident in how Howell peacefully handled his persecution and prosecutions by the British colonial authorities. Howell was arrested and convicted in 1934 and sent to prison for "sedition". Howell's imprisonment was a backlash by the colonial establishment to his creation of a positive black racial identity. This imprisonment did not deter Howell, who continued to preach Rastafari to fellow inmates. After his release from prison in 1936, Howell preached about Rastafari with greater fervour. He appropriated Hindu cosmology and took on the name Gangunguru Maragh (the Gong), and continued to spread the revelation of Rastafari to the black masses.[25] The first Rasta man, like his followers, faced discrimination because his religious and racial identities were stigmatized. The police sometimes incited people to attack Rastas. Howell imbued blackness with positive affect and meanings in the process of becoming black, because he had internalized black culture, history, achievements and heroes.[26]

The colonial authorities arrested Howell for "sedition" again in 1938, and sent him to the Bellevue psychiatric hospital for confinement for most of that year. Howell's inner peace and strong commitment to Rastafari in the face of official provocations and repression were indicative of his strong Afrocentric identity, which the colonial authorities found subversive. It was an anti-systemic identity that overturned the Eurocentric dogma that God is white, blacks are inferior and Africa is uncivilized. After his "psychiatric" incarceration, Howell focused on spiritually driven black empowerment because of his strong pro-black identity. This movement towards black empowerment was driven by the need of the early Rastafarians to become economically independent through communal living, collective self-help and black self-reliance.[27]

Howell's strong Afrocentric identity influenced him in 1939 to purchase the 153-acre Pinnacle property in St Catherine for twelve hundred pounds, to establish an independent commune to empower Rastafarians. The encampment at Pinnacle commenced in 1940. The commune had over three thousand members. Pinnacle was a successful economic venture which empowered the early Rastafarians. This was the kind of black economic empowerment that Garvey preached. The enterprising members of the commune owned a bakery, burned coal, and made white lime and shoes. The members also raised chicken and cattle and farmed crops such as vegetables, yams, cassava and peas, among others. The residents of Pinnacle sold some of their produce to members of the surrounding communities and saved their earnings. Howell and his supporters also had other communities in Kingston and St Thomas.[28]

The first successful Rasta commune was viewed as a threat by the colonial establishment, because the liberating ideas of Rastafari undermined white supremacy. The police destroyed Pinnacle in 1954. The security forces found the money saved by the commune members from their toils, but attributed these large sums to the illegal sale of marijuana. The Howellites were also accused by the authorities of keeping an insanitary camp, which was a public health threat, and also of attacking their neighbours. These "problems", among others, were used by the authorities as excuses to destabilize Pinnacle. Still, although Howell left the Pinnacle property in 1958, he never wavered in his commitment to Rastafari and black empowerment. The colonial authorities could not shake Howell's strong Afrocentric identity, even after he was again incarcerated in Bellevue psychiatric hospital in 1960. To date, Howell is the most persecuted and prosecuted Rasta man, having been arrested an alleged forty times or more by the police. Despite becoming a recluse until his death in 1981, Howell never flinched in his devotion to Rastafari and his commitment to black redemption. Pinnacle survived until 1981, when the remaining followers of Howell were expelled by a court order because of money allegedly owed on the property.[29]

Conclusion

This chapter has contributed to the sparse literature on Howell, the first Rastafari Gong, by using the psychological theory of nigrescence to track and explain his black identity conversion. However, there are limitations to the study. Several scholars have written about Howell, but there are many things we do not know about the first Rasta man, because the scholarship about him is limited and just emerging. The foregoing means that the information we have about Howell is incomplete, and some of it may be inaccurate; as such, nigrescence theory may be applied differently to the data in the future, when more is known. With future research, certain timelines and current "facts" may change, and a single encounter event for Howell may be identified, as well as a recycling process for Howell's black identity. Also, with more research, the emotions Howell experienced after the pre-encounter stage may be identified for the various stages of blackness, and this will help us to better understand the process of his conversion. Despite the potential changes of future research, the stages in Howell's process of becoming black will remain the same, because nigresecence is a well-validated theory that has been used to explain black identity conversion in Africa and the diaspora since the early 1970s.[30]

Positive black identity in Jamaica has historically been an anti-establishment identity, because the assertion of the psychic integrity and human dignity of the black self, particularly one with a spiritual awakening, overturns the denigration of blackness by colonial and neocolonial Jamaica. The Afrocentric identity of Rastafarians in general and Leonard Howell in particular is the most potent contemporary expression of a positive black identity that resists white oppression. At the core of this tradition of radical blackness, imbued with a spiritual awakening, is the manifestation of Rastafari. I recently witnessed a proud and confident articulation of this manifestation at one of the entrances to the University of the West Indies, Mona. I saw a young female student, Empress Natasha, entering the university with a Rasta button pinned to her blouse that bore the picture of a man who was not Haile Selassie I. I asked the student if the picture was of Prince Emmanuel, and she said yes. I saw the student a week later and introduced her to Jahlani Niaah, who told her about the Rastafari studies minor at the University of the West Indies. The young Bobo Shanti Empress revealed that reasoning with her brother was the encounter which triggered her conversion to a religious black identity. Rastafari has moved from being a negatively stigmatized identity, as it was in the 1930s, to become a positive exemplar of moral, religious and cultural blackness.

Notes

1. See William E. Cross Jr, *Shades of Black* (Philadelphia: Temple University Press, 1991).
2. Ibid.; William E. Cross Jr, "The Psychology of Nigrescence: Revising the Cross Model", in *Handbook of Multicultural Counselling*, ed. Joseph G. Ponterotto (Thousand Oaks, CA: Sage, 1995), 93–122.
3. I queried the starting point of nigrescence (adolescence and beyond) in the "Conceptualizing Black Identity" seminar in 2000 at the Graduate Center at the City University of New York, taught by William E. Cross Jr, the creator of nigresecence theory. I told Bill of my own experience as a child during my primary-school years

in Jamaica. I was an enraged child during the Heroes Weekend every year when the Jamaican Broadcasting Corporation showed documentaries or short films of the rebellions of captive Africans in Jamaica. I was enraged and upset with God for not allowing me to be born during slavery, so I could fight with the captive Africans against the murderous British. My knowledge of the inhumanity of African captivity on the plantations in the West as a child was my encounter that triggered my process of becoming black. Bill agreed in the seminar that the encounter stage of nigrescence can occur during childhood.

4. Cross, *Shades of Black*; Cross, "Psychology of Nigrescence"; William E. Cross Jr and Peony Fhagen-Smith, "Patterns of African American Identity Development: A Life Span Perspective", in *New Perspectives on Racial Identity Development*, ed. Bailey Jackson and Charmaine Wijeyesinghe (New York: New York University Press, 2001), 243–70; William E. Cross Jr and Beverly J. Vandiver, "Nigrescence Theory and Measurement: Introducing the Cross Racial Identity Scale", in Ponterotto, *Multicultural Counselling*, 371–93.
5. Cross and Vandiver, "Nigrescence Theory and Measurement", 371–93.
6. Ibid.
7. Ibid.
8. Ibid.
9. Ibid.
10. See Charles R. Price, "No Cross No Crown: Identity Formation, Nigrescence and Social Change among Jamaica's First and Second-Generation Rastafarians" (PhD Diss., City University of New York, 2002); Charles R. Price, "Social Change and the Development of a Black Antisystemic Identity: The Case of the Rastafarians in Jamaica", *Identity: An International Journal of Theory and Research* 3 (2003): 9–27; Charles R. Price, *Becoming Rasta: Origins of Rastafari Identity in Jamaica* (New York: New York University Press, 2009). These works by Charles Price, my graduate-student friend and now academic colleague, are timely. In the "Conceptualizing Black Identity" seminar taught by William E. Cross Jr at the City University of New York, I made the point to Bill that nigrescence did not account for religion as an encounter which can trigger conversion to blackness. I told him about the manifestation of Rastafari in Jamaica, and how it allowed "man and man" to become psychologically black. Bill agreed that religion was a trigger. Charles Price (the first African American Rasta I met) also shared this view. Price completed his doctoral dissertation on the nigrescence of early Rastafarians in Jamaica with Bill as his supervisor.
11. Christopher A.D. Charles, "Skin Bleaching and the Deconstruction of Blackness", *Ideaz* 2, no. 1 (2003): 78–105. I was influenced by Bill's research on blackness. I completed my psychology doctoral dissertation on skin bleaching in Jamaica at the City University of New York, under the supervision of Dr William E. Cross Jr and Dr

Martin D. Ruck. These co-supervisors, along with Dr Don Robotham, comprised the core members of my doctoral dissertation committee.

12. See Edward Brathwaite, *The Development of Creole Society in Jamaica, 1770–1820* (Oxford: Clarendon Press, 1978); Orlando Patterson, *The Sociology of Slavery: An Analysis of the Origins, Development and Structure of Negro Slave Society in Jamaica* (Teaneck, NJ: Fairleigh Dickinson University Press, 1969); Price, *Becoming Rasta*.

13. See Price, "Social Change"; Donald Robotham, *"The Notorious Riot": The Socio-Economic and Political Bases of Paul Bogle's Revolt* (Kingston: Institute of Social and Economic Research, 1984).

14. See Kenneth Post, *Arise Ye Starvelings: The Jamaican Labour Rebellion of 1938 and Its Aftermath* (The Hague: Martinus Nijhoff, 1978); Price, *Becoming Rasta*.

15. Rupert Lewis, "Garvey's Perspective on Jamaica", in *Garvey: His Work and Impact*, ed. Rupert Lewis and Patrick Bryan (Kingston: Institute of Social and Economic Research, 1988), 229–42; See also Price, *Becoming Rasta*.

16. Ibid.; see also Horace Campbell, *Rasta and Resistance: From Marcus Garvey to Walter Rodney* (New York: Africa World Press, 1987).

17. Carl Campbell, "Social and Economic Obstacles to the Development of Popular Education in Post-emancipation Jamaica", *Journal of Caribbean History* 1 (November 1970): 57–88; Hélène Lee, *The First Rasta: Leonard Howell and the Rise of Rastafarianism* (Chicago: Lawrence Hill, 2003). See also Price, *Becoming Rasta*; Eric Williams, *Education in the British West Indies* (New York: A&B Books, 1994).

18. Michael Hoenisch, "Symbolic Politics: Perceptions of the Early Rastafari Movement", *Massachusetts Review* 29, no. 3 (1988): 432–49. See also Lee, *First Rasta*; Price, *Becoming Rasta*.

19. See Campbell, *Rasta and Resistance*; G.G. Maragh [Leonard Percival Howell], *The Promised Key* (1935; repr., Kingston: Headstart, n.d.).

20. It is possible that Howell's argument that oppression is the same everywhere is an indication that he experienced white racial discrimination in the United States, which triggered his conversion towards a religious black identity. More research needs to be done to find out if this is so.

21. See Lee, *First Rasta*; Price, *Becoming Rasta*.

22. See Campbell, *Rasta and Resistance*; Howell, *Promised Key*; Lee, *First Rasta*.

23. See Hoenisch, "Symbolic Politics"; Howell, *Promised Key*; Lee, *First Rasta*; Rupert Lewis, "Marcus Garvey and the Early Rastafarians: Continuity and Discontinuity", in *Chanting Down Babylon: The Rastafari Reader*, ed. Nathaniel Samuel Murrell, William David Spencer and Adrian Anthony McFarlane (Philadelphia: Temple University Press, 1998), 145–58.

24. Lee, *First Rasta*; Post, *Arise Ye Starvelings*.

25. Leonard Howell was the first Gong, and Bob Marley was the second Gong. Both Gongs died in 1981.

26. See Hoenisch, "Symbolic Politics"; Lee, *First Rasta*; Price, *Becoming Rasta*.
27. Ibid.
28. See Lewis, "Marcus Garvey"; Miguel Lorne, introduction to Howell, *Promised Key*..
29. Miguel Lorne, introduction to Howell, *Promised Key*
30. Several black American scholars in the 1960s, including William E. Cross Jr were influenced by the Black Power movement in the United States. These scholars were confronted with the fact that many Americans who were physically black were becoming psychologically black by taking on a black identity. These scholars felt that it was necessary to explain the process of becoming black, so they developed theories of black identity. Cross's nigrescence theory is the most popular and widely used, and has been made into a scale (Cross Racial Identity Scale [CRIS]) to measure black identity development. Nigrescence and the CRIS are currently used with African Americans and other blacks in psychotherapy and research.

7

REORIENTING RASTA
Tracing Rastafari's Visual Roots

PETRINE ARCHER

In the *Daily Gleaner* of 18 January 1937, two pictures accompany a story headlined "St Thomas Wars on the Ras Tafari Cult". They are extremely detailed and embellished line drawings (figures 7.1 and 7.2). At the bottom of one image are handwritten notes in a cryptic language. Both images, along with the text, are used as evidence against Leonard Percival Howell, considered to be the leader of Rastafari and the source of recent disturbances in the parish of St Thomas, where locals have used "switches and lengthy sticks" to chase members in efforts to dismantle the Rasta's "cult" settlement. The special newspaper report, written by George B. Wallace, describes all this material as "photographic reproductions of the mystic signs of Ras Tafari" and a prayer of "unknown" tongue, which the reporter likens to Pukkumina.

These pictures represent some of the earliest visual evidence of the Rastafari movement, later renowned for its symbolism.[1] They are important artefacts for understanding the movement as well as the seminal ideas of its leader, L.P. Howell. As such, they have been written about by Robert Hill, Jake Homiak and Hélène Lee, from the disciplines of history, anthropology and journalism, respectively.[2] All have viewed these images as part of Howell's attempts to position himself as a mystical prophet or healer, with the aid of East Indian, Kongolese and cre-

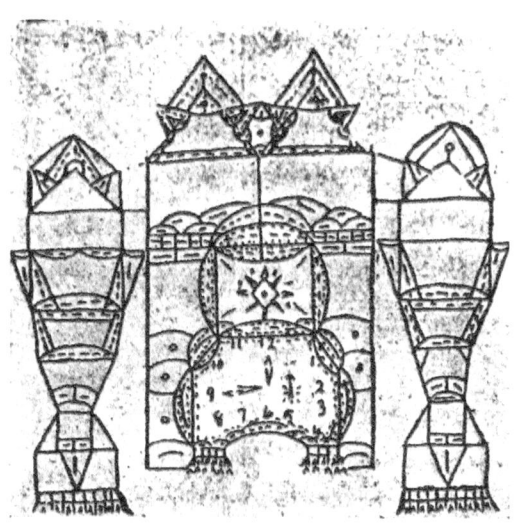

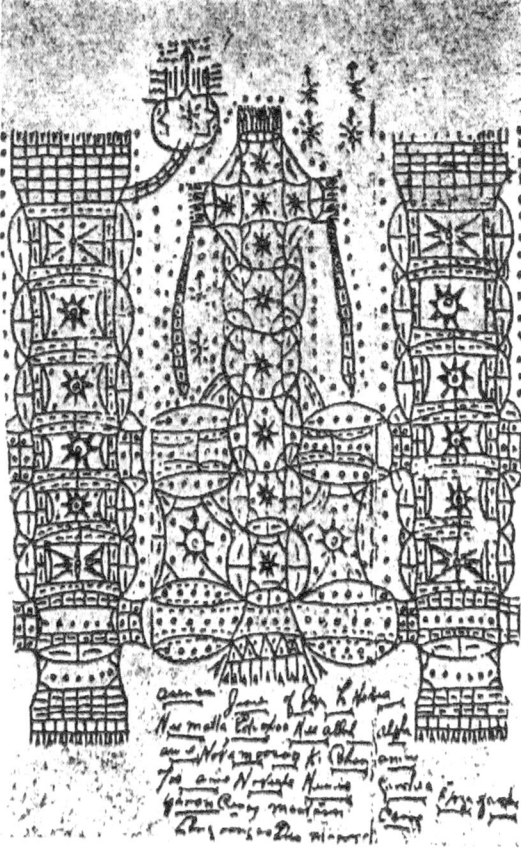

Figures 7.1 and 7.2. Line drawings showing "the Mystic Signs of Ras Tafari". Courtesy of the *Gleaner*.

olized cultural forms such as Kumina, Revivalism and Junkanoo, practised in St Thomas. Further, they have underscored the multicultural influences that informed the development of the movement during that era. In like fashion, this chapter will add to this "callaloo" by using art historical analysis to retrace this imagery's unique origins, and to suggest additional ways of viewing the past and, as a consequence, Rastafari's present.

The Images and Context

We can begin by examining the images themselves and the context that informed them. Howell described them as "a dream of what houses in future Abyssinia will look like", yet there is nothing particularly residential about them.[3] In fact, their tripartite form might even be suggestive of the Trinity. In the first image, the central form, topped by two pinnacles, appears to house a seat that might even be a throne. Within its centre is a timepiece, with hands showing that it is 9:00 a.m. or 9:00 p.m. A smaller clock to the right indicates the same time. Even though these are line drawings, the artist has created some depth of field, and background scenery is indicated. The second image is even more embellished. The same three forms appear to be studded with gems that shimmer. The central form is crucifix-like and topped with a crown. On the left, a chalice-like tube releases a cloud surrounding another timepiece, with more hands and arrows that point heavenward.

There is no doubting the surreal quality of this imagery, and a few explanations have been offered regarding their symbolism and the sense of imminence that black people felt during that time. The throne-like forms, the clocks and the references to transcendence all suggest that these images reinforced millenarian beliefs of that post-war era. Returning to the 1920s, it is possible to see how Howell's pictures were directed towards a black underclass, whose members harboured aspirations for transformation and change. As an early follower of Marcus Garvey, L.P. Howell came back to Jamaica around 1932 and began selling images of Emperor Haile Selassie I, professing him to be the long-awaited King of Kings, who would lead oppressed black people to victory over the white race and to a new land of Zion in Africa. Looking at the photograph of Haile Selassie I that Howell sold for one shilling, we can understand how Jamaica's downtrodden masses would have been seduced by its splendour (figure 7.3).

Taken from the pages of the *Illustrated London News*, the image is that of a

Figure 7.3. Image of Emperor Haile Selassie I sold by Leonard Howell, c. 1932.

dignified black monarch, bedecked in a jewelled crown that signifies both great wealth and his warrior status. Gems hang, pendant-like, around the fringe of the crown, while his forehead is covered by a golden Star of David. The theme of the crown is carried through to his brocaded robe, which bears golden medals of honour. Even though this image predates the imperial coronation, which featured even more splendid attire, Haile Selassie I already looks the part of an emperor. In contrast to Garvey's portraits of the same era, which are often self-conscious and even unflattering, this image (like so many more of the emperor) suggests a regent at ease with his station and power.[4]

Photographs taken during the period of HIM Emperor Haile Selassie's coronation can also be linked to Howell's heraldic drawings, such as the image of the emperor seated beneath a luxurious canopy, a fabric-covered, tent-like structure reserved for the monarch as a sort of sanctuary during the ceremony. If we compare the crowning feature of the emperor's abode with Howell's drawings, we see that they share the same highly ornate crest, shrine-like form and decorative pillars, although Howell's are far more opulent. With this, there is the suggestion that perhaps Howell was being quite truthful when he stated that his drawings were representations of what homes might look like in Abyssinia. His drawings might not depict homes built with bricks or mortar, but rather imagined tabernacles that house thrones reserved for the righteous alongside "Jah Rastafari". But if Howell's visual musings are not directly inspired by photographs of Haile Selassie's coronation, what else might they represent, and what more can we learn from the jumbled text that accompanied them? A return to Howell's life and its historical context might provide the clues.

The seminal research on L.P. Howell is a 1981 article by Robert Hill which provides a great deal of detail about Howell's earliest activities and his shaping of the Rastafari movement.[5] Howell, like Garvey, was a traveller, and although his journeys were not as well documented as Garvey's, we know that during the 1920s, he too visited Panama and also ended up in Harlem, running a tea house that might have even been a cover for other nefarious activities.[6] Hill tells us that Howell developed a reputation for being a "samfie-man", or at best a man of "science" or "Obeah", and he suggests that this might also have been a reason for Garvey's later rejection of Howell, once they both began "working the crowds" back in Jamaica. Garvey was deported from the United States in 1927, and Howell followed in 1932, initially trying to establish himself as a speaker at Garvey's Edelweiss Park in Kingston, but eventually giving up the city to develop his popularity in the countryside.[7]

That Howell moved to Trinity Ville, St Thomas, may be an accident of history, but it was also fortuitous, since few parishes could have proved a better seeding ground for his budding mystical beliefs.[8] As in Clarendon, the parish of his birth, St Thomas's economy was dominated by large sugar plantations and small farming communities, formed around free towns established after emancipation. The parish was noted for its radicalism, having been the site of the Morant Bay Rebellion back in 1865. Additionally, it was culturally diverse. In addition to the white landowners, Baptist missionaries and the mass of West Africans imported as slaves to work on the plantations, St Thomas had also hosted a large influx of East Indians, brought into the parish from 1845 to augment the labour supply after emancipation in 1838.[9] But its diversity was even broader as the parish experienced a second wave of Africans, who came to Jamaica from the Kongo region, now known as Angola.[10] They came not as slaves but as indentured labourers, beginning in 1841, and as such, they shared the same barracks and yards as their East Indian counterparts. The bonding arrangements for these labourers were such that by the time Howell arrived in St Thomas in the 1930s, these families had already worked off their time on the plantations, and those who stayed in the parish had become creolized and assimilated into the wider society. It was not unusual for Africans to intermarry with East Indians, or for the two groups to share and exchange their distinct cultural forms.[11] We now know that Howell associated with these Indians and even drew from their rituals and customs to reinforce his mystical charisma.

Although no firm evidence confirms Howell's sources for his pen name, G.G. Maragh, his use of the Hindi, Urdu and Bengali languages in prayers, or his adoption of Indian rituals related to food and vegetarianism as well as the smoking of kali weed (ganja), we can speculate that these derived from Howell's association with an East Indian called Laloo, who was his constant companion and bodyguard during these years.[12] Additionally, in the realm of music and religion, especially in forms such as Kumina, Revival Zion, Nyabinghi, Convince, Bongo and tabla drumming, as documented by the musicologist Ken Bilby, we begin to hear the influence of one cultural form on another.[13] In fact, much of what Bilby tells us about the relationship of these overlapping forms bears out in Robert Hill's conclusions that the emergence of Rastafari in this period needs to be viewed as "an integral aspect of the larger matrix of black religious nationalism, folk religious revivalism, and Jamaican peasant resistance to the plantation economy and state", and that there is "an urgent need to reintegrate the study of Rastafarianism into the dynamic flow of popular social movements", albeit with sensitivity to that historical process.[14] Hill underscores that Howell's grounding in the Garvey movement and the development of a black worldview has meant that his life and work have been framed within the context of Garvey's Afrocentrism. More recent scholarship, such as Homiak's "Pinnacle Redux: Remembering Leonard Percival Howell" and a rereading of

Hill's writings on Howell and millenarianism, however, suggest that both East Indian and Kongo influences as well as those of other contemporaneous movements, such as Revival Zion, may have played a more significant role in Howell's philosophical development than has initially been considered.[15]

With this in mind, perhaps we can view Howell's drawings within the context of contemporaneous East Indian and Kongo influences to better understand their mystical forms. In his article "Pinnacle Redux", anthropologist J.P. Homiak begins by remarking on issues related to selective memory, and why some aspects of Howell's rituals have been remembered and others are forgotten. By way of example, he looks at Howell's drawings, finding it curious that over the years since their publication, no one has noted the obvious resemblance between them and the central ritual object of Indo-Jamaican Hosay celebrations, known as the *tadjah*. Homiak writes, "Suffice it to say that [Hosay] is a tradition known in both St Thomas and Clarendon, both parishes with sizeable East Indian populations and both familiar to Howell and his followers", and goes on to remark that the segmented and layered structure of the *tadjah*, coupled with its peaked surmounting structure, "are far too reminiscent of [Howell's] future homes in Zion not to have served as the inspirational source for these drawings".[16]

Beyond the Images

Yet how many of us ever really look beyond what we expect to see? And to what extent is our vision blinkered by our own perspectives and a need to see the world in a particular kind of way? Looking again at the drawings and their relationship to Muslim *tadjahs* raises more questions than we may be fully prepared to answer. Is it possible that West African Islam, Junkanoo (also popular in the parish of St Thomas during Howell's time) or a latent East Indian culture could have been precursors for Rastafari's earliest Binghi rituals? Let's continue by comparing their imagery.

It is known that some West Africans who were taken to Jamaica in the earlier period of slavery were Muslims, but their Islamic practices faded "due to forced mixing of ethnic groups and the success of a Christianity-based anti-slavery process", according to Sultana Afroz. But "the advent of East Indian indentured labourers from the late nineteenth century saw a public rekindling of Islam in Jamaica".[17] What better occasion to play out hidden beliefs and identities than Junkanoo, the public holiday festivities afforded slaves during Christmas and independence celebrations? Junkanoo is a masquerade parade believed to be of West African origin and was regularly performed by slaves during festival holidays throughout the New World. In Jamaica, it took the form of small bands dressed in fanciful and outrageous costumes, which performed, often competitively, to display their skills in dancing, music and fearsomeness. Although little is known about the masquerade's origins, Junkanoo is generally understood to be a dynamic and eclectic practice that since slavery has reinvented itself with new characters and cultural influences. In fact, artist Isaac Mendes Belisario, who documented the practice between 1831 and 1837, lamented even then that many of the more traditional African characters, such as "Jack in the Green", were being replaced by new forms.[18]

The case of the "set girls" is a significant example of these newer forms; these were Haitian exiles who had arrived in Jamaica during the revolution of 1791–1804.[19] Even so, they injected their own aesthetic and even rivalry into the Junkanoo parade, sporting meticulously tied red, green and gold head wraps that denoted their Mabiales Kongo origins (figure 7.4). In retrospect, their Ethiopian colours make for interesting speculation on contemporary relationships to Africa and contemporary affiliations in Jamaica, especially

Figure 7.4. *French Set-Girls*, Kingston, Jamaica. Drawn from life by Isaac M. Belisario; printed by A. Duperly, 1837. Courtesy of the National Library of Jamaica.

given the rise of the first African Baptist Church under the influence of black missionary George Liele at that time.[20] Central to the masquerade band was Junkanoo himself, a figure carrying a house-like structure, again similar to Howell's "visionary drawings", constructed with card, fabric, tinsel and foil that allowed it to shimmer in the same fashion.[21]

Although the connection between Junkanoo and West Africa has long been accepted, Bilby tells us that Junkanoo was also favoured by the East Indians in Jamaica.[22] In fact, he identifies Junkanoo as an area of cultural exchange, stating, "In some areas, East Indians have taken up [Junkanoo] dancing, and have created their own unique costumes to go with it."[23] In light of the St Thomas New Year's celebrations that sparked Howell's 1937 arrest, is it possible that what Howell and his followers were planning was a creolized version of Junkanoo, with cultural influences that would have appealed to East Indians and West African descendants alike? Let's pick up on the *Daily Gleaner*'s description again, as special reporter Wallace described the planned event:

> From Thursday, Ras Tafari's New Year's Eve, his followers had been arriving to take part in a procession planned for the morrow, New Year's Sunday, when a cow in full Ras Tafari regalia [a horse head] would lead the Howellites about the town, and stupendous preparations were already made to accommodate the expected multitude, when a sheep would be burned [curry goat] as a sacrifice to their Alpha and Omega. A newly erected zinc fence skirted the meeting yard and home of the Ambassador, Councillor and Defender (as he titled himself) and on the ground directly before his residence scores of conch shells spelt the words "King's House". Attached to a pole above the gate was the artistic emblem of a Lion with a spear in his mouth, and beneath inscribed in bold letters "King of Kings and Lion of Judah".[24]

That Howell was arrested before this event could even take place should not be surprising, not because this event was just another harmless street masquerade but because, as Hill tells us, Rastafari followers were already under suspicion for what were perceived as more deviant activities linked to Revivalism and Shakerism.[25] These concerns had escalated with the popularity of personalities such as Alexander Bedward and Garvey, but they went back as far as the Haitian Revolution, which had rid white authority from what was then Saint-Domingue, and the Morant Bay Rebellion, which had destabilized British rule in Jamaica. In fact, ever since the establishment of France's famous *Code Noir* in 1685, any religious practice that flouted Christian rituals (read values) in favour of African ones was viewed as deviant and subversive.[26] To the government of the day, Rastafari represented a religion threatening political disruption, blasphemy and sedition.

But to what extent was this representation the result of a mere smear campaign? What was the relationship between Rasta and Revivalism, between Orthodox Ethiopianism and Kongo Spiritualism? These are questions still being considered and unravelled by historians and Rastas alike, even today. From an art historical perspective, I would like to re-examine Howell's drawings once again, comparing them with two more drawings that appeared in that same *Daily Gleaner* article of January 1937. These images are described as "ideographic diagrams" that were found on the inside of the cover of a minute book belonging to Joseph Nathaniel Hibbert, renowned man of science and one of Howell's earliest cohorts (figures 7.5 and 7.6).[27] We can assume that they were designed by Hibbert and that, like Howell's drawings, they represent ideas that informed his thinking during the developmental stages of Rastafari. In Hibbert's case, the symbolism is more cryptic, and whereas with Howell we can more readily discern tangible forms, these drawings are a combination of signs and symbols that bear no resemblance to a Western visual lexicon. But there is a reason for

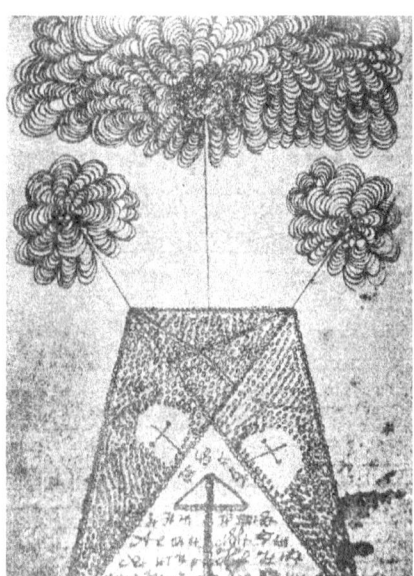
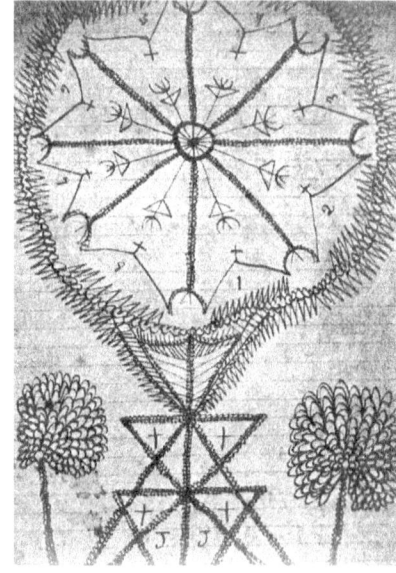

Figures 7.5 and 7.6. "Ideographic diagrams" taken from the inside cover of a minute book belonging to Joseph Nathaniel Hibbert. Courtesy of Robert Hill.

this: their detailed forms and tendril-like draughtsmanship share commonality with an African cosmology more readily seen in this hemisphere in the Haitian *veve* – signs and symbols that reference Kongo deities and African spirit forms. Specifically, Hibbert's images referenced the *lwa* of Simbi, a diverse family of serpent deities from the Kongo that, rather like Mercury, represent water and communication. Simbi are the messengers of Legba, the sun.

I do not practice Vodou, and my interpretation of this imagery may not be entirely accurate, but I make these allusions so that we can better appreciate the cross-fertilization of ideas and images that were in play when Rastafari was in its infancy and perhaps even before its birth.

Conclusion

Today, Rastafari has come to be characterized by its red, green and gold symbolism and its distinct garb, locks and livity, but these forms represent a way of seeing and a process of selection and rejection that have developed over decades, if not centuries. Although it may be useful for us to see Howell's first drawings as depicting a tabernacle, housing a throne where Emperor Haile Selassie I might sit in all his glory, as we have seen, it is also possible for us to see them as representing an Islamic *tadjah*[28] or the Junkanoo figure described by Belisario as "House John-Canoe". Even more curious is the resemblance of Howell's drawings to the Haitian *veve* of Damballa or Baron Samedi, with similar tripartite divisions – only now the two forms on either side are not thrones, but coffins.

I believe that what we are witnessing in these drawings are a range of choices that would determine Rastafari's future survival, and the visual forms that would more accurately come to depict Howell and Rastafari's belief over time – that is, a belief in a Jah ever-living and a life everlasting.

Acknowledgements

This paper would not have been possible without the research I completed at the Smithsonian Institution in April 2011. I wish to thank Jake Homiak, Shirley Samuels and Carolyn Cooper for supporting my application for the fellowship that made this research visit possible. I am further indebted to Jake Homiak for encouraging my curiosity about the influence of Jamaica's East Indians on Leonard Percival Howell.

Notes

1. Howell's book, *The Promised Key*, published earlier in 1935, featured two crossed keys, a Masonic symbol, on its cover.
2. Robert Hill, "Leonard P. Howell and Millenarian Visions in Early Rastafari", *Jamaica Journal* 16, no. 1 (1983): 24–39; Jake Homiak, "Pinnacle Redux: Remembering Leonard Percival Howell", *Reggae Festival Guide* 1 (2009): 62–69. The most extensive biography to have been written about Leonard Howell is by French journalist Hélène Lee. See *The First Rasta: Leonard Howell and the Rise of Rastafarianism* (Chicago: Lawrence Hill, 2003).
3. George B. Wallace, "St Thomas Wars on the Ras Tafari Cult", *Daily Gleaner*, 13 January 1937, 28.
4. For a detailed critique of Garvey's portrait, see Robert Hill, "Making Noise: Marcus Garvey Dada, August 1922", in *Picturing Us: African American Identity in Photography*, ed. Deborah Willis (New York: New Press, 1994), 181–205.
5. Hill, "Leonard P. Howell", 24–39.
6. For a more extensive discussion about symbolism and Marcus Garvey, see Hill, "Making Noise", 181–205.
7. See John Carradine, "The Ras Tafarites Retreat to Mountain Fastnesses of St Catherine", *Daily Gleaner*, 23 November 1940.
8. I owe my understanding of the importance of St Thomas as a seeding ground for Rastafari and Howell to my father, Gerald Ashley Archer, who was born in that parish in 1930. His grandmother, Irene Bryan, a.k.a. Miss Irene, was East Indian and lived all of her life in Golden Grove, St Thomas. My father spent a great deal of his youth moving between the small towns and villages of Dalvey, Duckenfield, Trinity Ville, Stokes Hall and Old Pera. He remembers the community of Africans, whom the locals called "Bongos", as well as East Indians, and their distinct lifestyles and celebrations. His maternal uncle, Xerxes Bryan, was a Junkanoo travelling entertainer, who performed in costume at Christmas and independence celebrations. Xerxes Bryan was also involved in Kumina. My father later became a good friend of L.P. Howell's son, Monty Howell, when they both lived in the United Kingdom during the 1960s. Interview with Gerald Ashley Archer, 1 June 2011.
9. This chapter is offered as a tribute to the late professor Ajai Mansingh (1931–2011), who provided me with a great deal of information about cultural continuities between East Indian culture in Jamaica and the Rastafari movement. Professor Mansingh, along with his wife, Laxmi, devoted a great deal of research to Rastafari as part of their interest in interfaith studies. See the following by Ajai and Laxmi Mansingh: *Home Away from Home: 150 Years of Indian Presence in Jamaica, 1845–1995* (Kingston: Ian Randle, 1999); "Rastafarianism: The Indian Connection", *Sunday Gleaner*, 18 July 1982; "Hindu Influences on Rastafarianism", in *Caribbean Quarterly*

Monograph: Rastafari, ed. Rex Nettleford (Kingston: Caribbean Quarterly, 1985), 96–115; and "The Impact of East Indians on Jamaican Religious Thoughts and Expressions", *Caribbean Journal of Religious Studies* 10, no. 2 (1989): 36–52.

10. See the liner notes for two album recordings: Ken Bilby, "From Kongo to Zion: Three Black Musical Traditions from Jamaica", in *Kumina and Revival Selections*, Folkways Records, 1979; and Ken Bilby, liner notes, in *Bongo, Backra and Coolie: Jamaican Roots*, vol. 1, Folkways Records, 1975.
11. Archer, interview, 2011.
12. Lee, *First Rasta*, 97–107.
13. See Bilby, "From Kongo to Zion"; Bilby, liner notes, *Bongo, Backra and Coolie*.
14. Hill, "Leonard P. Howell", 38–39.
15. Homiak, "Pinnacle Redux", 62–69.
16. Ibid.
17. Sultana Afroz, "Jamaica: The Muslim Legacy", www.geocities.com/mutmainaa/history/islamjamaica.html.
18. Isaac Mendes Belisario, *Sketches of Character, in Illustration of the Habits, Occupation and Costume of the Negro Population in the Island of Jamaica* (Kingston: I.M. Belisario, 1837), reproduced in Jackie Ranston, *Belisario: Sketches of Character, A Historical Biography of a Jamaican Artist* (Kingston: Mill Press, 2008), 244 and 254.
19. For my interpretation of these dancers, see Petrine Archer, "Art and Emancipation in Jamaica", *Jamaica Journal* 3, nos. 1–2 (2008): 74–77.
20. Mary Turner, *Slaves and Missionaries: The Disintegration of Jamaican Slave Society, 1787–1834* (Kingston: University of the West Indies Press, 1998), 11.
21. Junkanoo of Belisario's time has been documented extensively in two fairly recent publications. See Tim Barringer, Gillian Forrester and Barbaro Martinez-Ruiz, *Art and Emancipation in Jamaica: Isaac Mendes Belisario and His Worlds* (New Haven, CT: Yale Center for British Art, 2007); and Ranston, *Belisario*.
22. Bilby, liner notes, *Bongo, Backra and Coolie*, 1.
23. Ibid.
24. Wallace, "St Thomas Wars on the Ras Tafari Cult", 28.
25. Hill, "Leonard P. Howell", 30.
26. In this sense, Rastafari was tarred with the same brush. Hill describes "the gradual penetration of unrest in Jamaica in the two years preceding 1938 by the force of the Rastafari millenarian ideology of racial dominion", and notes that "it thus remains important to recognize the depth to which popular belief in the power of the occult played a formative role in the early stages of Rastafari consciousness". Ibid., 38.
27. Ibid., 34.
28. Homiak, "Pinnacle Redux", 68.

8

SOCIAL ENTREPRENEURSHIP AND RASTAFARI "LIVETY"
Pinnacle as a Successful Social Enterprise

K'ADAMAWE A.H.N. K'NIFE, EDWARD DIXON AND
ALLAN BERNARD

This paper is "livicated" to the Howellites, who we got a chance to speak to at Tredegar Park All Age School; their knowledge and time shared are invaluable and reflect the continuation of a philosophy of self-reliance through collective security . . . more life, joy and prosperity, Rastafari Lives.

I am convinced that the children we are teaching today will become vanguards and guardians to our freedom tomorrow and better citizens to defend our democracy and to ensure that generations to come will learn from the Holocaust of slavery, and keep the flame of remembrance burning. Help them to understand more about the past, that our history NEVER repeats itself, so that we can create a better future for all [of the] human race.
 –*Leonard Howell*[1]

The practice of social entrepreneurship is not new; however, the way in which it is expressed suggests that the scholarship on it is just emerging. The practice is becoming more important and generating significant attention as a way of addressing the myriad of problems facing many countries.[2] These ideas of social entrepreneurship are being seen as a meaningful approach to improving the quality of life of the people in an effective and sustainable way. While there has been a proliferation of research on the practice within many developed countries, few scholars have done any meaningful research on this subject in or among developing countries. Like developed countries, however, many developing countries face problems, sometimes even greater ones, which require the urgent attention and support of social entrepreneurs. Whether resulting from need or simply from the seizing of an opportunity, there has been a history of organizations and individuals who sought to meaningfully transform the lives of people within developing countries. Marcus Garvey, in the 1920s and 1930s, with the Universal Negro Improvement Association (UNIA), presents evidence of these activities within the early twentieth century.[3] One could go further to provide evidence of these practices from the period of enslavement, starting with the enslaved Africans who left the plantations to establish their own Maroon settlements. Subsequently, these ex-slaves, with support from some churches and abolitionists, established free villages, which it could be argued also operated like social enterprises. Note, however, that more detailed research must be done to explore and substantiate this claim. Nonetheless, the practices within contemporary Maroon towns provide some evidence that the idea was to establish a sustainable dynamic for community development among a free and independent people. Within these settings, the primary focus was not on generating profit but on improving the quality of the lives of the people in a self-sustained way. There are other communities, especially within Rastafari, which developed similar settlements that, we would argue, display characteristics of social enterprises. This essay therefore examines Pinnacle, the first Rastafari community, using a business model approach to reveal how the entrepreneurial practices of Leonard Howell, the community's founder, map onto the social entrepreneurial process, and how he applied a robust business model to create social value.

The remainder of the article will review the literature on entrepreneurship and the characteristics of an entrepreneur; examine social entrepreneurship and social value creation; discuss the context in which Howell was applying this model at Pinnacle; and look at the implications of these issues for entrepreneurship policy development, including recommendations for future research.

Leonard Howell, Social Entrepreneur? Definitions and Characteristics

> Howell became the most successful teacher of Rastafari doctrine. He enjoined black people to be PROUD of [their] heritage and culture, to have their own "Money" Banks, be self-motivated, strong, self-sufficient, where black economies would triumph and to hold high the value of education. Furthermore, he preached to show respect, love and honour. He said, "The white man's doctrine has forced the black man to forsake silver and gold and seek heaven after death. It has brought us to live in disgrace and die in dishonour."
> —*Barbara Blake-Hannah*[4]

It is becoming clearer that there is no one comprehensive and accepted definition of entrepreneurship. Stevenson et al. advise that entrepreneurship "is a process of creating value by putting together a unique package of resources to exploit an opportunity".[5] Timmons defines it as a "process of creating or seizing an opportunity and pursuing it regardless of the resources currently controlled".[6] Other definitions have emerged with the key terms of *value creation, seizing* and *opportunity, utilizing resources* and *creating value*. Regardless of which definition one subscribes to, examining the work of Leonard Howell at Pinnacle would reveal that he was an entrepreneur.

Howell's travels to the United States in the early 1920s exposed him to the harsh realities facing black people globally. This reinforced within him the importance of addressing these realities and the need to radically transform the lives of the people. Additionally, at the time there were other leaders, such as Marcus Garvey, whose actions influenced Howell and encouraged him to continue on this path when he returned to Jamaica in 1932. Blake-Hannah writes,

> During the 1920s, black men and women were living in an era of racial discrimination, bigotry, oppression, segregation and encountered brutality and endless violence. It was not easy for Howell who had fallen victim to hatred, bigotry and oppression to stand aside and look. He was convinced it was his responsibility that he committed his life by taking a personal stand against the forces of hatred, oppression and injustice. He travelled to many cities and countries, preached among all groups of people to help raise the conscience of the public. He encouraged Black Leaders so that every individual would work and create a world in which genocide will not occur again.[7]

A plethora of research has emerged in defining entrepreneurship. Schumpeter, Kuemmerle, Sarasvathy, McClelland, Timmons and other researchers have conducted extensive work in identifying the characteristics and traits of entrepreneurs.[8] Other researchers have examined entrepreneurship as a social process which is influenced by social networks, that is, driven by groups and not individuals.[9] This research best validates Howell as an entrepreneur with a social objective. Despite having adequate financing for himself, Howell never emphasized individual security but rather focused on collective security through cooperative enterprises. Kuemmerle's work presents five questions that he considers to be a litmus test for entrepreneurs:

1. Are you comfortable stretching the rules?
2. Are you prepared to make powerful enemies?
3. Do you have the patience to start small?
4. Are you willing to shift strategies quickly?
5. Are you a closer?[10]

It can be argued that Howell fit these criteria. Within the context of racial tension and class inequity in which he was operating, he would be considered to be stretching as well as breaking the rules. He advanced not only the idea of black nationalism in economic terms, but also the idea of God being black and a living man "trodding" creation. This contradicted all the ideals of the status quo and resulted in Howell being considered as one of the biggest enemies of the colonial government of Jamaica. The numerous occasions on which he was arrested, convicted and imprisoned are evidence of this. The recurring raids and destruction of property that Pinnacle endured up until the 1950s further attest to this fact. Howell displayed many characteristics of the entrepreneur, such as being a visionary, taking calculated risks, being persistent and developing networks.

McClelland points out that entrepreneurs tend to have a greater need for above-average achievement, and are calculated risk-takers. Timmons has advanced six general characteristics of entrepreneurs:

1. commitment and determination
2. leadership
3. opportunity obsession
4. tolerance of risk, ambiguity and uncertainty
5. creativity, self-reliance and ability to adapt
6. motivation to excel[11]

Leonard Howell's "livety" undoubtedly places him within the group characterized as entrepreneurs; specifically, and more importantly, he is part of the group referred to as social entrepreneurs. Additionally, the practices within Pinnacle, given its vision and how it was operationalized, substantiate the claim that it was not just a Rastafari settlement but an effective social enterprise led by a social entrepreneur.

The social entrepreneurship literature suggests that activities that fall into this category are generally intervention strategies, where the focus is on improving the quality of life of people, and not on profit. The emphasis of these strategies is to generate social value in critical but usually ignored sectors.[12] Scholars including Mair and Marti argue that the objective of this process is to effectively address social needs through innovation that will result in sustained social value creation.[13] Increasingly, the emphasis is on the social value generated from such innovations,[14] which in turn supports social change, occasioning the creation of psychological, social, political and economic capital among once-disempowered communities. Some of these intervention strategies have not been sustained; however, the efforts are noteworthy and have spurred increasing interest in this type of endeavour.[15] The increasing interest, research and practice have revealed that social entrepreneurship means different things to many practitioners.[16] However, these inconsistencies in theoretical development, meanings and definitions are to be expected, given that this area of study is in its developmental stage.

Social entrepreneurship is usually reflected in the attributes and practice of social entrepreneurs as change agents.[17] One key attribute tends to be their focus on creating value through innovation and applying good governance "best practices". When social entrepreneurs do not have all of the required resources, they will take calculated risks to develop models in order to significantly transform society.[18] It must be noted, however, that the traits of the social entrepreneur are present in groups and individuals to varying extents. No individual or group can claim to have all of these attributes. For this reason, groups and individuals with different qualities and approaches may be defined as social entrepreneurs. The literature has shown that there are several models that organizations employ in their endeavours to create social value. According to Alter, these are determined by the level of integration between an organization's social programmes and business activity, whether embedded, integrated or external. Regardless of the model, all such organizations have an enterprise component, which helps to sustain the interventions, and are expected to generate measurable social value, according to Tuan.[19] These social-sector actors are not like regular enterprises, whose effectiveness can be measured via traditional profits or returns on investment; the social enterprise's primary aim is not to make profit but to add social value in a sustainable way.

Howell and Pinnacle

Jamaicans of African descent have endured more than four hundred years of race and class oppression. This has resulted in high levels of poverty and an increasing sense of hopelessness among the population, in particular the youth. There is a sense of urgency to arrest this downward-spiralling trajectory, as the situation is becoming untenable. The quest is to find effective models to engage the over 140,000 youth who are at risk of being either perpetrators or victims of violent crime. More importantly, there is urgent need to reduce poverty among more than half a million nationals living below the poverty line. However, there is an opportunity to address concerns of food, health and nutritional security through high-growth agricultural social enterprises. Essentially, if the country is to attain the goals outlined in the Vision 2030 National Development Plan, wherein Jamaica is "the place of choice to live, work, raise families and do business", it cannot be business as usual. There is a need, therefore, to examine the attempts that have been made to alleviate these issues throughout the history of the country, and to ascertain why they have not worked.

This situation begs for a model from which insights can be gained as to how to effectively establish community-based social enterprises to make improvements in the lives of the people. Pinnacle presents such a model. Howell returned to Jamaica in 1932, after being exposed to the hardships black people faced globally. The socio-economic and sociopolitical situation in the years after the First World War was harsh enough to precipitate a worsening of international relations, culminating in the Second World War in 1939. At this time, black people were disempowered and disenfranchised, existing merely as cheap labour and as numbers for the frontlines of the battlefields for Britain and America. There was a low sense of self-pride and dignity among the members of the African diaspora, holding as they did the lowest place on the social ladder. Essentially, there had not been much change for the better since the slavery period had ended. It could have been successfully argued that slavery had not ended. It is within this context that Howell, driven by his characteristics as a social entrepreneur, persisted in his endeavours, despite the obvious risk and subsequent harm and persecution it brought to him, his family and friends. Undoubtedly, the societal context, both locally and globally, was not welcoming or conducive to Howell's vision of establishing a sustainable social enterprise at Pinnacle in the parish of St Catherine. However, it is clear that he had significant successes with this project, given the wealth it generated, the improvements it made in the livelihoods of its members, its rapid expansion in the community and its socio-economic activities. Through Pinnacle, Howell empowered the people by strengthening their social, political and economic capital. It was this strengthening that raised the alarm among those upholding the status quo, who were already becoming weakened from the effects of the Second World War.

What are the lessons that the current population could learn from Howell? How do his activities map out on the entrepreneurial process, and what was the business model he applied? These are critical questions to answer. Having entrepreneurial characteristics might be necessary, but these alone are not sufficient to implement and sustain a successful venture or a social enterprise. Entrepreneurial frameworks and business models have emerged as tools that strengthen the success of start-ups, moving through the process from idea generation to implementation and harvesting of the benefits.

The literature suggests that there are two primary ways in which entrepreneurs discover ideas: through systematic search or by alertness to emerging opportunities. James Fiet has produced a body of work which argues that successful repeat entrepreneurs employ systematic search "in opportunity discovery".[20] Prior to Fiet's work, the research suggested that idea discovery was based on the "alertness" of the entrepreneur to opportunities, as these opportunities cannot be anticipated and thus are accidentally discovered.[21] Regardless of the approach, there is a process through which ideas are developed and implemented. Within the process framework, there are six stages:

> The first two, "opportunity identification" and "business concept development", represent the ideation phase of the process. The entrepreneur is attempting to identify patterns or forces in the environment that represent profit potential, and to develop a creative means of capitalizing on that potential. The remaining stages are concerned with implementation. Thus, the entrepreneur assesses and acquires the necessary resources, implements the concept, manages the business, and eventually harvests the venture.[22]

While this outlines the process for traditional ventures, the process is similar for social enterprises (see table 8.1). This process starts with the ideation stage and is outlined as follows:

1. Idea (vision)
2. Opportunity recognition (identifying social problems and unmet need)
3. Concept development (identification of social rewards and new products and markets)
4. Resource determination and acquisition (financial, human and physical resources)
5. Launch and venture growth (measurement of returns, expansion and change)
6. Goal attainment (succeed in mission and shut down; succeed in mission and find new opportunity; and attain a stable service equilibrium then integrate into another venture)

During the entrepreneurial process, particularly at the ideation phase, the development of a business model is critical. However, like most definitions within entrepreneurship, that of a "business model" varies. According to Morris, Kuratko and Schindehutte, there are three broad categories for such a model: strategic, operational and economic. At the strategic level, value creation for stakeholders (suppliers, customers, investors and/or partners) is the focus. At the operational level, emphasis is on the operations that enable the organization to present a unique value proposition, its source of competitive advantage. At the economic level, the emphasis is on how to generate and sustain profits (see table 8.2). Morris details six broad questions that a business model should address, two at each level, as outlined below:

Strategic Level
1. How does the firm create value?
2. For whom does it create value?

Operations Level
3. What are the internal sources of advantages?
4. How does it differentiate itself?

Economic Level
5. How does it make money?
6. What are its time, scope and size ambitions?

Table 8.1. Framework of the Entrepreneurial Process

Stages	Key Decision Variables or Alternatives
Identify an opportunity	• **Changing demographics** • **Emergence of new market segments** • Process needs • New technologies • Incongruities • Regulatory change • **Social change**
Develop the concept	• **New products** • **New services** • **New processes** • **New markets** • **New organizational structure/forms** • New technologies • **New sales or distribution channels**
Determine the required resources	• **Skilled employees** • **General management expertise** • **Marketing and sales expertise** • **Technical expertise** • **Financing** • **Distribution channels** • **Sources of supply** • **Production facilities** • Licences, patents and legal protection
Acquire the necessary resources	• Debt • **Equity** • **Leveraging** • **Outsourcing** • Leasing • Contract labour • Temporary staff • Supplier financing • Joint venture • **Partnership** • **Barter** • Gifts

(Table 8.1 continues)

Table 8.1. Framework of the Entrepreneurial Process (*continued*)

Stages	Key Decision Variables or Alternatives
Implement and manage	• **Implementation of concept** • **Monitoring of performance** • Payback of resource providers • Reinvestment • **Expansion** • **Achievement of performance goals**
Harvest the venture	• Absorption of new concept into mainstream operations • Licensing of rights • Family succession • Sell venture • Go public • **Shut down venture**

Note: Elements in bold reflect the areas applied to the model at Pinnacle.

The table above reflects the six stages of the entrepreneurial process. The first two, opportunity identification and business concept development, represent the ideation phase of the process. The entrepreneur is attempting to identify patterns or forces in the environment that represent profit potential, and to develop a creative means of capitalizing on that potential. The remaining stages are concerned with implementation. Thus, the entrepreneur assesses and acquires the necessary resources, implements the concept, manages the business and eventually harvests the venture. While creativity is perhaps most associated with the beginning of the process, and especially with the development of the concept, in practice it is the subsequent stages that often require the most innovative and risk-taking behaviours on the part of the entrepreneur. The table also provides key decision variables or alternatives that come into play at each stage in the process (Morris, Kuratko and Schindehutte, "Towards Integration", 35–49).

Table 8.2. The Core Components of a Business Model: Foundation, Proprietorship and Rules

Foundation Level	Proprietorship Level	Rules
Component 1 (factors relating to the offering): How do we create value? (select from each set) • **Primarily products/primarily services/heavy mix** • **Standardized**/some customization/high customization • **Broad line**/medium breadth/narrow line • Deep lines/medium depth/**shallow lines** • Access to product/**product itself**/product bundled with other firm's products or services • **Internal manufacturing or service delivery**/outsourcing/ licensing/reselling/**value added** • **Direct distribution**/indirect distribution (if indirect: single or multi-channel)		
Component 2 (market factors): Who do we create value for? (select from each set) • Type of organization: **buyer to buyer/buyer to consumer/both** • **Local/regional/national/international** • Where customer is in value chain: upstream supplier/downstream supplier/government/institutional/**wholesaler/retailer/service provider/final consumer** • **Broad or general market/niche market** • **Transactional/relational**		
Component 3 (internal capability factors): What is our source of competence/advantage? • **Production/operating systems** • **Selling/marketing** • Information management/mining/info. packaging • Technology/R&D/creative or innovative capability/intellectual • Financial transactions/arbitrage		

(Table 8.2 continues)

Table 8.1. The Core Components of a Business Model: Foundation, Proprietorship and Rules (*continued*)

Foundation Level	Proprietorship Level	Rules
• Supply chain management		
• **Networking/resource leveraging**		
Component 4 (competitive strategy factors): How do we differentiate ourselves?		
• **Image of operational excellence/consistency/dependability**		
• **Product or service quality/selection/features/availability**		
• Innovation leadership		
• Low cost/efficiency		
• **Intimate customer relationship/experience**		
Component 5 (economic factors): How do we make money? (select one from each set)		
• Pricing and revenue sources: fixed/**mixed**/flexible		
• Operating leverage: **high**/med/low		
• Volumes: **high**/med/low		
• Margins: high/med/**low**		
Component 6 (personal/investor factors): What are our time, scope and size ambitions? (select one)		
• Subsistence model		
• Income model		
• **Growth model**		
• Speculative model		

Note: Elements in bold reflect the areas applied to the model at Pinnacle.

The table above outlines three levels for consideration when developing a robust business model: foundation, proprietorship and rules. First, it details the six core components to be addressed in the foundational level of the business model. Second, proprietorship, which reflects innovation that is unique to the particular entrepreneur and venture, is a key determinant in the sustainability of the organization. The final level, rules, reflects "the basic set of operating rules ... these are guidelines that ensure the foundation or core components of the business model are reflected in the on-going strategic actions in the firm" (Morris, Kuratko and Schindehutte, "Towards Integration", 35–49).

Strategy, Operations and Economics

On returning to Jamaica, Howell had a clear vision as to what he wanted for his disempowered people. His aim was to establish a self-sustaining community based on the principles of self-reliance through collective security. Its activities would be guided by solid spiritual practices, which identified Haile Selassie I as God in flesh and earth's rightful ruler.

Howell recognized that there were significant social, economic and political problems facing the African descendants in Jamaica, emerging from the changing social conditions and demographics of the period after the First World War. Not only were they socially, politically and economically disempowered, but they were also psychologically and spiritually decapitated. It was urgent to instil a sense of self-worth and determination among this group, especially in the context of increasing hardship. He recognized that significant needs existed that were unmet, and essential services were not being provided. There was a significant shortage of access to education and health facilities. There was increasing homelessness; there were infants in need of care, the aged in need of protection, the shelterless in need of shelter, the naked in need of clothes and the hungry in need of food. Essentially, Howell sought to fulfil what has today emerged as the creed within Rastafari. The presence of these problems and unfulfilled needs indicated that there was a good opportunity for Howell to establish a successful social enterprise, given that there were untapped markets, especially among African descendants in Jamaica. That enterprise became Pinnacle.

With the changing social conditions and demographics, coupled with the unmet needs of Africans in Jamaica, Howell developed a unique concept of a self-sustaining community anchored in social agricultural entrepreneurship. However, agricultural produce was not the only product generated by Pinnacle; the community became a centre for the production of goods and services which would today form part of the creative and cultural industries. The community comprised various skilled artisans, educators and farmers. New products were being created through minimal processing; new services were being offered; new techniques were being applied to production, in particular farming; and new markets were being developed, with new sales and distribution channels. The most novel of all was Pinnacle's organizational structure, which was that of the self-contained social enterprise. As stated earlier,

They lived a natural way of life, in harmony with the universe, showed love and peace to all races and colours, lived in unity, worked collectively, upheld culture, heritage, freedom and justice. Many who were farmers planted organic food, others who were skilled in arts and craft made household items. In addition, herbal medicines, roots, tonics and other produces were supplied and sold to the local government, private and public sectors.[23]

All organizations depend on four factors of production to generate goods and services: land, labour, capital and entrepreneurship. Clearly, land was essential for Pinnacle, and using his own resources (equity), Howell purchased approximately two to three hundred acres of land to establish the community. The disenfranchised people who joined the community provided the labour (skilled and semi-skilled) that was required to manufacture the goods and provide the services being offered to the market. Howell provided the entrepreneurial competence to guide such an operation, and the effectiveness of his stewardship was reflected in the profits generated and in the threat this structure posed to the established order. Howell employed a number of techniques to secure resources, including equity, leveraging his land to get support from interested persons to join the community, developing internal partnerships and bartering systems, and offering gifts. Howell had successfully diversified his resource pool, so as to ensure the sustainability of the enterprise.

There is clear evidence of the launch and growth of the Pinnacle community and its entrepreneurial activities. Timing was a key factor in the launch of the venture. Howell's return to Jamaica in 1932 and his acquisition of the property in 1940 presented a unique opportunity for African descendants to be a part of a promising process, which he detailed in *The Promised Key*, his small book published in 1935. This process promised to unlock the social, political, psychological and economic potential of the people, and it did. The 1930s marked a turbulent period in Jamaica, as evidenced by the labour protests in St Thomas, Westmoreland and other parishes. Howell, because of his work and its impact, was charged by the state for sedition, imprisoned for two years and released in 1936. Pinnacle grew and reached its zenith between 1940 and 1954. During this period, the community suffered several raids and theft by the state police. However, the residents of Pinnacle were not deterred by these actions, and they continued their efforts to build their community. The last major raid took place in 1958. Blake-Hannah describes this event and its aftermath:

During the last raid on Pinnacle, the police burned to the ground homes belonging to thousands of Rastafarians. Included in the fire were furnishings, personal items and clothing. Having no place to live and their leader in jail, most Rastafarians relocated throughout Kingston, St Catherine, Clarendon and St Thomas. That was the beginning of the Rastafari dispersion and relocation in groups of churches and mansions. . . . In the 1970s, a small flock of Rastafarian elders took refuge in Tredegar Park, St Catherine, [and] continued to support the teachings of Howell until his death in 1981. Until today, the Rastafarians of Pinnacle were never compensated for their loss of property, homes, lives and [the] humiliation suffered.[24]

The wealth that Pinnacle generated attested to the growth of the community. Even after its members were displaced, the philosophy which had guided them persisted, and they applied the same practices they had used at Pinnacle wherever they went. Today, these practices remain within the Rastafari community.

Undoubtedly, despite the many obstacles it faced, Pinnacle attained its primary goal, which was to establish a self-sustaining community that would bring a sense of self-worth and black pride to disempowered African descendants in Jamaica. It also succeeded in planting the seeds of Rastafari within the Jamaican people, seeds that have become a rainforest for the world, promoting truth, rights and equality among all humans. This is evidenced by the universalization of Rastafari and its philosophy of one love. However, the growth of the community at Pinnacle was handicapped by a number of factors, including the raids and persistent harassment and the subsequent illegal sale of the property by the state to private developers during the 1980s. Despite these attempts, the spirit of Howell and Pinnacle prevails in the area, and Pinnacle is now considered a national heritage site. This is by no means enough; however, the legacy of Howell has triumphed, and Pinnacle will always remain one of the earliest and most successful community-based social enterprises within Jamaica, the diaspora and, by extension, the world.

Eventually, the operations at Pinnacle were forced to close down, and the members dispersed to Coral Gardens and various other parts of the island. The dispersion, however, has had the positive impact of the further spreading of the message and "livety" of Rastafari throughout the island and the world, which was a part of the vision of Leonard Howell. The remaining question is, what was the business model that he applied that led to this success? Although there are no written documents which answer this question, review of the literature and of accounts from Howellites provides some meaningful insights on Howell's business model. These are presented below.

1. *How did Pinnacle create value?*

The community generated a mix of goods and services, most of the products being standardized, with minimal customization. Customization was specific to goods and services that included some kind of processing, like roots and artisan services. There was a broad line of goods and services, but not much variation in types of the same product (shallow line). These goods and services could be accessed alone or in a bundle, usually at some kind of discount. All products were manufactured internally, with some value added through the process. Products were distributed directly on site, as well as indirectly through external retailers. Pinnacle became the place that various persons, from wholesalers and retailers to direct customers, would visit to purchase goods and services. However, community members would also go to the markets to sell their products.

2. *For whom did Pinnacle create value?*

Pinnacle had an open-door policy and would sell to anyone who wanted to buy a product or service. It offered its wares to wholesalers and retailers as well as directly to consumers. As such, its customers were both upstream and downstream. The operations, however, were confined to Jamaica, targeting a niche made up of African descendants and a broader market of whoever wished to purchase. The focus was on establishing livelihoods for the community members, while providing access to high-quality goods and services to the general population. Through this process, the residents developed transactional associates as well as lasting relationships with customers. Inherently, given that there was an internal community market which operated on a bartering system, meaningful relationships also developed among various producers, bolstering the level of trust and cooperation within the community.

3. *What was Pinnacle's internal source of advantage?*

The setup of Pinnacle created natural internal advantages. Given its interdependent structure, Pinnacle was able to develop an efficient and effective production and operating system. One element of this was the use of shared labour and resources. Persons who produced similar products would benefit from economies of scale by bundling and selling, thus allowing them to meet growing demand. This also supported ease of sale and marketing. Additionally, Pinnacle itself served as a marketplace, thus reducing the cost of transportation and other associated transactions, which resulted in more profits for the sellers. The community setting also facilitated greater networking and resource leveraging, which served to increase access to resources while simultaneously reducing operational costs. Pinnacle provides a model for classic modern-day clustering, in which producers of similar and complementary products collude for efficiency gains.

4. How did it differentiate itself?

The elements that generated internal advantages for Pinnacle within the market were also the source of its differentiation strategy. Pinnacle had developed an image of operational excellence, which allowed it to supply consistent, high-quality goods and services in a dependable way. Additionally, given the variety of goods and services offered, customers would find a "one-stop shop" for the majority of their needs, reducing both search time and transaction costs. The shared space and economies of scale allowed the production and operational costs to be greatly lowered, coupled with the fact that the community served as a direct sales point, and hence there was no transportation cost to the seller, who, over time, developed meaningful relationships with the buyers. It must be emphasized that this was also a result of the innovation employed in production, operations and distribution, setting Pinnacle apart from other suppliers in terms of efficiency and effectiveness.

5. How did Pinnacle make money?

Undoubtedly, Pinnacle was a very successful venture strategy and made substantial profits for its community members. The pricing and revenue sources represented a mix between fixed and flexible sources. Sellers had the option of changing prices to support bargains and had diversified revenue sources from the selling of various goods and services. Given that they also controlled their operations, their leverage tended to be high, with the ability to adjust operations given the changing demands of both internal and external customers. The nature of the products also influenced the volumes produced. For agriculture and agro-processing, the volumes were generally high, with low margins. However, for specialized services, the volumes were demand-driven and thus offered on demand, with margins again being low. Essentially, Pinnacle operated on a model of medium to high volumes, with low margins – a low-cost, low-price leadership strategy. This highlights the intent of the project, as while it had to be sustained by enterprise, its primary aim was to improve the quality of life of African descendants, whether or not they were a part of the Pinnacle community. The goal was to supply high-quality goods and services at reasonable prices.

6. *What were Pinnacle's time, scope and size ambitions?*

Howell's vision was big yet pragmatic, and he seized the opportunity which presented itself. While Pinnacle started out as a subsistence model, it quickly emerged into an income model. Here, the entrepreneurs would reinvest in their ventures until they were able to support a good standard of living, not just "hand to mouth". The Pinnacle entrepreneurs were able to accumulate savings, as evidenced by the accounts of money found and stolen during the police raids. Clearly, however, Pinnacle was emerging into a high-growth model, as the businesses as well as the community were expanding. This was what posed the greatest threat to the status quo. At the time of Pinnacle's establishment, there was a state of economic hardship and increasing inequity, and the need for a solution. However, the solution was emerging from the grassroots and not from the colonial leadership. With the calls for change from various sectors, including Marcus Garvey and the newly formed political parties, people were seeking meaningful alternatives to support themselves. Pinnacle was very attractive as it provided social, political and economic security to its members, thus presenting a serious threat to the status quo.

Conclusion

The historical experience of Jamaica and other countries has been one of hardship for African descendants. This hardship has forced many of these populations, out of necessity, to become very creative and innovative in order to eke out a living. Today, innovation and creativity are seen as the two critical pillars of entrepreneurship. Entrepreneurship has become the accepted approach to advancing consistent growth and development for both developed and developing countries. Social entrepreneurship, in particular, is seen as one of the most effective vehicles to facilitate this transformation in a deeper and more selfless way. The need to effect systemic and structural changes with the primary focus of improving the quality of people's lives has increased the importance of developing robust social entrepreneurship models for communities. Undoubtedly, a careful examination of the Jamaican landscape can unearth such examples. It is clear that such models – of effecting change through the entrepreneurial process and a business model approach – exist, Pinnacle being one of the most notable.

Howell was an entrepreneur – but specifically, and more importantly, he was a social entrepreneur. Pinnacle was not just a settlement; it was a thriving and effective social enterprise. It presents a pragmatic approach to addressing many of the problems facing communities across Jamaica, in both rural and urban areas. Many foreign models and strategies have been "cut and pasted" onto the Jamaican landscape, with few positive results; however, successful examples of what Jamaica needs are already here. It is important for more research to be carried out on this historical experience so that more examples can be unearthed. It is critical that we learn from these examples, not only to "tun yuh hand an mek fashion", but also because "one hand caan clap" and "many hands mek the wok light". We should follow the lead of those who have gone before, beginning with our ancestors who burned the plantation to set up their societies: the Nannys of the Maroons, the Bedwardites, the Marcus Garveys, the Howellites and many others whose work the status quo has continued to ignore. Self-reliance through collective security must be the philosophy upon which Jamaica's developmental agenda is anchored, if the country hopes to become "the place of choice to live, work, raise families and do business".[25]

> Wherever there is African blood, there is a basis for unity.
> – *Haile Selassie I, Jamaica, 1966*

Notes

1. See Barbara Blake-Hannah, "Pinnacle: History and Current Status – Position Paper", Ministry of Information, Culture, Youth and Sports, Kingston, Government of Jamaica, 23 July 2008, 5.
2. Densil A. Williams and K'adamawe K'nIfe, "The Dark Side of Social Entrepreneurship", *International Journal of Entrepreneurship* 16 (2012): 63–82; S. Shane and S. Venkataraman, "The Promise of Entrepreneurship as a Field of Research", *Academy of Management Review* 25, no. 1 (2000): 217–26.
3. K'adamawe K'nIfe, Allan Bernard and Edward Dixon, "Marcus Garvey the Entrepreneur? Insights for Stimulating Entrepreneurship in Developing Nations", *Journal of Liberty Hall: The Legacy of Marcus Garvey* 2 (2011): 37–59.
4. See Blake-Hannah, "Pinnacle", 2.
5. Howard Stevenson, Michael Roberts and H. Irving Grousbeck, *New Business Ventures and the Entrepreneur* (Chicago: Irwin Publishing, 1992), 38.

6. This definition emerged from the Harvard Business School, according to J.A. Timmons in *New Venture Creation: Entrepreneurship for the 21st Century* (Burr Ridge, IL: Irwin Press, 1994). Cited in Tom Byers, Heleen Kist and Robert I. Sutton, "Characteristics of the Entrepreneur: Social Creatures, Not Solo Heroes", in *The Handbook of Technology Management*, ed. Richard C. Dorf (Boca Raton, FL: CRC Press, 1997), 1–6.
7. See Blake-Hannah, "Pinnacle", 4.
8. See Joseph A. Schumpeter, *The Theory of Economic Development* (Cambridge, MA: Harvard University Press, 1934); Walter Kuemmerle, "A Test for the Fainthearted", *Harvard Business Review* (May 2002): 4–8; Saras D. Sarasvathy, "What Makes Entrepreneurs Entrepreneurial?" Available at http://ssrn.com/abstract=909038; David C. McClelland, *The Achieving Society* (Princeton, NJ: Van Nostrand, 1961); Timmons, *New Venture Creation*.
9. See Byers, Kist and Sutton, "Characteristics of the Entrepreneur"; J. Freeman, "Venture Capital as an Economy of Time" (working paper, Haas Business School, University of California at Berkeley, 1996); R.S. Burt, *Structural Holes: The Social Structure of Competition* (Cambridge, MA: Harvard University Press, 1992); K.M. Eisenhardt and C.B. Schoonhoven, "Organizational Growth: Linking Founding Team, Strategy, Environment, and Growth Among US Semiconductor Ventures, 1978–1988", *Administrative Science Quarterly* 35 (1990): 504–29.
10. See Kuemmerle, "Test for the Fainthearted".
11. See Timmons, *New Venture Creation*.
12. A. Peredo and M. McLean, "Social Entrepreneurship: A Critical Review of the Concept", *Journal of World Business* 41, no. 1 (2006): 56–65; and M. Pomerantz, "The Business of Social Entrepreneurship in a 'Down Economy'", *Business* 25, no. 3 (2003): 25–30.
13. J. Mair and I. Marti, "Social Entrepreneurship Research: A Source of Explanation, Prediction and Delight", *Journal of World Business* 41, no. 1 (2006): 36–44.
14. Williams and K'nIfe, "Dark Side of Social Entrepreneurship", 63–82; David Bornstein and Susan Davis, *Social Entrepreneurship: What Everyone Needs to Know* (Oxford: Oxford University Press, 2010).
15. Mair and Marti, "Social Entrepreneurship Research", 36–44; and Sarah H. Alvord, L. David Brown and Christine W. Letts, "Social Entrepreneurship and Societal Transformation", *Journal of Applied Behavioral Science* 40, no. 3 (2004): 260–82.
16. C. Ramirez, T. Hernandez, A. Cardenas, L.C. Calcedo and M.A. Gonzales, "Social Entrepreneurship Education for Engineers" (paper presented at the NCIIA 16th Annual Conference, 2012); J.G. Dees, "The Meaning of Social Entrepreneurship" (draft report for the Kauffman Centre for Entrepreneurial Leadership, Stanford University, 1998), 1–6.
17. Dees, "Meaning of Social Entrepreneurship", 1–6.

18. Peredo and McLean, "Social Entrepreneurship", 56–65; Roger L. Martin and Sally Osberg, "Social Entrepreneurship: The Case for Definition", *Stanford Social Innovation Review* 5, no. 2 (2007): 28–40; and C. Seelos and J. Mair, "Social Entrepreneurship: Creating New Business Models to Serve the Poor", *Business Horizons* 48, no. 3 (2005): 241–46.
19. S.K. Alter, "Social Enterprise Models and Their Mission and Money Relationships", in *Social Entrepreneurship: New Models of Sustainable Social Change*, ed. Alex Nicholls (Oxford: Oxford University Press, 2006), 144–68; Melinda Tuan, "Measuring and/or Estimating Social Value Creation: Insights into Eight Integrated Cost Approaches" (Seattle: Bill and Melinda Gates Foundation, 2008).
20. See James O. Fiet, "The Informational Basis for Entrepreneurial Discovery", *Small Business Economics* 8 (1996): 429–30; James O. Fiet, *The Systematic Search for Entrepreneurial Discoveries* (Westport, CT: Praeger, 2002); James O. Fiet, Van G.H. Clouse and William I. Norton Jr, "Systematic Search by Repeat Entrepreneurs", in *Opportunity Identification and Entrepreneurial Behavior*, edited by John E. Butler (Greenwich, CT: Information Age Publishing, 2004), 1–28; James O. Fiet, Alexandre Piskounov and Pankaj C. Patel, "Still Searching (Systematically) for Entrepreneurial Discoveries", *Small Business Economics* 25 (2005): 489–504; and James O. Fiet, "A Prescriptive Analysis of Search and Discovery", *Journal of Management Studies* 44, no. 4 (2007): 592–611.
21. K'nIfe, Bernard and Dixon, "Garvey the Entrepreneur?", 37–59; W.J. Baumol, "Formal Entrepreneurship Theory in Economics: Existence and Bounds", *Journal of Business Venturing* 8 (1993): 197–210; I. Kirzner, "Entrepreneurial Discovery and the Competitive Market Process: An Austrian Approach", *Journal of Economic Literature* 35 (1997): 60–85.
22. Michael H. Morris, Donald F. Kuratko and Minet Schindehutte, "Towards Integration: Understanding Entrepreneurship through Frameworks", *International Journal of Entrepreneurship and Innovation* 2, no. 1 (2001): 35–49; Michael H. Morris and Minet Schindehutte, "Teaching Entrepreneurship Students the Concept of a Business Model" (paper presented at Experiential Classroom XI, Oklahoma State University, 2011).
23. See Blake-Hannah, "Pinnacle", 5.
24. Ibid., 6, 7.
25. Planning Institute of Jamaica, *Vision 2030: Jamaica National Development Plan*, 2009.

9

BIBLIOGRAPHICAL ESSAY
Howell in the Studies on Rastafari

LOUIS E.A. MOYSTON

This chapter explores some of the major studies on Rastafari with a view to locating Leonard P. Howell, the founding prophet and philosopher of Rastafari, in the setting of their related stories. It is observed that some of the earlier studies of Rastafari, designed from the settings of western Kingston and St Andrew, have neglected or made limited mention of Howell. These studies relied on interviews from certain sects of urban-based Rastas and employed widely related sociological theories to explain the emergence of the early Rastafari. The 1970s were a sort of golden age in Jamaica, as they relate to Rastafari studies. This quality was reflected in a growing scholarship that slowly integrated reasonable use of primary and secondary data. These studies progressively revealed the history of Howell, including the emergence of the early Rastafari in St Thomas and its exodus to the Howell-built community of Pinnacle, near to Sligoville in St Catherine, in 1940. This study dispels the notion of Garvey as the founding prophet of the idea and movement of Rastafari, and exposed the pioneering role of Leonard P. Howell.

The Early Scholarship

The earliest scholarly work on the Rastafari movement was conducted by the American sociologist George Eaton Simpson in the early 1950s. In his seminal work, Simpson relies heavily on sociological theory to explain the emergence of the Rastafarian movement as that of a violent and aggressive group.[1] The slum of western Kingston is the setting of the story. In his interpretations of interviews with Rastafari brethren, Simpson locates the origin of the foundational idea of Rastafari in the prophecy of Marcus Garvey and selected passages from the Bible.[2] Howell is not mentioned in his works, but in his 1985 reflections, Simpson suggests the need to explore the rural origin of the movement that occurred three decades before his seminal study.[3] This approach would permit the researcher to uncover Howell in his pioneering state.

Five years after the first scholarly work on Rastafari was done, the University of the West Indies at Mona, Jamaica, conducted an action research on the topic. The institution responded to a request from some of the brethren-leaders within Rastafari to assist with providing greater understanding of the movement after the violence related to the Back-to-Africa events in 1959. According to the resulting report, written by Rex Nettleford et al. and published in 1960, "the movement [was] rooted in unemployment", and Marcus Garvey was the prophet who had inspired the idea and doctrine that Ras Tafari was the Messiah returned to earth. The report notes that the "prophecy was revealed" by four leaders independently after the coronation of Haile Selassie I in 1930. It continues, "Of these, Mr Leonard P. Howell is genuinely regarded as the first to preach the divinity of Rastafari in Kingston." The study argues that "the most successful preacher was undoubtedly L.P. Howell[,] who moved between Port Morant and Kingston until 1940". It further states that "from 1933 Howell had been preaching violence" and that Pinnacle was a ganja farm.[4] There is no evidence to support the theory of four preachers, but this researcher was informed that it was the orientation towards pluralism of one of the authors, M.G. Smith, that inspired the notion.[5]

Two years after the 1960 report, Katrin Norris published the book *Jamaica: The Search for an Identity*. H. Orlando Patterson's novel *The Children of Sisyphus* and his short journal article entitled "Rastafari: The Cult of Outcasts" were both published in 1964. Norris dedicated a chapter in her book, entitled "The Call of Africa", to the African aspect of the Jamaican political scene in 1960, emphasizing the character of Millard Johnson and his resurrection of Garvey's People's Political Party, along with Sam Brown and his ideas about black politics.[6] In the article "Rastafari: The Cult of Outcasts", Patterson describes the "millenarian cult of Rastafari" as "bizarre" and as "fantasy", characterizing it as a group that functions as an outlet for "frustration", as opposed to making its members the agents of revolutionary change.[7] Leonard P. Howell is not mentioned in any of these texts.

As previously mentioned, the 1970s were, in my view, the golden period for the study of Rastafari. Two of the significant sociological studies of the period, both from 1977, are *The Rastafarians* by Leonard Barrett and "Millenarian Movements and the Politics of Liberation: The Rastafarians of Jamaica", a doctoral study by Klaus de Albuquerque. Barrett provides extensive coverage of Ras Sam Brown in the politics of the 1960s, at the eve of independence. In looking at the wider society, Barrett illustrates the consciousness inspired by Garvey and rooted in a new era of Ethiopianism from George Liele to Paul Bogle. Barrett nonetheless describes the movement in terms of "hatred" and "violence" and links a brief story of the sedition arrest and trial of Howell to the "first glimpse of the doctrine" that launched the movement. According to Barrett, Garvey inspired the movement and Howell developed the doctrine.[8]

De Albuquerque emphasizes the history of religious-political insurrection in Jamaica. Also interesting is his account of the influence of Rastafari in the politics of the 1970s, in particular its association with Michael Manley and the national elections of 1972. The writer's short but important history of Howell in St Thomas credits the latter for the creation of a "new awareness" informed by moral justice that began in the "minds of men". This new awareness, according to de Albuquerque, unleashed a "political awakening".[9] Unlike the authors of the earliest studies, de Albuquerque made reasonable use of the limited number of primary and secondary sources that were available, enabling him to uncover the central role of Howell in the emergence of the early Rastafari. Howell is thus characterized beyond the role of the first preacher. As described in this study, Howell is a significant thinker whose ideas penetrated the colonial situation and awakened a sleeping majority.

"The Lions in Babylon: The Rastafarians in Jamaica as a Visionary Movement" is an anthropological study and the doctoral dissertation of the Canadian scholar Carole Yawney, done in 1971. "The Rastafarian Brethren of Jamaica", also published in 1971, was another anthropological study, by Sheila Kitzinger.

Dread: The Rastafarians of Jamaica by Father Joseph Owens, published in 1976, is an equally important anthropological work on the Rastafari. These anthropologists immersed themselves in the setting of the movement to gain firsthand information in order to examine Rastafari practices and inform readers of their meanings. Yawney conducted her research in Kingston and worked primarily with Mortimo Planno on the politics of the repatriation movement.[10] Regrettably, Howell was depicted nowhere in this setting. Kitzinger, who visited urban and rural Rastas from the Nyabinghi, writes in her opening remarks that she defines the Rastafari as a "social problem for Jamaica ever since 1933", and links this claim to Howell's selling of Emperor Haile Selassie's picture as a passport to Ethiopia.[11]

In 1976, Joseph Owens, a Roman Catholic priest and social worker, published his anthropological study, in which he argues that Rastafarian theology is radically different from that of Christianity, and that it consistently promoted "race consciousness" in Jamaica. The Rastafari's view of the Bible, Owens argues, generated a critique of the very foundation of Christian civilization, capitalism and imperialism, promoting a new, anti-imperialist trend in the wider Caribbean. As in some of the earlier studies on Rastafari, Owens identifies Garvey as a prophet of the movement. However, making limited use of secondary sources, namely newspaper articles, Owens locates the origin of the movement in St Thomas, where Howell in 1933 said that His Imperial Majesty Haile Selassie I "is [the] Messiah" returned to earth. In making sense of Howell's 1934 sedition trial, Owens writes, "Howell's trial in 1934 set the precedence ... which Rastas would later follow." In spite of his earlier charge that Garvey was a prophet of the movement, Owens authoritatively states that Howell was, indeed, "the Rastafari prophet".[12] Owens acknowledges Howell's central role in the emergence of Rastafari and opens the door for deeper studies to explore Howell's contribution to the idea of Ethiopianism.

The anthropological studies of Barry Chevannes have contributed an array of insightful perspectives to Rastafari scholarship, by way of three major works. These are his 1977 master's thesis, "Jamaican Lower Class Religion: Struggles against Oppression"; his 1989 doctoral dissertation, "Social and Ideological Origins of the Rastafari Movement in Jamaica"; and his 1994 monograph, *Rastafari: Roots and Ideology*. Chevannes, in his works, introduces a framework for exploring the idea of Rastafari as a renewal of the Myalist and Revivalist traditions, and of these as foundations of the movement. He argues that Rastafari emerged out of the "Africanization" of the Myalist and Revivalist traditions. Against this background, he lionizes Alexander Bedward for the Africanization of the older traditions and discusses the Reverend Claudius Henry as providing the "prophetic leadership of the Rastafari movement". Garvey is elevated to a prophetic status as well, because of his dramatic statement that blacks should "look to Africa for the crowning of a Black King".[13] Chevannes also declares that Robert Hinds was among the panoply of prophets who inspired the early Rastafari.[14]

It is important to note that Chevannes does provide some background information on Howell, his New York experience and his relationship with Marxist and radical pan-Africanist George Padmore. Similar to the 1960 report by Nettleford et al., Chevannes informs his readers that "Howell is universally credited with being one of the first if not the very first preacher of Rastafari". He identifies several prophets of the movement but defines Howell as the first preacher. Chevannes also suggests that he was reliably informed that Howell selected the parish of St Thomas as the place to establish "his community of followers" as a result of the tradition of "anti-colonial resistance" in that parish. This tells us that Howell was a man with an extraordinary understanding of history. While Howell is characterized as a ganja farmer by Chevannes, he is nonetheless granted leadership qualities, shown especially at Pinnacle, which itself inspired important social and cultural formations.[15]

John Paul Homiak's 1989 doctoral dissertation, "The 'Ancient of Days' Seated Black: Eldership, Oral Tradition and Ritual in Rastafari Culture", is another anthropological reflection, but of extant Rastafari through the voices of its leadership, namely the elders of the Nyabinghi mansion. Homiak suggests that Rastafari emerged as an anti-colonial and anti-imperial response to European oppression and slavery, and that nationally, the political influence of Howell set off a tension between the lower classes and the colonial leadership. Garvey is identified as the prophet of the movement, but Homiak notes that the "new Ethiopian religion emerged out of Howell's manifestations" which began in April 1933, and that Howell's preaching "clearly formed a corpus of ideas from which others drew and elaborated upon". It is this "act", he writes, that led to "a Rasta awakening worldwide", guided by the new philosophical centre of power described as "black supremacy . . . the crux of Rasta eschatology". The Nyabinghi movement has a unique basis from which it emerged, and it is not surprising that interviews from this group consistently point to Garvey as the prophet of the movement. Homiak complements his interviews with the use of primary and secondary archival materials, from which he is able to illustrate Howell's "corpus of ideas", which became the basis for the doctrine of Rastafari.[16]

Ken Post, in "The Politics of Protest in Jamaica, 1938: Some Problems of Analysis and Conceptualisation" (1969), *The Bible as Ideology: Ethiopianism in Jamaica, 1930–38* (1970), his more famous work *Arise Ye Starvelings: The Jamaican Labour Rebellion of 1938 and Its Aftermath* (1978) and *Strike the Iron: A Colony at War; Jamaica, 1939–1945* (1981), examines the background of the 1938 uprisings from March to June of that year. But in neglecting the important events that took place from 27 December 1937 to early January 1938, Post largely overlooks Howell's role in the later uprisings. In his 1969 study, an otherwise incisive analysis, Post illustrates, for example, the leading characters and the masses who participated in the radical developments leading up to 1938, but does not count Howell as a notable contributor. His study reveals the weakness of using Marxism to describe and analyse this activism in the context of the colonial situation. Like some of the previous studies of Rastafari, Post declares Garvey a prophet, but he also notes that it was the poorest and most exploited who were attracted to Howell's preaching and that although Howell "went far doctrinally[,] he did not build an organizational form".[17] The strength of this study is Post's portrayal of Howell's mission in St Thomas, not in terms of the manifestation of prophecy, but rather in terms of how this activated the parish into a scene of vibrant struggles. Post argues that Howell had a doctrine and a following, but due to his lack of an organizational form, he and the early Rastas did not contribute much to the struggles of 1938.

Contrary to Post's studies, Jimmy Carnegie, in *Some Aspects of Jamaica's Politics, 1918–1938* (1973), makes reference to the role of the early Rastafari in the political activities in St Thomas that culminated in the 1938 protest at the Serge Island sugar estate. Carnegie notes that these functions took place outside of "the sphere of the colonial government". In articulating his understanding of the emergence of the idea of Rastafari, the writer describes Howell's early missionary role and his clashes with the police, and argues that the philosophy associated with the movement is "distinctly unorthodox [despite having] some 'educated' men behind it". Carnegie includes the critical recognition that in early January 1938, there was a massive strike and confrontation with an "army" of police from Kingston at the Serge Island estate in Seaforth, St Thomas, "the parish in the centre of the Rastafari activity".[18] Howell is defined as an intelligent person with a history of conflicts with the colonial authorities, whose influence may have been important in the January 1938 events at Serge Island.

Centralizing Howell

Robert Hill, in his 1981 historical study "Dread History: Leonard P. Howell and Millenarian Visions in Early Rastafari Religions in Jamaica", makes Howell the central character and prophet of the early Rastafari. Howell, according to Hill, requires special attention due to his leadership qualities, which can be seen partly in the presentation of Howell as ambassador and president general of the Kings of Kings Mission and in his prophetic role in the revelation of prophecy of the divinity of Ras Tafari. Hill illustrates Howell's revelation of prophecy from Trinity Ville to Port Morant in St Thomas as "systematic statements of the doctrine", and he provides vivid details of the meetings, speeches and flyers bearing his message and a picture of Haile Selassie. He also details the roles of the planters and the police, who described Howell's lectures as seditious in nature. Noted as important is the political impact of *The Promised Key*, Howell's 1935 book, on the basis of the report by a retired resident magistrate who "was worried of the political threat of Rastafari; and so too was the planter Major Cawes of Trinityville, who declared that the book was dangerous because of the bitter hatred it stirred among certain strata of the lower class in Jamaica". Hill concludes that "these reports point to the very real likelihood that Rastafarian millenarian ideology functioned as an active catalyst in the development of the popular consciousness that led to the labour uprisings of 1938". Hill also highlights Howell's founding and prophetic role in Rastafari, as this was articulated in his political influence in St Thomas.[19]

The most extensive study on the Rastafari movement was conducted by Frank Jan van Dijk and published in *Jahmaica: Rastafari and Jamaican Society, 1930–1990* (1993). This study examines the rise of Garvey, his Universal Negro Improvement Association and his role in the process of resistance and change. Central to this study is the role of prophets and prophecy. In looking at the period from 1930 to 1939, van Dijk provides a detailed account of Howell's mission to St Thomas. Relying on newspaper articles, he develops a sterling portrait of Howell, recounting his meetings in St Thomas, the revelation of his prophecy and how the nature of his seditious utterances led to Howell's arrest. The study gives excellent details of the arrest and trial of Howell and positions him as the central character in the story of the emergence of the early Rastafari. Van Dijk illustrates the radical nature of Rastafari thought, its global reach and its influence on the politics of Jamaica during the 1960s and 1970s. The lessons from this study point to the political influence of the ideas of Rastafari and, by extension, the political qualities of Howell's thinking that informed the emergence of that idea.[20]

I am of the view that in *The First Rasta: Leonard Howell and the Rise of Rastafarianism*, published in English in 2003, Hélène Lee may have been on the hunt for the source of Bob Marley's music, when she encountered Leonard P. Howell. This book is very strong in providing personal details about Howell: his life at home, some of the inspiration from abroad that may have influenced Howell's development of an Ethiopianist perspective, his "Marxist animosities", his mission to St Thomas and his exodus to the Pinnacle community. Lee portrays Howell as a well-dressed character, who was fond of women. Her vivid illustration of his fiery sermons and how they provoked serious responses from the colonial elite in Port Morant, leading to his subsequent arrest and trial, is instructive. So too are her accounts of the scene at Howell's trial, both inside and outside of the Morant Bay courthouse, including the size of the crowd and the prophet's articulation of his defence against the sedition charge. In examining the importance of his role in the 1938 protests, Lee asserts that Howell was influenced by his association with the Marxist and pan-Africanist Padmore, and his own reading of *The Negro Worker*. Lee claims that Howell made a significant contribution to the politics of decolonization in Jamaica. Her book also shows Howell's influence at the community level in Seaforth, one of the main centres of Rastafari activity in St Thomas.[21]

Anthony Bogues, in his 2003 book *Black Heretics, Black Prophets: Radical Political Intellectuals*, provides a new approach to Howell and the early movement in his conceptualization of the thought of Rastafari into the "politics of Jah" and "redemptive politics". In looking at Howell's anti-colonial political qualities, Bogues argues that Howell created a "symbolic world" to displace the "Anglo-Saxon's Kingdom with another King and Kingdom". Bogues pays careful attention to the role of prophets in prophecy, and notes that Howell was deliberate in what he was doing in pioneering the redemptive "politics of Jah". He justifies this claim in his analysis of Howell's thought and foundational doctrine, and he illustrates three important moves by the prophet or philosopher. First, his thought was located outside of mainstream politics. Second, his thought was advanced in terms of the political language that Haile Selassie I was the Messiah, which brought out the conflict with domesticated Christianity and the colonial situation. Third, Howell's rejection of Christianity, seen as "idolatry", gave black people a black God, which was Howell's fundamental departure from the traditional thinking in Ethiopianism. Bogues shows that at his trial in 1934, Howell not only advanced a new political thought but also set forth the "early enunciations of Rastafari theology . . . following a stream of black radical thinking which centred on Africa".[22] Howell is defined in prophetic and philosophical proportions.

Conclusion

The earlier studies on Rastafari neglected or provided limited information on the founding thinker of the idea that Ras Tafari is the Messiah returned to earth. Howell has been characterized as a violent person and as a ganja farmer, but also as the first preacher of Rastafari. Due to the reliance of some studies on oral testimony, Garvey, in spite of his rejection of the Rastafari movement, has been identified as the prophet of the early Rastafari. Some of the studies provide mixed conclusions by declaring Garvey the prophet and Howell the first preacher. However, Hill, Lee and Bogues locate Howell as the central character in the story of the early Rastafari, as both prophet and philosopher. These writers have dispelled the long-held misconception of Garvey's role as the prophet. Lee goes further to declare Howell an anti-colonial champion against the background of his political influence in St Thomas. Indeed, Howell is one of the finest organic scholars in the history of Jamaica, the most influential advocate of black consciousness among the lower classes. Today, what began as a rural-based politico-religious movement has proliferated as a new philosophy all over the world.

Notes

1. George Eaton Simpson, "The Rastafari Movement in Jamaica: A Study of Race and Class Conflicts", Social Forces 34, no. 2 (December 1955): 167–71.
2. George Eaton Simpson, "Political Cultism in West Kingston, Jamaica", *Social and Economic Studies* 5 (1955): 133–49.

3. George Eaton Simpson, "Religion and Justice: Some Reflections on the Rastafari Movement", *Phylon* 46, no. 4 (1985): 286–91.
4. M.G. Smith, Roy Augier and Rex Nettleford, *Report on the Rastafari Movement in Kingston, Jamaica* (Kingston: Institute of Social and Economic Research, 1960), 5–9, 28.
5. This researcher, at a conference in June 2008 on M.G. Smith at the University of the West Indies, Mona, asked Roy Augier how the idea of the four preachers emerged. He replied, "It was M.G. Smith's idea."
6. Katrin Norris, *Jamaica: The Search for an Identity* (New York: Oxford University Press, 1962), 57.
7. H. Orlando Patterson, "Rastafari: The Cult of Outcasts", *New Society* 4, no. 3 (November 1964): 14–16.
8. Leonard E. Barrett, *The Rastafarians* (Boston, MA: Beacon Press, 1977), 64, 85, 86.
9. Klaus de Albuquerque, "Millenarian Movements and Politics of Liberation: The Rastafarians of Jamaica" (PhD diss., Virginia Polytechnic Institute and State University, 1977), 113, 118.
10. Carole Yawney, "Lions In Babylon: The Rastafarians in Jamaica as a Visionary Movement" (PhD diss., McGill University, 1971), 15.
11. Sheila Kitzinger, "The Rastafarian Brethren of Jamaica", in *Peoples and Cultures of the Caribbean: An Anthropological Reader*, ed. Michael M. Horowitz (New York: Natural History Press, 1971), 580.
12. Joseph Owens, *Dread: The Rastafarians of Jamaica* (Kingston: Sangster's Book Store, 1976), 7, 14, 58, 63, 221.
13. Alston Barrington Chevannes, "Jamaican Lower Class Religion: Struggle against Oppression" (MSc thesis, University of the West Indies, 1971), iii, 54.
14. Alston Barrington Chevannes, "Social and Ideological Origins of the Rastafari Movement in Jamaica" (PhD diss., Columbia University, 1989), 17.
15. Ibid., 93, 193, 194, 195.
16. John Paul Homiak, "The 'Ancient of Days' Seated Black: Eldership, Oral Tradition and Ritual in Rastafari Culture" (PhD diss., Brandeis University, 1985), 4, 134, 162, 164.
17. Ken W. Post, "The Politics of Protest in Jamaica, 1938: Some Problems of Analysis and Conceptualisation", *Social and Economic Studies* 8 (1969): 380, 195.
18. James Carnegie, *Some Aspects of Jamaican Politics, 1918–1938* (Kingston: Institute of Jamaica, 1973), 95, 101, 127, 187.
19. Robert A. Hill, "Dread History: Leonard P. Howell and Millenarian Visions in Early Rastafari Religion in Jamaica", *Epoché: Journal of the History of Religions* 9 (1981): 24, 35, 199, 201.
20. Frank Jan van Dijk, *Jahmaica: Rastafari and Jamaican Society, 1930–1990* (Utrecht, Netherlands: ISOR, 1993), 2, 3, 80, 91, 196, 224.

21. Hélène Lee, *The First Rasta: Leonard Howell and the Rise of Rastafarianism* (Chicago: Lawrence Hill, 2003), 71, 117, 161.
22. Anthony Bogues, *Black Heretics, Black Prophets: Radical Political Intellectuals* (New York: Routledge, 2003), 16, 165.

Part 2

REMEMBERING LEONARD HOWELL

10

GROWING UP IN PINNACLE
An Interview with Monty and Billbert Howell

CLINTON A. HUTTON

This interview with Leonard Howell's sons, Monty and Billbert, was conducted in 2010 by Clinton A. Hutton in his Department of Government office at the University of the West Indies, Mona, Jamaica.

Monty: [They arrested us,] a twelve-year-old and a fourteen-year-old. Because they couldn't get my father, they arrested us.

Clinton: They arrested you?

Monty: Arrested me, fourteen years old and he [Billbert] was twelve years old.

Clinton: The police?

Monty: Yes, because we couldn't show them receipts for the watches [we were wearing].

Clinton: You know that there is a long history of that?

Monty: Yeah.

Clinton: During the Morant Bay Rebellion [of 1865], the British soldiers, and Maroons and other people, went around . . .

Monty: Yes.

Clinton: . . . and plundered people houses; "thief dem" money and all of that.

Monty: Right.

Clinton: The people found with jewellery and watches [were] asked to account for them.

Monty: Yeah.

Clinton: Because people like them [were] not supposed to [be able to] *own* jewellery.

Monty: Right. Yeah. So that's what happens. But little did they know that we might have the original receipt. But as I said, at different occasions, the police, the authorities, would come in and take whatever paperwork was [available]. But it was traceable back to Church Street, where we bought the watch[es] from Hamilton Jewellery in the first place. They gave the lawyer a substitute receipt, or a copy of the receipt. But in the process that day – because we were taken to Spanish Town jail – we were too young for them to put us in the jail itself because you have to be a certain age where you could actually be locked up. So they kept us outside in the sun, all day. And we got bail about nine o'clock at night. I mean, it was one of the most embarrassing, agonizing thing[s] you could imagine for two kids.

Figure 10.1. Leonard Howell and his wife, Teneth Bent. Courtesy of Monty Howell.

Clinton: Two boys.

Monty: There were other kids there as well, you know, but we were the only two that got bail. But before that, they sent a note to my father through Mullings, a shopkeeper at the last shop at Thompson Pen, before you get to the crossroad that goes into Kingston, that if he didn't give them seven hundred pounds, they would put a pound weight of ganja to my name, and a pound weight of herb to his [Billbert's] name. And naturally, my father, although I told him not to do it, he went ahead. I was sort of strong-willed, you know. But that would really hurt us today and we couldn't have gotten any papers to go to the United [States].

Clinton: You would have got a police record.

Monty: We would have had a police record, even at that early age. I have the *Gleaner* report on it [the incident].

Billbert: In the *Gleaner* report, I see something about it. There is a misspell-

Figure 10.2. Billbert Howell. Photograph by Clinton Hutton.

Figure 10.3. Monty Howell. Photograph by Clinton Hutton.

ing. They said "Cilbert", and the name was Billbert. That is my official name, Billbert Howell. And his name wasn't even [spelled] Monty, it was . . . misspelt.

Clinton: Okay.

Monty: But the "Howell" was there.

Billbert: They say "two [of] Howell sons arrested".

Monty: Yeah.

Billbert: Howell two sons arrested; Cilbert which was to be Billbert; and Mortinale or something to that [effect].

Monty: The fact that he paid the money and everything, there were no mention of herb, of ganja at the time, within the [newspaper] article; only that the police had acquired the legitimate papers, receipts, in that case and the case was dismissed. There is another article about our mother in 1941. They were looking for my father, and they interviewed her, and she was crying and everything. There was this little baby hanging on to her coattail. That was me because he [Billbert] wasn't born at the time. He was born in 1942 – January 1942.

Clinton: (*addressing Monty*) And you were born in . . . ?

Monty: Thirty-nine, December. I'll be seventy-one December coming...

Clinton: You could have fooled me. (*Loud guffaw.*)

Billbert: The years go by so fast.

Clinton: Yes, I know, I know. But he [Monty] looks like forty . . . So [in] what year were both of you arrested?

Monty: 1954.

Billbert: You remember the month? I don't remember the month, you know. It was a great raid. I mean, that would be in the [news]paper, the actual month.

Monty: And another thing they did, they separated these people, the mother and father. Some of them had young kids that they left behind. And because people were traumatized, you know, nobody was taking care of the kids, because they had their own problems, you know. Everybody was in a daze. The following day, when you look at the people, they [were] just looking around. . . . The harassment was going on from 1932 [*sic*]. . . .

Clinton: From St Thomas?

Monty: From St Thomas. You know: thirty-two, thirty-three, every year on, there was a different story, different incident, you know. And one of the big one[s] was the sedition, you know, when he called Queen Victoria a harlot. . . . I mean, these British soldiers, they were mad, really mad. But you know . . . I expect . . . that the old man would back down from the harassment and stuff like that. But he just went on like nothing happen[ed] before. And they brutalized him again and again and again and again. He just kept going. I don't know another man that could take that type of punishment. . . .

Clinton: A man of fortitude?

Monty: He took some punishment that [was] unbelievable. And then we in the background, it was just one embarrassment after the other. Because we were kids, kids see things the way it supposed to be. Seeing all this harassment and the persecution, the embarrassment. I remember after 1954, me and Billy used to hide from people, because they took away everything. The bank account, everything. Over three thousand pounds that the old man had in the bank, it was frozen. They took away his two cars. Three cars! Two Studebaker and a Ford pickup that was seized and they sold it. They kept the money.

Clinton: For what reason?

Monty: The lawyer was another so-and-so. Because I found out that he had this money through some sources. And when I [went] and asked him, "Why didn't you return this money to my father?", he [gave] me all type of cock and bull story. And I think just to sort of quiet me, he gave me enough money to buy a motorcycle and stuff like that. But it was . . . if I didn't do it, he would have gone with everything.

Clinton: Who was the lawyer?

Monty: Lawyer Record from Dais, Record and Nash . . . on Duke Street. . . . I remember the last time I went there for money – because every so often I [would] go down and he would give me like a forty pounds, or a ten pounds, or whatever. First it was a little bit high, then it got less and less. The last time I went there, his little niece – I was there waiting for about an hour, and when she came in the room for whatever reason, he asked her if she had any change in her wallet. Now, I am sitting there admiring this young lady. She was about my age. And when she looked in her wallet and find a couple of pounds and some shillings and stuff like that and gave me, I felt like disappearing.

Clinton: Embarrassing.

Monty: So because of that, and that reason alone, I did not go back. Because it was totally embarrassing for me for this little girl to take money and give me, because I'm not accustomed to that type of thing, you know. But as I say, we were devastated. We didn't have anything, you know. And the thing about my father, he didn't ask for the money. He knew that he had the money. He wouldn't fight! He'll fight in his own way, like [with] the police. He would do his thing, he [was] not afraid of them. But to defend himself, he would not defend himself.

Billbert: Money.

Monty: He wouldn't ask for the money. It's like money didn't mean anything to him, you know.

Billbert: And that's how he was. Most of his things were done [that way]. He might have bought the property [Pinnacle]. He trust[ed] people. He paid the money. Everything he thought was legally taken care of, he allowed other people to do that. That's one explanation. Another explanation is that the [land] papers were there and they were taken when the police raid[ed], and [during] the different raid[s] they probably destroyed [them], or gotten rid of [them]. But that property I know was legally ours for sixteen years. No one questioned our authority. Tax[es] were being paid. Now they say that all those papers are all gone because the archive was burned.

Monty: One of the thing[s] that I would really like [of] the so-called owners today is a paper trail of the transaction with the deed, where they got the money from, who they paid the money to; that so-called owner that they bought this land [from], and a transmittal of the cheque that they gave. Because although it's fifty years or sixty years, whenever, or forty years they acquired this land, there should be a paper trail in terms of a transmittal. The bank should have a copy of the cheque. It is called a transmittal. They should produce this. If you check the entire record, it is a systematic harassment of Howell, that started in the thirties, and they wanted to eliminate him. They had people in the Home Office in England that were doing things and saying things; that they should put a stop to Howell, you know. All his action – it's like he was a threat to them. I never believed that the Home Office was involved until I got some of the minutes that came from London in the archives and stuff like that. I have a lot of copies of stuff [that I] can furnish. I can give you copies of it as well. It's unbelievable that little Jamaica with this little man, Howell, could [have] created such controversy where the Home Office in London would get involved. So it wasn't just [Alexander] Bustamante and so on. And another thing, I heard that one of the architects of the raid on Pinnacle acquired land [there] after. . . . His name [was] Watt from St Catherine.

Clinton: He acquired land where?

Monty: He acquired land at Pinnacle.

Billbert: He had the adjoining land. We had two properties.

Monty: He had the adjoining lot. After the raid, he acquired the land. But he was also very friendly with Bustamante, and Bustamante was the arch-enemy of Howell, you know. There are articles that Bustamante wrote to the Home Office, saying that Howell should be neutralized.

Billbert: The most dangerous man on the island.

Monty: The most dangerous man in the island in that time, in the thirties, okay. [And] why was Watt visited by Bustamante several times?

Clinton: Oh yeah?

Monty: They [Pinnacle residents] saw [a] car drive up with security system and everything, with Bustamante coming out, meeting Watt. . . . They were so surprised. So the connection was there, where everything was arranged. Plus the commanding officer of Spanish Town in 1954 – I also have that article; it came out in the *Gleaner* – where they were asking permission to go and clear

Pinnacle of the Rastas. "Do you want us to go up there and clear them, get them off the land?"

Clinton: So Watt was in the police force?

Billbert: No, no, no.

Monty: He was a rich landowner. He [had land] adjoining Pinnacle. Another story now, where the commanding officer of the force in Spanish Town was asking the authority in the government – I can't remember what the article say, if it was the governor of Jamaica at the time – some authority he wanted to get permission from to go and get rid of all the people, the thousands of people [who were] on Pinnacle. He wanted to push them off. Now, you have a community, Pinnacle – I'll give you a little story about Pinnacle – where you have all these people, self-sufficient. They planted fields, various type[s] of food produce. They made cabinets and desks, these carpenters. The bricklayers would go to Caymanas and work, [also] the stonecutters. . . . And we had all the trades up there. I've seen men gone in the bushes, cut down [a] tree, like an oak tree, and got a piece of metal, bent it into a certain shape, put the oak wood tightly unto these shaped metal and made a violin. All the strings for the violin were vines that you got from the bush. [When] you heard him play the violin, you would never believe it. . . . Even the glue that he used, they made [from] cow hoof and all type of stuff, you know. These were some of the most brilliant minds you ever saw, that was in Pinnacle. And you have this community living together in harmony, thousand[s] of people, self-sufficient, uplifting people that [you] meet on the streets in terms of: be brave, be dignified, respect yourself. Because at the time, black people, before my father came [back] to Jamaica, black people were just running around like they [were] lost, because they were second- and third-class citizens. He [told] them they should respect [them]selves, have love for [them]selves, show love to other people and so on.

Billbert: "Peace and love, brother man" was the slogan.

Monty: Peace and love, you know. To see all of this destroyed, or attempted to be destroyed, was hard. It was hard. That's why I went away. I couldn't take the embarrassment. I couldn't fight.

Clinton: What year you went away?

Billbert: Fifty-nine first.

Monty: Between fifty-nine and sixty-one. I can't remember clearly. We're talking about a long time ago. I would have to look at the papers. But more like

1959. But to see somebody who could motivate black people – that was what he did with a lot of people, motivated them. Just imagine, fresh out of slavery and people looking on you and telling you that you [were] no good, you [were] subhuman and stuff like that. For him to motivate people where they became strong mentally, you know, I lift my hat to him. To me, he was just a father, but to a lot of his followers he was like the supreme. He held a very, very high position in their minds. He was their leader. And to see the powers that be tried to hurt him in the way they did – and when I say tried to hurt him, to the end they sent some goons over Pinnacle, because he was still living [there]. He built a small house at the foothill of Pinnacle and was living there and they sent about twelve people one night. And they beat him up real bad, wanted to cut his tongue out. Wanted to cut his tongue out, and they cut him and everything. They hit him in the head. It was nine months before he died, actually. He never really recovered from that beating. That was the finale where they really put it on him.

Clinton: When they beat him up, the seventies?

Monty: No. He died eighty-one, so it had to be eighty. Nine months before he died, he got the beating that was nine months to the day almost – he got that cutting up and that beating....

Clinton: [And what of the breaking up of Pinnacle?]

Monty: To break up that community was a disaster. I have never seen anything like it in Jamaica again, that those people living together in harmony. And if this [had] gone on until today, Jamaica would have been better off, because you would have a community that people could emulate. They could say, look at those people, look how they live. But instead, they sent the police in. Every so often the police was there. Until finally in 1954 they have this big raid and put ganja on everybody, because [some] had fields that they planted with herb. And you tell me: nobody had herb in their house, but everybody, about three hundred people or close to that, were arrested and they put ganja on them.

Billbert: They found a lot of ganja.

Clinton: On their person?

Monty: They didn't have any in the house. But the field had ganja in it. All some of the little teenage kids that was old enough to send to prison, they send them to prison. Gave them a record.

Billbert: And they didn't have anything on them.

Monty: I mean, what sort of human being are you when you're living in a society where you can brutalize teenagers? Not only the ganja field, even the field where the cassava and stuff like that [were], they just destroyed it. Pull up the cassava and the yam.

Clinton: So they have cassava, yam?

Monty: Yam, cassava . . .

Billbert: Banana. Plantain.

Monty: You name the stuff that you can grow in Jamaica.

Clinton: Potato?

Billbert: We had mango.

Monty: We had places where you have hundreds of mango trees. We have places where you have hundreds of pear trees; some of the nicest pears you could ever find.

Billbert: Guinep also.

Monty: Guinep! You name the fruit, it was on that property. You name it.

Billbert: Anything you can name.

Monty: Because they went up there and they planted, they plant these things. [Police] destroyed [them]. If Pinnacle did survive, Jamaica itself would [have] been a better place, because as I said before, you would be emulating that setting there. Look how this bunch of people . . . lived in harmony. They [were] self-sufficient because if they didn't have the taste for, say, codfish or something like that, they wouldn't have to go out to buy anything. They have their chicken, their goats there. I used to sell goats to a butcher in Spanish Town name[d] Shaw, a big, red white man that was living in Thompson Pen. He used to come around and buy goats. I sold him a goat [that] weigh[ed] almost two hundred pounds, a ram goat, you know. We had hundreds of goats on the property. We had cows, we had donkeys, we had mules, we had horses.

Clinton: I heard your father used to ride a horse.

Monty: Yeah.

Billbert: This little idiot Watt talk about the old man was riding donkey!

Monty: Why should he ride a donkey when he had horses to ride?

Billbert: He could have ridden on a donkey.

Monty: Why would you ride a donkey? A big man riding a donkey with saddle looks like an idiot. There's no reason for you to ride a donkey, but he had to debase him, by saying he saw Howell riding a donkey with a saddle on it, when we had horses and mules!

Billbert: Cars.

Monty: We had cars. We had trucks. We even had about three dray carts, because some of the men used to burn coal and load it unto the drays and took it to Coronation Market and sold it. Some of them used to get car tyres, and cut the car tyres and made sandals.

Billbert: Something like slippers.

Monty: Slippers and sandals, and stuff like that. You used to have stockpiles of sandals made of rubber going to the Coronation Market.

Billbert: That's how Rasta spread, too. Because it spread from the Coronation Market to those people [at] Back-a-Wall [Back-o-Wall].

Clinton: Yes?

Billbert: They came into contact with these poor people, but they were so intelligent and so much aware of themselves that they made a difference in the crowd of people in the Coronation Market. So people would see these people who act with such respect towards each other and other people. And they would try to emulate them, and that's one of the things that [caused] the Rasta doctrine to spread.

Monty: Brothers and sister. Everybody was brother and sister. You never called a person by their name. You say brother so-and-so, sister so-and-so. And the love [was] always there. They always end with the love.

Billbert: Peace and love, brother man.

Monty: Peace and love. There was a lot of love. They used a lot of love, not only by expression, but by physical kindness. It was a beauty.

Billbert: You never [had] a murder. Never a crime reported to the police. People fight, they might have arguments, but it was settled. There was always a wiser head [t]here to intervene if things got out of control. You know, people know bounds just by living peacefully among each other. And that was like an addiction, it spread.

Clinton: How was the education of the children?

Billbert: That was the part that was neglected more than anything else.

Monty: They were at a distance away from school, and that create[d] a problem in terms of them going to school. But in the most part, the kids them that grow up in the forties got the worst of it. The other kids that were born inside like the late forties and early fifties, they used to go to school [even though] they used to get some [harassment] from them [the people from the surrounding areas].

Billbert: They were antagonistic towards the Pinnacle, the community, when we first moved there.

Clinton: The community?

Billbert: Right. Very violent at times. They used to attack the Rastas. But over the years, we developed a very good friendship, and then they came to respect the Rastas, because they knew that there wasn't any violence. They weren't violent people. They wouldn't come out or steal their goods or create any fuss, so the Rastas were accepted. The position reversed where they like envied the Rastas. Several times you would have people come up and want to come in the commune. There were instances like that. Now, schooling; I would say of all the things that we didn't do good there was schooling....

Clinton: What were some of the cultural things taking place there?

Monty: They [had the] drums. And they have different names for the different drums, like the bass drum and the Kbandu.

Billbert: The playing drum. These sounds were like...

Monty: These people used to dance on Saturday nights and they started to...

Billbert: People would get in spirit. The drum was working hypnotic...

Monty: And they fell down and people had to hold them and comforted them in that state of mind; they [were] not themselves. I used to wonder how the drum could give them that sort of high. It's like a high, a real high from the music. ... I don't think any other instrument can [do that] to the mind; intoxicated or whatever terms you want to use. I don't know if I'm using the right term when I say they were intoxicated by the music, just listening to those drums. As a matter of fact, I have some drums that this American went to Tredegar Park and got these people together, and they played these drums, and they [recorded the music and] took it back to the United States, and were selling it in CD form. I paid forty dollars for it, and [it] was my people, the Howellites, playing it. But although it was very, very good, it was nothing like those drums that the original elders used to play, but it is good....

Clinton: You remember any of the names of the drum players?

Monty: Oh, yeah. They were Toots, Swaby, Berry Man, Chilbert Black. All of these guys died. Most of the people that I'm calling were ten and fifteen and twenty years older than me, and I'm seventy-odd. The only one that['s] alive today is Louis. Louis is the only one.

Billbert: And he was a young kid then. He wasn't the master.

Monty: You could get some good beat from Louis today. But all of the real professionals, and these were guys, I don't know, they seemed to get it from their ancestors that came down from Africa, ancestors right down; they actually taught them . . .

Clinton: The Kumina people?

Monty: Yes.

Clinton: [From] St Thomas?

Monty: Because most of his people were from St Thomas.

Billbert: The majority of his people.

Monty: He had some from Clarendon, some from Kingston, some from all over the place. But majority of them was from St Thomas, you know. I have such good memories. When you're up Pinnacle and you looked at the sun going down, it was like a gallery. You see everything; every day is a new photograph with the clouds and the sunshine and everything.

Clinton: On top of the hill there? Where the Great House was?

Monty: Yes. [You] saw the sun going down and the clouds. The formation of the clouds, you saw human faces, you saw horse, man riding; you name it. You used to see things. I'm not a spiritual person per se, but people had their own interpretations of looking at it. I only saw it from the beauty. You saw the thatch trees and the palm trees when the sun hit them and how they glittered. And it's like they danced sometimes. . . . And you looked down and you saw the Rio Cobre river running down and then you looked across, you saw Port Royal, you saw Port Henderson, you saw parts going into Bog Walk area. You saw Kingston, Spanish Town. Three hundred and sixty degrees you saw. Jamaica – we have gold in our hands right now, Pinnacle. And the international Rastas are all over the place, in every country. And it would be unwise for us not to have Pinnacle. We need a base for Rasta. We need a foundation for Rasta. For us to ignore the fact that Pinnacle is in the hands of people who have no respect for the culture, this alone is embarrassing. It shouldn't be happening. Not in Jamaica, not now, not today; it shouldn't. Pinnacle belongs to you. You think like a Rasta. Somebody asked me to define Rasta and I said if your mind is clean and you believe in beauty and respect and love, you have all the attributes ... you're a Rasta. I even go to the point to say some people are Rastas and they don't even know that they [are] Rastas. Growing your hair or beard, that doesn't make you a Rasta. It's what you have up here [pointing to his head]. If you are proud of being black, you're proud of being a human being; you love people on a whole; you respect people, you're a kind person, you're a gentle person, you're a humble person, then you are a Rasta. I don't have any hair on my head. I want to grow it. I can't grow any hair, but that doesn't take away from the fact that I'm a Rasta. I born one and I will die one, you know. I know a lot of Rastas that don't have hair. The fortunate ones can grow hair. It's up to the individual. And they have a lot of people that grow hair and you'd think that they Rastas, but they not Rastas, they [are] rascals.

Billbert: Some people just like the style.

Monty: Yeah. It's a style.

Clinton: Was there a bakery at...

Monty: Oh yeah! We had a big oven there and we used to put out a lot of bread. As a matter of fact, I was up Pinnacle yesterday and when Curline was talking about Ingrid and you said you going take Ingrid to show her where the bakery was, because it is in ruin now. You only have the foundation left there and some bricks that used to be the top of oven. Anyway, when Ingrid was away there, I remember an incident. Well, it was several incidents, where they put the bread out to raise – you know, after you make the bread they put it in a lacquer, and you put it out there to expand – and the bloody goat them come and was eating the dough, the raw dough, from the lacquer there, you know. And I remember – what-her-name was chasing them away – this happened about sixty-odd years ago – and she was chasing them away.

Clinton: So you used to sell the products from the bakery outside of Pinnacle as well?

Monty: No, no. Most of the bread was consumed...

Billbert: Some was sold, but not on a broad scale.

Clinton: About how many dwelling houses were there?

Monty: I think roughly about three hundred, maybe four hundred dwelling houses, over East Avenue. But you see, each house will take a family of X amount because they had some two bedrooms.

Billbert: They attached all the houses.

Clinton: They were attached together?

Monty: Yes.

Clinton: All three hundred?

Monty: No, no. You have a row of houses going down here. You have this [one] belonged to one person and he'll have three or four compartments in that one [house].

Billbert: And somebody can build another house beside his house ...

Monty: Yeah. It stopped them from building a wall ...

Billbert: And behind you would have the same arrangement.

Monty: But in the early forties when they went there, they acquired the land with these very big pots. As I say, I don't know if they bought them or they acquired the land with them. I think most likely he would [have] bought them, because the owner of the property wouldn't have that many people to feed with these giant pots. They are like five feet in diameter. And you have a big place that they built with cement and stone that underneath you could push the firewood to cook these pots. And there were about four big ones that [we] would [be] able to feed more than, say, two thousand people [from]. And they used to cook, like, curry goat. I hear that they used to slaughter a lot of goats and different, different things to feed these people. That's in the early part of the forties, before they settled.

Clinton: A lot of people started to come in?

Monty: Oh, yeah. In 1940 a lot of people came in. ...

Billbert: Right.

Monty: At that early time. The infrastructure wasn't there, you know. A few of them died of different [things] like fever and stuff like that. I see some of the minutes [documents] ... from Spanish Town. Minutes they get from the hospital itself. This would happen anyway in any society where you have hundreds of people or thousands of people. Some will die.

Clinton: When did it actually start? Because you were born in thirty-nine. Were you born there?

Monty: No, he [Billbert] was born there.

Billbert: Pinnacle started ...

Monty: 1940.

Clinton: Because he was previously in Trinity Ville?

Monty: Yes.

Billbert: He was in St Thomas, different places in St Thomas.

Monty: Trinity Ville.

Billbert: And main office, and also in Kingston. He was operating from different areas in St Thomas. Port Morant, Seafort, Trinity Ville and probably I [am] missing some other [places]. But he wasn't at one static point. He was at different places.

Monty: At different time[s].

Billbert: And different locations in Kingston as well. Until he was being harassed so much both in Kingston and in St Thomas that he decide[d] that he want[ed] to get all his people together. He want[ed] a safe place.

Clinton: St Catherine?

Billbert: Right, so that's why Pinnacle came about. And he acquired the property and then people start[ed] to come there. . . .

Clinton: So you say there were craftspeople there?

Monty: Oh, yes.

Clinton: Skilled?

Billbert: Skilled people. All the trades, tailors . . .

Monty: All the trades were there.

Billbert: There weren't any professionals. I don't think there were the engineers or doctors. I don't know. They were poor people. Crossroads people, basically. When it comes to . . . carpentry or stone-making or stone-laying or stonecutting, [they were there] . . .

Monty: They had a few scholars as well; very educated people there as well.

Billbert: Yes.

Monty: Most of his lieutenants and so on.

Clinton: Who were some of his lieutenants?

Monty: Edgar Reid, Walker, Penny, Catherine's grandfather, Malabe. He was one of them as well.

Clinton: Catherine was born there?

Monty: Yes. Catherine was born in Pinnacle but she wasn't born in the Great House. . . .

Clinton: That is where you used to live?

Billbert: Yeah, that's where Dada lived. But you had a village that had all these people. That's East Avenue. Plus you had houses all over and little settlements all over the place, but the main village was East Avenue. Let me see if I can think of another name. Shine was one.

Clinton: So you would say that the governing structure was – at the top would be your father?

Monty: Oh, yeah. He was the head.

Clinton: Who were the lieutenants?

Monty: The names that we gave you a while ago would be people that have a dialogue with him daily. About the running of the place itself, it wouldn't be a day-to-day affair in terms of "you should do that" or "you should [do this]". People very much did their own thing, but they did it on a corporate basis. Because if you have something and you want something, you ask around and anybody that have that thing that you want, they would give it to you.

Billbert: They would barter with you, and you'd get it.

Monty: You'd get it. It was a very, very, very good community.

Clinton: And all the adults took care of all the children?

Monty: Yes. If they see them doing something wrong they would talk to them, or get in touch with the parents and . . . it's corrected.

Billbert: Everybody knew everybody and nobody was going to abuse anyone. You lived right in front of everyone, as I said.

Monty: The closest thing I've seen to that, like outside in my travels, is the kibbutz in Israel. They [were] very protective of each other, especially when they travelled to Kingston, travelled outside, you know; extremely protective of each other.

Clinton: More than one person would go at a time?

Monty: Oh, yes. As I say, they were very protective of each other. It was part of their culture. They referred to the people not living there . . . as the outside people. . . .

Billbert: And referred to themselves as the Pinnacle people.

Clinton: They called themselves the Pinnacle people?

Monty: Yeah.

Billbert: And the outside people referred to them as the Pinnacle people.

Monty: I have this friend, Bunny, and I was talking to him the other day, and he was telling me that he had a couple of kids. But he and this lady that he had a common-law [relationship with] were not living together because she didn't believe in Howell, and that type of Rasta [thing], you know. He says he is too old to change, and he knows he's not going to get a woman within the community. He is about seventy-six years old. But if you see him, you would never believe that he is seventy-six; strong and active. And he's saying that because he can't find a woman that thinks like him in the Howell community, and he is old now anyway, he's not going to live with anybody, or even think about finding one. And he devotes his whole life [to the cause]. There are a lot of those people. Even today – although the old man is gone and everything – they devote their entire lives to the cause. They live for their memory, a lot of them. Right now, although a few of them live on the property still, is basically those that can't [live] without the property. They have nothing outside there. At least on the property they can make the little field. The property is so big and so mountainous that even the [present] "owners" don't even know where these places are, and to get at these places you would have to do a lot of climbing with honeycomb rock and stuff like that.

If the so-called owners know where they are, they would probably go and chase them off or do something. But on the top there [where Howell lived], I don't think they would try to do anything with the top ... because at the top you have a few [Rastas] who live up there and they [are] up there all the time. And these people, they are the type ... willing to even die for it. Nobody [is] going to chase them off there. I'm afraid that if it comes to a test where we don't, for whatever reason, acquire the land, there's going to be a confrontation there. It could be deadly as well. . . . I hope we get some sort of satisfactory conclusion, because it would seem to be a waste, a missed opportunity not to [allow] the Rastas. . . . I hope that we get the place and we have a base there, somewhere where people can come and learn about Leonard Howell, the history about Jamaica, the history about Howell, the history about Rasta. They could stay there if they want, for a week [or] so. Like a hotel where they could stay and you have entertainment, whether religious or whatever entertainment we decide that's appropriate that would be there, because we have to think in terms of the one that passed, and show him some respect as well. Nothing rowdy would be tolerated there in terms of loud type[s] of music that's not appropriate and so on. We would have food there. In other words, to maintain the site, and the structure that I'm thinking about having there, it would have to be capable of maintaining itself. You would have people working there. They would have to be paid. So this community would have to generate enough money to take care of all the business aspects of the whole affair, including the archive or the museum of the old man, and so on. We have certain stuff between me and Billy, like his old suit, that you could put up on display and stuff like that. We have pen[s]. I even have an old watch that he gave me – a Rolex watch. I'll have to fix it up good. I was wearing it and it dropped from me, and the stem – you can see the stem is missing. . . . It's . . . probably eighty or ninety years old.

Billbert: What surprises me is something that we didn't keep more of.

Monty: What? I have two suitcase leather grips, and I had them up until the eighties and then a girlfriend of mine took mine and I had one. Then I threw it away because the stitch was getting [bad] . . . I threw it away.

Clinton: You shouldn't. . . .

Billbert: I had a trunk. A lot of his personal papers, all his photographs that you see around of him, that really came from out of this trunk I had.

Clinton: So you had photos of him?

Billbert: Yes, but most of the stuff I have, I think you have seen, right. You see all these photographs of the emperor on the throne. All those photographs came out of this trunk that I had. And you know what happened to that thing? I went to America in sixty-nine, and I left that trunk beside the bed. And when I got back in seventy, they said there was a lot of weevil or something like that that got inside of it and they ate up everything. So they threw it out. I had a book in there called *The Book of Knowledge*, a massive thing like that. I mean, just reading that is an education. And that [and] all of the [other] books . . .

Clinton: That was one of his books that he used to read?

Billbert: Yeah, one of his books . . .

Clinton: He used to have a lot of books?

Billbert: Yeah.

Monty: Lots of literature.

Billbert: And writing.

Monty: The police destroyed [that] as well; took them away.

Clinton: They used to destroy his books?

Monty: Yeah, they used to destroy a lot of papers because he used to hand out a lot of papers, you know. They figured more or less, [to] destroy the literature would be a way of keeping him in check. So they used to do a lot of destruction of his work, you know.

Billbert: If you talked to him and asked him to tell you his occupation, he would tell you a writer.

Clinton: So he used to write a lot?

Monty: He did a lot of writing.

Clinton: Do you have any of his original writings?

Billbert: [I am not sure.] I might have some. I also have a little suitcase that I had from him as well. But surprising we didn't keep it better.... To tell you the truth, I wanted to get away from it.

Monty: That happened to all of the kids that [were] especially close to him: at one point we just wanted to get away.... In the fifties there was nothing, no article about Howell that was positive; none, period! You did not have a single human being in Jamaica saying positive [things] about the old man. Never! Every striking day you see his name in the paper is something negative. And not only that, the *Gleaner* was saying something negative and the *Star*; the people around was saying something negative; outsiders were saying something negative. In Spanish Town: "See Gong son there." I was tired of hearing that. "Gong son". "That's Gong son." And the way they said it, *"Gong son"*.

Billbert: A girl broke off with me, Marguerite Chevannes. I used to see this girl from Golden Spring. She used to go Alpha [School] at the time, and she used to be a very fair girl. And then her father found out who I was, and he said no way he'll have his daughter talk to Howell's son.

Monty: They [the Pinnacle people] had ganja, they sold ganja! One day, I was going to Kingston and on the road near Ferry Police Station – you know that big cotton tree across the street – it was drizzling slightly and a car passed me. I'll never forget. It was a Morris Oxford passed me, and I could see a red seam [policeman] was in the back seat of the car, and when the car passed me in the rain, the police looked back on me. And in the distance, it pull[ed] into Ferry Police Station. He came out of the car, and when I got close to the station, he flagged me down, but he sort of did it late so I passed the station. But because he flagged me down, I turned back [and] parked up in the station yard there. He said to me, "You're Howell son, right?" I said, "Yes." He said, "Well, I want you in the guard room; I'm going to search you." I said, "No, I'm not going in the guard room." And he said, "I'm not asking you, I'm telling you, you have to go in the guard room." And I said, "I'm telling you that I'm not going in the guard room." And I start[ed] up my motorcycle to go – the little 250 at the time – the year I think was 1955.... So... I turn[ed] on the motorcycle, and he turned it off and took the key. When I look[ed] at him, I saw this giant of a person. I got mad and I rip[ped] my shirt open and I dropped my pants and I started crying. And he was just there and he freeze [sic] like that and he just handed me back the key, you know.

Billbert: If they had taken you in that guard room, you'd leave there with probably two ounces of ganja.

Monty: Every time I think about that incident, I... [He fades into silence trying to hold back the tears.]

Clinton: When you remember your father, what [do] you remember? What comes to your mind immediately?

Monty: Pride, respect, love, strength, honour, a protector, somebody that you can rely on. Somebody you want to be around you for the rest of your life.

Clinton: What you think, Bill?

Billbert: Yeah... the same things. Also somebody I still don't yet understand. Now I'm even appreciating him more than when I was around him. When I was around him, he was just my father. Now I have the chance of – you know, not being with him for all these years – but now appreciating what he did, and what he tried to do, and what he accomplished. I realize that, to be honest, I have to think of him as a great person. I think his accomplishment in starting a philosophy, a religion, a movement that is going to live on its own for probably through the centuries. I think that's an accomplishment. I have very good feelings towards him.

Clinton: Your memory of Pinnacle?

Monty: Just beauty, longing to see some of those evenings where you could relax and watch a show from nature, have some of the fruits them that we had up there. It's just a place of beauty and love, and as far as I'm concern[ed], paradise. This is history that will not go away. This is something that is growing. It's not a matter of if [but] when Pinnacle becomes a place, a shrine for... Rasta. This is inevitable that it will happen. It might not happen in my lifetime, but it will happen. It will come to pass, regardless [of] who's living there or who is doing what. It is something that is growing. Christianity didn't take nuh [any] big root until five hundred years after the death of Christ, when King Constantine, the monarch, introduced it to the rest of the world. So is just a matter of time.

Clinton: Apart from playing the drum, usually every night, on a Saturday night? When was...

Billbert: Usually on weekends.

Monty: Because there was activity during the week... that would prevent them from playing the drum. But some evenings they would, like, do a rehearsal type thing.

Billbert: There were also other musicians there as well.

Monty: Guitarist.

Clinton: Guitarists?

Monty: Yes, the best guitarist in the entire world. I think he's better than anything that I've heard: Ernie Ranglin, Chet Atkins or anybody like that. This man could play and strum at the same time. Pick and strum at the same time.

Clinton: Who was that?

Monty: A man name Barrett.

Billbert: He could make the one guitar sound like you have five different instruments going at the same time. He would be picking something and he's strumming, and then his fingers were like doing different things at different times. To me, I wish I could hear that man play again.

Clinton: So drummers, guitarists?

Billbert: And you had fifes too.

Monty: Yeah.

Clinton: Violin too?

Billbert: This man made his own violin. Got his tree and soaked the wood with hot water and thing and bent it into shape, and made his own bow. That man was so good.

Clinton: What was his name?

Monty: Wood.

Billbert: [And this fife man.] This guy would put the fife in his nose, and play it [with] his nose – probably not the most sanitary thing to see – but someone had a fife in his nose and playing real melody.

Clinton: So what kind of music?

Billbert: It would be more than the Kumina.

Monty: It's more Mento.

Billbert: I'll tell you a similarity, you know the Kumina music.

Monty: And Mento.

Billbert: Well, yeah, some Mento . . . we had very good banjo players too. So their basic sound would be more like the Mento type.

Clinton: They had rumba bax [box] with them too?

Monty: Yes.

Billbert: But not much rumba bax. . . .

Clinton: And you have the grater?

Billbert: Yes.

Monty: And they used to knock something like a wooden thing.

Clinton: And you have the . . .

Billbert: You have the shaker. And some have the same cymbal thing here, too. They do it in a religious type thing. It was done to . . . it wasn't done basically for dancing. A lot of times it would be like a religious service, uplifting type of music where – how should I put this now – it wasn't anything like calypso. When our young people would play calypso and wine, the elders . . .

Clinton: Tell me something. I know St Catherine is a place where you have a drumming tradition called Burru. They used to play Burru drum there?

Monty: Quite possible, but maybe they didn't call it that name.

Billbert: It is a strain of drumming I guess that comes out of St Thomas, and some from Clarendon.

Clinton: Kumina would be from St Thomas and Burru would be from Clarendon. They probably try to combine both of them.

Billbert: Exactly. So there was a fusion of all the great players from the different places.

Monty: And you see the name of what they [were] playing would only apply to the ones that [were] playing in that thing. They wouldn't be saying this to people like us that don't know anything about music. Some of it would flow to us, like, but all we could hear is that beat.

Clinton: And those played late into the night?

Monty: Oh, yes.

Billbert: On weekends.

Growing Up in Pinnacle 241

Clinton: On weekends?

Billbert: I think that was like Friday night and Saturday night that would go on. Later on, it kind of went off because people get busy. First time you could say [it used to be] every night....

Monty: Is something that wind up.... [T]he drumming continued with the elders. What stopped the drum [was] the raid in fifty-four.... After fifty-four, everything died. It was... downhill from fifty-four. And then fifty-six [was] the final raid. This was the way it happened. They [had] been persecuting him from the early thirties, come right up until fifty-four. And then they really knocked him out in fifty-six. That's the big raid where they tried to turn everybody off the property.

Billbert: Burned the houses.

Clinton: Burned the houses?

Billbert: Oh, yeah. Literally burned all the houses...

Clinton: They burned down the Great House?

Billbert: Yes. The entire house!

Figure 10.4. Destruction of Pinnacle, 1954. Photograph published by the Jamaica Constabulary Force.

Clinton: How big was the Great House?

Monty: It was big. It was big.

Billbert: It was big.

Monty: It had probably about six bedrooms, I would say. And you have a dining area, kitchen area and then the old man had an outside kitchen as well, because he didn't like the heat inside the house. We had a big stove. It was when he got this big stove that worked with coal, and you could use wood as well. It had an oven by it. It [was] made of cast iron. So when he got that, he build an outside kitchen 'cause once that got going, there was a lot of heat! And you know the sun hot in Jamaica and you have a stove running at a hundred and odd degrees, it used to get hot. A small goat could hold inside that oven, inside that stove that we had there. And we used to have a lot of baked mutton. You remember all those times we used to bake? I can smell some of it right now. When it cools down, you get a knife and you cut a piece off stuffed with pimento and garlic and stuff like that. Oh god.

Billbert: Another thing we used to do a lot was cure meat. We would kill a cow...

Monty: Smoked it.

Billbert: And not only smoked, but corned it. What they did, they cut up the meat in little pieces, put some salt at the bottom, put the meat on top of the salt, then put more coarse salt, rock salt on top of that. Then put more meat, then put more rock salt, and keep doing it like that. They would eventually [pack] it and then put a lid unto the barrel ... [a] wooden barrel. But for some reason, sometimes they said if it was not sealed totally and air got in or maggots got in, that thing would start to rot inside, and that was one of the worst things that could ever happen. Because sometimes that thing inside there and it got so stink.... When you take it out – somebody would have to periodically go around, not every day, but people who know this, know when one is bad – and they take one out and when they go outside and when they open it, you see the maggots inside of it.... So it haffi [had to] be done properly.... And over the time, that meat got so dried out that when you took it out, you could eat that meat. It's like jerky. And that's how it's cured. Just put the fresh meat on top of the salt, put the salt and keep doing [that], and then you make sure you pack it. I think they used to use – was it crocus bag or flour bag? Something to make it airtight [so] that nothing get down inside of it and out the lid and then, you know, knock down the side.

Monty: I remember they had these places where they hang the meat and they smoked. And it [was] there until it [got] cured, you know. . . . And it was so delicious when it was cooked. . . .

Clinton: About how many people lived in Pinnacle, in your estimation?

Billbert: I would say . . . three thousand. I've heard numbers as much as five, but I'm not going to call that.

Clinton: 'Bout three thousand? But that was pretty big still. If you have three thousand, that's big.

Billbert: Plus there were other people that was all over, behind us, [and] were at times counted among [us]. You [would] see them every six month because they were so far away, those people that used to live down close to the river. You hardly see these people because the property is so big that these people don't, like, interact. They just come over to the village. We mostly know the people that live in the East Avenue. That was where our town was.

Monty: [Howell] had people [who weren't] at Pinnacle. They were still in St Thomas; they were still in Kingston. They were still in Clarendon, so the exact numbers . . .

Billbert: The exact number of the followers, we just didn't have a . . .

Monty: I think Walker . . .

Billbert: There were folks that probably could tell.

Monty: Walker told me that he had five ledgers filled with people. And you know, the ledgers, they have multi sheets, and they were like twelve by eight inches.

Billbert: Legal is fourteen inches.

Monty: And he told me that one time he had five full with names of people. That's what Walker told me.

Billbert: But there was so many of those books, and it's like they just disappeared off the face of the earth. If you can get the police to go through their archives, you probably could get [a] lot of stuff that they – I know that they must have burned [and] thrown out some – but something must be left there in their archives. Now these police have a different outlook on it. I don't think they want to hide anything now. I don't see why they should, I mean if they really want to be genuine. So they could go through their archives. Even photographs, because in some of those raids, the police were there with cameras. So there are archives [photos] of probably those buildings; I don't know what they were shooting. If somehow, some way, we can get somebody to look at things from within the police archives . . .

Monty: Even the *Gleaner*. The *Gleaner* should have photos of some of the . . .

Billbert: There is an incident that happened after [Hurricane] Charlie in fifty-one. The front part of the house where Monty and myself used to be, the windows broke and we put some boards and things [over the damage]. One of the raids when the police came up, they came up with someone – I guess he was from the newspaper, from the *Gleaner*. And the next day we saw a thing in the newspaper. And I know because I saw the picture [with] Monty and myself. And it was the night when they came there. And the photograph came out so plain: Monty and myself looking through this broken window.

Monty: You could see my face.

Billbert: It was very plain.

Monty: I wish I could find that paper, because [it had] the youngest photograph of myself, I was about nine or eleven, and I can't find it. I haven't seen it in years. I would love to see those photographs as well. And another photograph that I would love is the one that they took with my mother in 1941 that they had in the *Gleaner* – the front page there. Billy wasn't born then. I would love to get that one as well, you know.

11

LEONARD HOWELL VERSUS ROBERT WILLIAM LYALL-GRANT

MIGUEL LORNE

Adapted from the keynote address at the Leonard Howell Symposium, University of the West Indies, Mona, Jamaica, 17 June 2011

G**reeting and** blessings. Give thanks to JAH RASTAFARI!
How I have postulated the topic tonight is Leonard Howell versus Robert William Lyall-Grant, chief justice of Jamaica in 1934. Why I put it this way is because I am certain if Leonard Howell knew some of the things we now know about Robert William Lyall-Grant, there would have been a bigger uproar and objection to him being the judge in the Morant Bay courthouse in March of 1934.

Now, to understand the man Leonard Howell in 1934, it is important to look at some of his writings and the writings of others within that era. It was a creative time in Jamaica and the diaspora, with the publication in the 1920s and early 1930s of books such as *The Holy Piby*, written by Robert Athlyi Rogers of Anguilla, *The Royal Parchment Scroll of Black Supremacy* by Reverend Fitz Balintine Pettersburgh, *The Edicts of God Jehovah's Perfect Law of Liberty* by Joseph Solomon Ashby, *The Hamitic Church Hymn Book* by the Bahama Athlyi Rectory and Leonard Howell's 1935 work, *The Promised Key*. Many of these writings and songs emphasized and referred to the black God or the God of Ethiopia or the black man heaven. Leonard Howell, who at the time called himself Gangunguru Maragh or the Gong, coalesced all of the earlier thinking and writings, and not only pointed to the black God but taught that the black God was King Rastafari, the returned Messiah, and this was what made him different from the other movers of that era of the 1920s, 1930s and 1940s.

On 10 December 1933, Leonard Howell made a speech to over three hundred people at Seaforth in the parish of St Thomas, for which he, along with Robert Hinds, was charged for sedition. It was alleged that in his speech, Leonard Howell abused the sovereign Queen Victoria, the governor of Jamaica and both the governments of Great Britain and Jamaica, "thereby intending to excite hatred and contempt for His Majesty the King and for those responsible for the Government in this island and to create disaffection among the subjects of His Majesty in this island and to disturb the public peace and tranquillity of this island" – the words of Robert William Lyall-Grant. The main evidence against Howell and Hinds came from two policemen, Corporal Ebenezer Brooks and Constable Enos Gayle, both of whom claimed to have made written notes of the so-called sedition remarks. Both were cross-examined and discredited by Leonard Howell, who represented himself. Both were unable to say exactly what Howell had said that was seditious or abusive.

Leonard Howell testified that "Ras Tafari is the Messiah returned to earth" and urged the people to "Go back to Africa, the home of their forefathers". Chief Justice Lyall-Grant and the jury found Howell and Hinds guilty. Howell was sentenced to two years' imprisonment, while Hinds was given one year. Jephet Wilson, a brother converted by Howell to the faith, and who was present in court, stated that "when they were trying him [Howell] at Morant Bay . . . he told the Judge that if he found him guilty, to give him the maximum of the law because when the day came when I shall sit around my radiant throne and judge you, I am going to judge you, so give me the full maximum". Leonard Howell was always full of confidence that he would be liberated by the coming King – King Rastafari – and that the tables would turn and he, Howell, would be sitting in judgement over these wicked judges one day. Thus, the words attributed to Howell by Wilson at the Morant Bay courthouse in St Thomas were to be repeated at the Sutton Street courthouse in Kingston in April 1937, when he told the magistrate, "Have no mercy on me, because I will not have mercy on you, when I sit in judgement."

In October 1937, Howell was sent to the Bellevue Mental Hospital by the court, and stayed until 11 January 1938, when he was discharged. However, on 15 February 1938, he was readmitted into Bellevue, where he stayed until the end of the year. Many times the judiciary in Jamaica adopted that approach; where the evidence was not sufficient to convict and send you to the general penitentiary, they would deem it sufficient to send the accused to the Bellevue Mental Hospital. Thus, it is either the general penitentiary or Bellevue.

So we have Leonard Howell on one hand and Sir Robert William Lyall-Grant on the other hand. Leonard Howell, described as the Doctor of Divinity, the Counsellor, the Gong, the Mystic Man and, to his personal family, Uncle Percy. He was the first announcer of the Rastafari faith. The core of the Rastafari philosophy is that Haile Selassie I is the returned Messiah, the black God, the black majesty. In his book, *The Promised Key*, Leonard Howell emphasized "Black Supremacy", stating, "His Majesty Ras Tafari is the head over all man for He is the Supreme God". He further describes the "Pope of Rome" as "Satan the devil" and says that "Black must not marry white nor white black, race enmity".

Sir Robert William Lyall-Grant was a white man born in Scotland. He first served as the attorney general in England until he was promoted to a judge of the Supreme Court in Nyasaland, which is today Malawi. In Nyasaland, the Africans resented and resisted the Scottish Presbyterian missions that constantly imposed and forced the white God concept on them. John Chilembwe was the leader of the African armed resistance, which started in 1913. The Africans objected to the racism and exploitation that was practised by the whites in Nyasaland. At the time, the British were recruiting thousands of Africans to fight for them in Tanganyika (now Tanzania) against the Germans as part of the First World War. Chilembwe encouraged the people to resist this level of obvious exploitation.

Chilembwe, who had studied in the United States and had returned as a pan-Africanist and Baptist preacher, had built many schools and churches. These were burned down by the white Presbyterians and their black house-slaves. Chilembwe himself was shot and killed on 3 February 1915, as he was trying to cross the Nyasa River. Many of his followers were captured and tried. The judge who tried and sentenced most of them to death or to long terms of imprisonment was Robert William Lyall-Grant. Until this day, the people of Malawi still complain of the kangaroo trials and the railroading of justice that took place under Lyall-Grant. John Chilembwe is now regarded as an international hero, and 15 February is annually celebrated as John Chilembwe Day in Malawi.

In August 1932, Robert William Lyall-Grant was appointed the chief justice in Jamaica. By March 1933, he appointed himself to preside over the most religiously and politically charged trial in the island, *Rex v. Leonard Howell, et al.* At the Supreme Court on King Street, the number one court is called the Chief Justice Court. It is the most spacious, with the best setting and with the chief justice chambers adjoining. Occasionally, the chief justice, if he or she chooses, travels out to other circuit courts. William Lyall-Grant chose to try Leonard Howell. It did not take him long after being made chief justice to decide that something needed to be done not only to "cool" Howell, but to stop the spread of the Rastafari movement.

It is not without significance that Robert William Lyall-Grant succeeded Fiennes Barrett-Lennard, who was the chief justice between 1925 and 1932. Fiennes Barrett-Lennard was the judge who made it his business to find Marcus Garvey guilty and imprisoned him for contempt of court. It is also important to note that like Leonard Howell, Marcus Garvey was convicted for contempt of court on the main evidence of a policeman, who claimed to have attended the meeting at Cross Roads and took notes of what Garvey said. The colonial system was ensuring that Garveyism and the Rastafari were dealt a double blow by Barrett-Lennard and Lyall-Grant.

In such an atmosphere and with such a judge, Leonard Howell could never get a fair trial. Leonard Howell was the architect of black supremacy and the black God concept. Lyall-Grant was a Presbyterian and part of the system of imposing the white God concept, the seizing of African lands and the exploitation of Africans to fight in a white man's war. I am certain that if Leonard Howell had known his background he would have asked Lyall-Grant to recuse himself. However, if Lyall-Grant had been a fair and just judge, he would have declared his past and his behaviour in sentencing many rebel Africans at the start of Howell's trial and thus given Howell an opportunity to either go through with Grant as the judge or apply for his removal. As a lawyer, I have experienced quite a number of occasions where a judge recused himself or herself from a matter because of personal or other connections or knowledge.

I am of the view that the Howell family should take legal action, either locally or internationally, for this obvious travesty of justice. The malice of Robert

William Lyall-Grant was borne out not only by his overwhelming summation in favour of "guilty", but by his comments prior to sentencing. Hinds was called "ignorant" and described as having been "led away" by Howell. Howell was called "a fraud" for merely advocating his loyalty to and claiming the divinity of his black God, Jah Rastafari.

12

LEONARD P. HOWELL
A Portrait

LOUIS E.A. MOYSTON

Adapted from an address at the Leonard Howell Symposium, University of the West Indies, Mona, Jamaica, 15 June 2012

Good evening, fellow panellists, friends, the Howell family. The occasion somewhat reminds me of some years ago in New York – I think around 1998. I started to work on Howell from about 1994 with some early encounters in New York City. And we had this one hundredth anniversary that was a meeting and a kind of exhibition. It was significant and it really reminds me of this occasion that we are celebrating – yet another anniversary, but of the birth of Leonard P. Howell.

In any other country, Leonard P. Howell would have been a national hero in a significant way. I think one of the major problems in this country is that we are living a big lie. We have been living that lie from 1938 and 1962. And there isn't anything in the terms of freedom, any kind of inclusion either in the constitution or independence, for the victories that black people have really made in this country. It is the black people in this country who have struggled for freedom and liberation, and they are totally left out of the picture in a significant way.

What I would like to do this evening is to look at the character Leonard P.

Howell, of course. Leonard P. Howell returned to Jamaica in 1932, December, and by June 1933, he became a political subvert – a national political subvert. The police reported, *St Elizabeth, St James: look out for this mischievous person, Leonard P. Howell*. Now, the early studies of the Rasta movement did not mention anything about Howell. We start from George Simpson, to H. Orlando Patterson and a few more works, and there was no mention. The 1960 *Report on the Rastafari Movement in Kingston, Jamaica* characterized Howell as a violent person, and also as a ganja planter. There is also the study by Barry Chevannes in which he states that he had an interview with Z. Munroe Scarlett, who was a member of the Garvey movement in New York, who knew and portrayed Howell as a "con man". It was in the late 1970s and early 1980s that some new studies started to recognize the role of Leonard P. Howell. And probably it was the work of Robert Hill looking on visions in Rastafari that really put Howell into this prophetic and philosophical role in terms of foundation leader. Other studies include the works of John Homiak, Klaus deAlbuquerque and Frank Jan van Dijk, and the new studies right up to the 2003 study by Anthony Bogues, who centred Howell as the foundation and prophetic leader of the movement.

It was Jimmy Carnegie who in the 1970s said that this Rastafari movement must have been started by somebody who was intelligent, and that, by implication, is the suggestion that Howell himself was a significant person. I would like to portray Howell to you as a teacher, as a lecturer and as an organic scholar. Howell knew what he was doing. Howell was deliberate in what he was doing. The way in which he presented himself – of course, he could have easily been the best-dressed man in Jamaica. He was also a ladies' man, I understand. And in politics, if you are not a ladies' man, you will not be all that effective. I learned that. But he did not have thirteen wives at Pinnacle, as the *Gleaner* said, and as reported in some other reports. Now, I am talking about being a teacher. It is not just good to say that Howell was charismatic. But here is a man who comes into the rural town meeting, size from three hundred to five hundred people, presenting himself as a representative of His Imperial Majesty. And someone would introduce him with a song – a song about himself, Howell – and at the end of the meeting, they would sing the new national anthem, in which they would replace King George with King Selassie. At his trial, when they asked him about it, Howell said, *I wanted the people to stamp the picture of His Imperial Majesty into their hearts*. He wanted to teach the people something new. And it was that new awareness that helped to bring a significant togetherness during the 1930s. Of course, the entire St Thomas was on mobilization. And there are many – sometimes they call it Nazi propaganda – who say that the early Rastafari movement had no rolling anti-colonial struggles. Howell himself was an anti-colonial and anti-imperialist leader, and that I will illustrate.

So he armed himself with all the pictures, with flyers on *His Majesty's Service, King of Kings and Lord of Lords of Ethiopia. Let our generation of Ethiopia hear the voice of Leonard P. Howell, for in his hands the law is given.* He now established himself as somebody who had a divine mandate to present to the people. *Woe be unto a race who seeks not for their own foundation. I strongly appeal to you to seek and learn your own foundation. The White men gave the Black men the wrong doctrine.* Now, Howell is speaking to the lowliest of the lowly. And the distinction between himself and Garvey is that Howell had a closer identification with Claudius Henry in the 1960s than he had had with Garvey. Both persons seem to attract cane-cutters and cane-loaders, and people who work on the wharves and this kind of thing. And here was Howell taking his divine mandate to people who could not read and write. But he would use the street meetings as a forum to recruit people. And you had to be a significant person to talk to somebody one time and that person becomes your follower. I liken Howell to the market person, the one who goes to market one day, and is expected to sell off the goods in one day. In one encounter with Howell, many people were changed.

Now, during much of the 1934 trial, Howell deliberately used that forum to illustrate what he did on the street. When they asked him about his travel – that is very important, because we need to know what encounters Howell had in America prior to 1932. That he could land in Jamaica in December, and by June become this national subvert – he drove fear from West St Thomas to East St Thomas. I have always said that Howell was a man of history, because to go to St Thomas and then to go to Pinnacle in Sligoville is not by chance. Of course, both places are of historic proportions when it comes to resistance in Jamaica, and freedom. Sligoville is of course the first free village, and St Thomas has its history of struggle. In fact, some people see it as the cradle of black nationalism – in St Thomas. Not my voice, but I am repeating what some people say. Of course, you know I am from St Thomas, right? Good.

Now, how do we measure the impact of a person like Howell? Whenever Howell speaks, it is that pyramid leadership in the colonial authority that all comes out in chorus. It begins first with the planters. It was a planter who first took the report to the police that this was a man that was anti-church, anti-state and anti–the society. The planters in St Thomas – and you would have to be able to imagine St Thomas in 1933, 1934. A place like Morant Bay had about three wharves. You had probably two more wharves in Port Morant. Port Morant was a hell of a production society. You had people like Mr Warfinger, who was the head of the Jamaica Producers Association. You had people like Mr Robinson, who was the head of Bowden Wharf. You had M.C. Surgeon, who was the head of the Wesleyan Church in Morant Bay and Seaforth, and a few more church persons. But what you begin to see now is that Howell's work started to take effect, and the employers started to see the effects in their employees. So the Producers Association and the wharf person said, *We cannot allow this man to continue or we will not get any work done*. The church leader described Howell in terms of *rank atheism, direct teaching against ministers, exciting rebellion and bloodshed. The movement is spreading. It is growing, and it is there to undermine the church and the authority of the state.*

In a profile of Howell in the leftist newspaper *Public Opinion*, published in 1938 but based on an interview done in 1938, the article's author, R.A. Leevy, illustrates the political power of *The Promised Key*. And Hill also describes the concern of another planter coming near up to 1938, talking about the dangers of Leonard P. Howell. Their problem is that the poor people could not think for themselves, and here is a man who is coming to mislead them, to create problems in the society. Hence, what we see now is not just Howell as the agitator, but Howell as someone who created a new awareness, and this new awareness led to action.

I will take on the history of 1938. The 1938 struggle began in Seaforth in St Thomas, Serge Island. As a matter of fact, it began from December 1937. And it came head on, that massive struggle with the cane-cutters and the cane-loaders. And it is very significant that when the newspaper people were reporting it, they said it was as if the entire St Thomas was on mobilization. *The white people are moving out of the parish because they fear return to another 1865*. You must understand that Seaforth was the bastion of the Rastafarian community in St Thomas. So Howell was there.

Now, speaking about how we perceive him, speaking about getting the wrong doctrine. One thing many people do not know is that Howell was very big on education. Sometime after his release from prison in 1936, he was at the Cotton Tree Cross Roads in Port Morant, and Howell laid a treatise on education. The first thing he did was that he condemned the church. The colonial government gave the church authority to conduct education in this country, and he condemned them for the miseducation of black people, one. Two, he said that we in Jamaica, we need a new board of education. Howell now was calling for a new philosophy of education in Jamaica, prior to 1938. Up to this day, we do not have any new philosophy in education. From the Negro Education Act of 1834–35, we have not seen a new philosophy of education. And that was a promise, but it is something that people do not see because they tend to see Howell and Pinnacle in terms of ganja production, and it is a serious mistake.

Just an aside: you can't see the 1954 raid out of the context of the Red Rasta fear, within that Cold War event. The British had anti-red and anti-black radicals. You can go to Gerald Horne, an African American writer, two books. I can't recall the names now. And he located that 1954 raid within the context of the anti-red, anti-Rasta alliance because the bauxite was coming in. New investments were coming in for tourism, and we couldn't bother with this black radical thing anymore. And another black radical that suffered was Ferdinand Smith, a real serious black conscious trade union leader who got destroyed in that period by Alexander Bustamante.

So back to Howell; in a letter from the Colonial Office in England, Colonel Sir Vernon Kell said that he had intercepted communication between Howell and his ally in London, George Padmore, and he said that Howell had now formed this Ethiopian Salvation Union for the total liberation of Africa. Really, the colonial authorities now see Howell beyond just anti-colonialism and in this sphere of anti-imperialism.

I salute Howell as a significant teacher, as an anti-colonial fighter, and as someone who has contributed a new thinking in Jamaica. Rex Nettleford, I think, in his 1983 work – looking at twenty-five years after independence, I think – he converged with G.K. Lewis (*The Growth of the Modern West Indies*) in his argument that the only new idea we have since independence is Rastafari. And it is very important that what we need to do is to do our studies. Very few Jamaicans have studied things that are Jamaican. And sometimes I wonder how these foreign researchers translate the Jamaican language when they come to deal with brethren, especially in the Rastafari movement. And think about it. We need to examine the history of modern Jamaica, especially a return to 1938, because we are living a big lie. I salute Howell as a teacher, an organic scholar and a significant Jamaican in the twentieth century.

Epilogue

THE NECESSITY TO NEVER FORSAKE OR FORGET GANGUNGURU MARAGH

I-NATION

Adapted from an address at the Leonard Howell Symposium, University of the West Indies, Mona, Jamaica, 18 June 2011

It is the opinion of this speaker that the Rastafari family should never forsake Leonard Percival Howell, the first Rastafari and original Gong, who was also known as Gangunguru Maragh. When one becomes more knowledgeable of the life, legacy and works of Leonard Howell, one not only becomes personally inspired, but one gets a clearer "overstanding" of the trajectory of the Rastafari movement and the works it has yet to achieve.

It is not the fault of Rastafari that Leonard Howell has so far remained a mystery. The same forces that made Bob Marley popular and through him gave the world its knowledge of reggae and Rastafari were the same powerful forces that tried to demonize and obliterate Howell and his works. Why was this anti-Howell campaign seen as necessary, you might ask? It could be argued that Howell was considered as a greater threat to the colonial regime in Jamaica than was Marcus Garvey.

Garvey had been petitioning the established order for land on which to build a new and strong black nation. Howell was actively building that nation within colonial Jamaica in the 1940s. The experiment which Howell called Pinnacle was the manifestation of independence long before Jamaica's independence was acknowledged by the British colonizers. Howell was on record for promoting the ideas of self-reliance, self-sufficiency and self-government. Pinnacle thrived on the principles of food security and cooperation that postcolonial nations such as Jamaica are still trying to accomplish.

Howell is the foundation of Rastafari and its entire works. Included in this are the legendary Marley and the poetic music of resistance known as reggae, which is one of the most successful inventions of the twentieth century. Rastafari has reappeared in the idea of "Brand Jamaica", which signals renewed interest in using the unique cultural inventions of the people to create fresh economic opportunities within the country. Howell needs to be recognized for his foundational role in bringing forth the philosophy of Rastafari. He was among the first to profess the divinity of His Imperial Majesty Haile Selassie I, inspiring the peasantry and working class. Howell is to be credited for bringing together the millenarian ideas of Kumina and Revivalism alongside the Black (Native) Baptism of predecessors Sam Sharpe, Paul Bogle and Alexander Bedward into one holistic prophesy, known today as Rastafari.

Howell showed that the black man and woman have power. He reinvigorated the philosophy of black supremacy to counteract the destabilizing efforts of white supremacy. Black supremacy was premised not on hatred but on love of self, history, culture and the prospect of prosperity. Yet Howell's value is not confined to Rastafari. His unrelenting courage and vision introduced concepts of black manhood and womanhood to restore dignity to blacks in Jamaica and elsewhere. Howell's work inspired the 1938 labour marches in Jamaica and across the Anglo-colonized Caribbean, the events generally credited with initiating the final days of British colonialism in the region. Though Pinnacle was attacked by the colonial police in 1941 and 1954, and the multitude scattered on each occasion, this also facilitated the spreading of Rastafari into other communities, especially those in the city of Kingston. Today Rastafari is worldwide.

The conclusion is that Howell is the embodiment of service. He showed the value of being proactive. He has left us with the essence of Rastafari and is the root of Rastafari's works. His idea that personal salvation is self-supremacy is instructive. It is the way in which we will actualize collective endeavour and reap its benefits. He has shown us that Rastafari is self-service, and self-service is the starting point of social responsibility.

Long live the Gong, Jah Rastafari.

BIBLIOGRAPHY

Archival Records

Jamaica Archives, Spanish Town

Acting inspector general to private secretary, 18 July 1936. JA 5073/34.
Activities of the UNIA, 1926–28. JA 5/79/15.
A.D.F. Lidley to J.D. Lucy-Smith, 18 July 1936. No. 283. JA 5/77 – 1934.
Alexander Bustamante to colonial secretary, 6 July 1939. JA 5/79/735.
Altamont Reid, Philip Walker and R.N. White to Governor Edward Denham, June/July 1937. No. 283. JA 5/77.
Attorney general: Labour Unrest, St Thomas, 15 January 1938. JA 5/77/30.
Attorney general to colonial secretary, 5 February 1940. No. 42. JA 5/79/735.
Attorney general to colonial secretary, 15 February 1940. No. 42. JA 5/79/735.
Attorney general to colonial secretary, 2 July 1941. JA 5073/34.
Centenary Celebration of the Emancipation of the Negroes: Universal Negro Improvement Association (UNIA), Kingston. No. 159. JA 5/77.
Circular from inspector general of police to all divisions warning them to keep a strict watch on Howell, 5 June 1933. JA 5/79/735.
Colonial secretary to E.V. Lockett, Unemployment Commission, 14 November 1935. JA 5/77 – 1935.
Commissioner Owen Wright to colonial secretary, 15 July 1939. No. 37. JA 5/79/735.
Commissioner Owen Wright to colonial secretary, 15 January 1940. JA 5/79/735.
Commissioner Owen Wright to colonial secretary, 29 January 1940. JA 5/79/735.
Commissioner Owen Wright to colonial secretary, 13 February 1940. No. 50. JA 5/79/735.
Commissioner Owen Wright to colonial secretary, 17 July 1941. No. 283. JA 5/77 – 1934.
Commissioner Owen Wright to colonial secretary, 25 March 1944. JA 5073/34.
Commissioner Owen Wright to colonial secretary, 17 July 1944. JA 5073/34.
Crown solicitor to attorney general, 11 July 1933. JA 5/79/735.

Draft dispatch to secretary of state for the colonies, April 1940. JA 5/79/735.
E.B. Smith to W.C. Adams, 15 September 1933. JA 5/79/735.
E.B. Smith to W.C. Adams, 31 October 1933. JA 5/79/735.
E. Holt Wilson for Colonel Sir V.G.W. Kell to Sir Arthur Jelf, 16 April 1934. JA 5/79/735.
Elder W.E. Barclay to W.C. Adams, 15 October 1934. JA 5/79/735.
Ethiopian-Italian War: Joining Up of West Indians to Fight for Ethiopia. No. 232. JA 3/77 – 1935.
General secretary, Kingston and St Andrew Civic League, to Colonial Office, London, 23 January 1937. No. 283. JA 5/77 – 1934.
G. Henry Clarke (crown solicitor) to colonial secretary, 2 January 1934. No. 8. JA 5/79/735.
Information regarding Rastafarian cult in St Catherine, 1934, 1936–37, 1940–41 and 1944. No. 283. JA 5/77 – 1934.
Inspector general of police to the colonial secretary, 11 November 1938. No. 28. JA 5/79/735.
Inspector L.P.R. Browning to Commissioner Owen Wright, 18 June 1941. JA 5/77.
James Nelson to the sergeant major, Spanish Town Police Station, 14 June 1941. JA 5073/34.
Krell to colonial secretary, 14 September 1938. JA 5/79/735.
Leonard Howell: Charge of sedition in St Thomas, 1933–34, 1939–40. JA 5/79/735.
Leonard Howell to George Padmore, 12 March 1939. JA 5/79/735.
Letters from Timothy Heath, Wilfred Grizzle and Alan Woodly, October 1935. No. 232. JA 3/77 – 1935.
Marcus Garvey to governor of British Guyana and associated correspondences, 20 February 1934. JA 5/77 – 1934.
Marcus Garvey to governor of British Somaliland, 19 February 1934. Item 37, No. 159. JA 5/77 – 1934.
Pinnacle Papers on Rastafari Followers Information. No. 387/36. JA 5/77/283.
Reparations to Africa, vol. 1. No. 394. JA 5/77 – 1933.
Repatriates: Number for 1930–34. No. 291. JA 5/77 – 1935.
Report on political meetings in Kingston by acting inspector in charge, 4 January 1926. JA 5/79/17.
Return Coolie Ship, 1935. No. 274. JA 5/77.
Ronald Robinson, J.P., to Inspector W.C. Adams, 4 September 1933. JA 5/79/735.
Rules and Constitution of the Ethiopian Salvation Society, Friendly and Benevolent Society, Kingston, Jamaica, 11 January 1939. JA 5073/34.
"Secret" report, 23 March 1934. JA 5/79/735.
Secretary of State to Governor: In-bound Telegrams, Secret and Confidential. 2 January 1940–27 August 1940. JA 5/76/68.
Spanish Civil War: Non-intervention of British Subjects. No. 239. JA 5/77 – 1937.
Statement of Madalin Kildare, district constable Thomas Kelly, John A. Ross and Corporal Leonard Moulton Thomas, 19 April 1933. JA 5/79/735.

Telegram from governor of Northern Rhodesia to secretary of state for the colonies (copy), 19 April 1934. No. 159. JA 5/77 – 1934.
Telegram from police, Trinity Ville, to inspector, Morant Bay, 17 November 1933. JA 5/79/735.

The National Archives, Kew

"Ethiopian Salvation Society", 24 March 1940. CO 137/840/6.
Minutes, Sir George Gates, 6 May 1940. CO 137/840/6.
Governor Richards to Malcolm Macdonald, 9 April 1940. CO 137/840/6.

Newspapers and Magazines

"Camera Record of Police Raid on Ras Tafaris at 'Pinnacle'". *Daily Gleaner*, 16 July 1941.
Carradine, John. "The Ras Tafarites Retreat to Mountain Fastnesses of St Catherine". *Daily Gleaner*, 23 November 1940.
"Charges against Howell to Be Heard Saturday". *Daily Gleaner*, 4 August 1941.
"Chief Justice Denounces Leonard Howell as a Fraud". *Daily Gleaner*, 17 March 1934.
"Chieftain of Camp Pinnacle before Court". *Daily Gleaner*, 19 August 1941.
"Cult Followers Sent to Prison". *Daily Gleaner*, 31 July 1941.
"Cult Leader Held by Police in His Home". *Daily Gleaner*, 26 July 1941.
"Dearth, Disease and Death". *Daily Gleaner*, 22 December 1940.
DePass, R. "Mass Meeting Spanish Town". *Plain Talk* 1, no. 22, 12 October 1935.
"Duke of Aosta Surrenders, Many Prisoners". *New York Times*, 22 May 1941.
"Emperor Beheads Stone Roman Eagle at Palace and Thanks Britain". *New York Times*, 11 May 1941.
Frater, Adrian. "Rastas Remember Massacre – 1963 Coral Gardens Riot Brings Back Bitter Memories". *Daily Gleaner*, 17 April 2003.
Garvey, Marcus. "The Failure of Haile Selassie as Emperor". Editorial, *Black Man*, March–April 1937.
Garvey, Mrs Marcus Jacques. "My Husband's Back to Africa Idea Was Right". *Plain Talk* 1, no. 24 (19 October 1935).
"Gunmen Terrorise Rastas Demanding 'the Weed'". *Daily Gleaner*, 23 May 1979.
"Home Circuit Trial List". *Daily Gleaner*, 20 March 1971.
"Home Circuit Trial List". *Daily Gleaner*, 26 August 1973.
Homiak, J.P. "Pinnacle Redux: Remembering Leonard Percival Howell". *Reggae Festival Guide*, 2009.
"Hon. Ehrenstein Answered". *Plain Talk* 4, no. 1, 15 January 1938.
"Howell before R.M. Court in Spanish Town". *Daily Gleaner*, 29 July 1941.
"Jamaica's Great Rastafari Kingdom Comes to an End". *Sunday Gleaner*, 14 October 1945.

"Judge's Summing Up at the Treason Felony Trial". *Daily Gleaner*, 31 October 1960.
Leevy, R.A. "The Laird of Pinnacle". *New Negro Voice* 2, no. 28, 10 April 1943.
———. "The Laird of Pinnacle, Chapter II". *New Negro Voice* 2, no. 29, 17 April 1943.
———. "The Laird of Pinnacle, Chapter III". *New Negro Voice* 2, no. 30, 24 April 1943.
———. "Ras Tafarianism". *Public Opinion*, 20 February–13 March 1943.
"Leonard Howell Being Tried for Sedition in St Thomas". *Daily Gleaner*, 14 March 1934.
Mansingh, Ajai, and Laxmi Mansingh. "Rastafarianism: The Indian Connection". *Sunday Gleaner*, 18 July 1982.
Mantle, L.F.C. "The Italo-Ethiopian Conflict: 'Things That Affects Us Here'". *Plain Talk* 1, no. 25, 2 November 1935.
Moyston, Louis E.A., "Sligoville Heritage". Letter to the editor. *Gleaner*, 28 February 2007.
"A New Religion". *Daily Gleaner*, 6 June 1927.
"No Trace Yet Found of Howell, Chief of 'Pinnacle'". *Daily Gleaner*, 17 July 1941.
"Police Raid 'Pinnacle', Ras Tafarian Den, Seize Seventy, But Miss Chief". *Daily Gleaner*, 15 July 1941.
"'Ras Tafarian' Head Convicted at Spanish Town". *Daily Gleaner*, 26 August 1941.
"Robbed, Tried, Found Guilty, Flogged by Ras Tafarians". *Daily Gleaner*, 9 July 1941.
"Selassie to Ease British Army Task: Intends to Release Troops Engaged in Ethiopia and Lend Aid Elsewhere". *New York Times*, 13 May 1941.
"Serge Island St Thomas Strike". *Plain Talk* 4, no. 1, 8 January 1937.
Thompson, H. "One Million Jamaicans below Poverty Line". *Jamaica Observer*, 2 July 2012.
"Three Freed in Pinnacle Camp Cases". *Daily Gleaner*, 23 July 1941.
Wallace, George B. "St Thomas Wars on the Ras Tafari Cult". *Daily Gleaner*, 13 January 1937.
Wynter, T.N. "Blatant Swindle Being Carried On in Parish of St Thomas". *Daily Gleaner*, 16 December 1933.

Books and Book Chapters

Afari, Yasus. *Overstanding Rastafari: Jamaica's Gift to the World*. Kingston: Senya-Cum, 2007.
Alexander, Robert J. *A History of Organized Labor in the English-Speaking West Indies*. Westport, CT: Praeger, 2004.
Alter, S.K. "Social Enterprise Models and Their Mission and Money Relationships". In *Social Entrepreneurship, New Models of Sustainable Social Change*, edited by Alex Nicholls, 144–68. Oxford: Oxford University Press, 2006.
Andrew, Christopher. *The Defence of the Realm: The Authorized History of MI5*. London: Alan Lane, 2009.
Austin-Broos, Diane J. *Jamaica Genesis: Religion and the Politics of Moral Orders*. Chicago: University of Chicago Press, 1997.

Barrett, Leonard E. *The Rastafarians*. Boston: Beacon, 1997.
Barringer, Tim, Gillian Forrester and Barbaro Martinez-Ruiz. *Art and Emancipation in Jamaica: Isaac Mendes Belisario and His Worlds*. New Haven, CT: Yale Center for British Art, 2007.
Baxandall, Michael. *Painting and Experience in Fifteenth-Century Italy: A Primer in the Social History of Pictorial Style*. Oxford: Oxford University Press, 1972.
Beckford, George. *Persistent Poverty: Underdevelopment in Plantation Economies of the Third World*. New York: Oxford University Press, 1972.
Beckles, Hilary. "Black Masculinity in Caribbean Slavery". In *Interrogating Caribbean Masculinities: Theoretical and Empirical Analyses*, edited by R.E. Reddock, 225–43. Kingston: University of the West Indies Press, 2004.
Beckles, Hilary, and Verene Shepherd, eds. *Caribbean Freedom: Economy and Society from Emancipation to the Present*. Kingston: Ian Randle, 1996.
Belisario, Isaac Mendes. *Sketches of Character, in Illustration of the Habits, Occupation and Costume of the Negro Population in the Island of Jamaica*. Kingston: I.M. Belisario, 1837.
Bilby, Kenneth. "The Holy Herb: Notes on the Background of Cannabis in Jamaica". In *Caribbean Quarterly Monograph: Rastafari*, revised edition, edited by Rex Nettleford and Veronica Salter, 135–51. Kingston: Caribbean Quarterly, 2008.
Birthwright, Eldon V. "Reggae as a Rastafari Poetic of Disenchantment". In *Readings in Caribbean History and Culture: Breaking Ground*, edited by D.A. Dunkley. Lanham, MD: Lexington, 2011.
Bogues, Anthony, ed. *After Man, Towards the Human: Critical Essays on Sylvia Wynter*. Kingston: Ian Randle, 2006.
———. *Black Heretics, Black Prophets: Radical Political Intellectuals*. New York: Routledge, 2003.
Bolland, Nigel O. *The Politics of Labour in the British Caribbean: The Social Origins of Authoritarianism and Democracy in the Labour Movement*. Kingston: Ian Randle, 2001.
Bornstein, David, and Susan Davis. *Social Entrepreneurship: What Everyone Needs to Know*. New York: Oxford University Press, 2010.
Brathwaite, Edward. *The Development of Creole Society in Jamaica, 1770–1820*. Oxford: Clarendon, 1978.
Brodber, Erna. *The Second Generation of Freemen in Jamaica, 1907–1944*. Gainesville: University Press of Florida, 2004.
Brown, Vincent. *The Reaper's Garden: Death and Power in the World of Atlantic Slavery*. Cambridge, MA: Harvard University Press, 2008.
Bryan, Patrick E., and Karl Watson, eds. *Not for Wages Alone: Eyewitness Summaries of the 1938 Labour Rebellion in Jamaica*. Kingston: Social History Project, University of the West Indies, 2003.
Burt, R.S. *Structural Holes: The Social Structure of Competition*. Cambridge, MA: Harvard University Press, 1992.

Byers, Tom, Heleen Kist and Robert I. Sutton. "Characteristics of the Entrepreneur: Social Creatures, Not Solo Heroes". In *The Handbook of Technology Management*, edited by Richard C. Dorf. Boca Raton, FL: CRC, 1997.

Campbell, Horace. *Rasta and Resistance: From Marcus Garvey to Walter Rodney*. New York: Africa World Press, 1987.

Carnegie, James. *Some Aspects of Jamaica's Politics, 1918–1938*. Kingston: Institute of Jamaica, 1973.

Carver, Michael. "Wavell and the War in the Middle East, 1940–1941". In *Adventures with Britannia: Personalities, Politics and Culture in Britain*, edited by Wm. Roger Louis, 217–33. Austin: University of Texas Press, 1995.

Charlesworth, James H. "Messianology in the Biblical Pseudepigrapha". In *Qumran-Messianism: Studies on the Messianic Expectations in the Dead Sea Scrolls*, edited by James H. Charlesworth, Hermann Lichtenberger and Gerbern S. Oegema, 121–52. Tübingen: Mohr Siebeck, 1998.

Chevannes, Barry. *Betwixt and Between: Explorations in an African-Caribbean Mindscape*. Kingston: Ian Randle, 2006.

———. "Garvey Myths among the Jamaican People". In *Garvey: His Work and Impact*, edited by Rupert Lewis and Patrick Bryan, 123–31. Trenton, NJ: Africa World Press, 1991.

———. "The Origin of the Dreadlocks". In *Rastafari and Other African-Caribbean Worldviews*, edited by Barry Chevannes, 77–96. New Brunswick, NJ: Rutgers University Press, 1998.

———. *Rastafari: Roots and Ideology*. Syracuse, NY: Syracuse University Press, 1994.

Cross, William E., Jr. "The Psychology of Nigrescence: Revising the Cross Model". In *Handbook of Multicultural Counselling*, edited by Joseph G. Ponterotto, 371–93. Thousand Oaks, CA: Sage, 1995.

———. *Shades of Black: Diversity in African American Identity*. Philadelphia: Temple University Press, 1991.

Cross, William E., Jr, and Peony Fhagen-Smith. "Patterns of African American Identity Development: A Life Span Perspective". In *New Perspectives on Racial Identity Development*, edited by Bailey Jackson and Charmaine Wijeysinghe, 243–70. New York: New York University Press, 2001.

Erskine, Noel Leo. *From Garvey to Marley: Rastafari Theology*. Gainesville: University Press of Florida, 2005.

Fiet, James O. *The Systematic Search for Entrepreneurial Discoveries*. Westport, CT: Praeger, 2002.

Fiet, James O., Van G.H. Clouse and William I. Norton Jr. "Systematic Search by Repeat Entrepreneurs". In *Opportunity Identification and Entrepreneurial Behavior*, edited by John E. Butler, 1–28. Greenwich, CT: Information Age Publishing, 2004.

Fleming, Ian. *The Man with the Golden Gun*. New York: New American Library, 1965.
Friere, Paulo. *Pedagogy of the Oppressed*. New York: Continuum, 2003.
Hart, Richard. *Towards Decolonization: Political, Labour and Economic Developments in Jamaica, 1938–1945*. Kingston: University of the West Indies Press, 1999.
Haughton, Suzette A. *Drugged Out: Globalisation and Jamaica's Resilience to Drug Trafficking*. Lanham, MD: University Press of America, 2011.
Hill, Robert A. *Dread History: Leonard P. Howell and Millenarian Visions in the Early Rastafarian Religion*. Chicago: Research Associates School Times Publications and Frontline Distribution International, 2001.
———. "Making Noise: Marcus Garvey Dada, August 1922". In *Picturing Us: African American Identity in Photography*, edited by Deborah Willis, 181–205. New York: New Press, 1994.
———. ed. *The Marcus Garvey and Universal Negro Improvement Association Papers*, vol. 10, *Africa for the Africans, 1923–1945*. Berkeley: University of California Press, 2006.
Homiak, John P. "Dub History: Soundings on Rastafari Livity and Language". In *Rastafari and Other African-Caribbean Worldviews*, edited by Barry Chevannes, 127–81. New Brunswick, NJ: Rutgers University Press, 1998.
Howell, Leonard Percival [G.G. Maragh, pseud.]. *The Promised Key*. 1935. Reprint, Kingston: Headstart, n.d.
Hutton, Clinton A. "The Articulation of El Tucuchean Eldership". In *Voice of a Smouldering Coal*, edited by LeRoy Clarke, 76–85. Trinidad and Tobago: De Legacy House of El Tucuche, 2010.
———. "Esclavage et origines cosmologiques de l'art afro-caribéen" ("Slavery and the Cosmological Roots of African Caribbean Art"). In *Art contemporain de la Caraïbe: Mythes, croyances, religions et imaginaires*, edited by Renée-Paule Yung-Hing, 14–21, 356–58. Paris: HC Éditions, 2012.
———. "From Douens to El Tucuche: Becoming and the Meaning of Being in LeRoy Clarke's Art". In *LeRoy at 70: The Art, the Poetry, the Man*. Trinidad and Tobago National Commission for UNESCO, Port of Spain: Trinidad and Tobago National Commission for UNESCO, 2011.
———. "La splendeur ésthetique du Revivalisme: L'art liturgique des festins chez les ancêtres et les esprits" ("The Aesthetic Grandeur of the Revival Table: Invocational Art and Feasting with Ancestors and Spirits"). In *Art contemporain de la Caraïbe: Mythes, croyances, religions et imaginaires*, edited by Renée-Paule Yung-Hing, 66–73. Paris: HC Éditions, 2012.
———. "Leroy Clarke: Des yeux pour voir derrière le zéro des choses et apprendre à reconstruire les ruines" ("Leroy Clarke's Art: Eyes to See Behind the Zero of Things to Reinvent Self and Rechart the Ruins"). In *Art contemporian de la Caraibe: Mythes, croyances, religions et imaginaries*, edited by Renée-Paule Yung-Hing, 332–53, 391–93. Paris: HC Éditions, 2012.

———. *The Logic and Historical Significance of the Haitian Revolution and the Cosmological Roots of Haitian Freedom*. Kingston: Arawak, 2005.

James, Winston. *Holding Aloft the Banner of Ethiopia: Caribbean Radicalism in Early Twentieth-Century America*. 1st. ed. London: Verso, 1998.

Kitzinger, Sheila. "The Rastafarian Brethren of Jamaica". In *Peoples and Cultures of the Caribbean: An Anthropological Reader*, edited by Michael Horowitz, 580–88. New York: Natural History Press, 1971.

Lacey, Terry. *Violence and Politics in Jamaica, 1960-70: Internal Security in a Developing Country*. Manchester: Manchester University Press, 1977.

Lachmann, Richard. "Agents of Revolution: Elite Conflicts and Mass Mobilisation from the Medici to Yeltsin". In *Theorising Revolutions*, edited by John Foran, 73–101. London: Routledge, 1997.

Lee, Hélène. *The First Rasta: Leonard Howell and the Rise of the Rastafarianism*. Translated by Lily Davis. Chicago: Lawrence Hill, 2003.

Levi, Darrell E. *Michael Manley: The Making of a Leader*. Kingston: Heinemann Caribbean, 1989.

Lewis, Rupert. "Garvey's Perspective on Jamaica". In *Garvey: His Work and Impact*, edited by Rupert Lewis and Patrick Bryan, 123–31. Kingston: Institute of Social and Economic Research, 1988.

———. *Marcus Garvey: Anti-Colonial Champion*. Trenton, NJ: Africa World Press, 1988.

———. *Marcus Garvey: Anti-Colonial Champion*. London: Karia, 1987.

———. "Marcus Garvey and the Early Rastafarians: Continuity and Discontinuity". In *Chanting Down Babylon: The Rastafari Reader*, edited by Nathaniel Samuel Murrell, William David Spencer and Adrian Anthony McFarlane, 145–58. Philadelphia: Temple University Press, 1998.

———. *Walter Rodney: 1968 Revisited*. Kingston: Canoe Press, University of the West Indies, 1998.

———. *Walter Rodney's Intellectual and Political Thought*. Kingston: University of the West Indies Press, 1998.

Mack, Douglas R.A. *From Babylon to Rastafari: Origin and History of the Rastafarian Movement*. Chicago: Research Association, 1999.

Mansingh, Ajai, and Laxmi Mansingh. "Hindu Influences on Rastafarianism". In *Caribbean Quarterly Monograph: Rastafari*, edited by Rex Nettleford, 96–115. Kingston: Caribbean Quarterly, 1985. Reprint, 2000, 43–66; revised edition, 2008, 105–33.

———. *Home Away From Home: 150 Years of Indian Presence in Jamaica*. Kingston: Ian Randle, 1999.

Maragh, G.G. *See* Howell, Leonard Percival.

Marcus, Harold G. *Ethiopia, Great Britain, and the United States, 1941-1974: The Politics of Empire*. Berkeley: University of California Press, 1983.

Martin, Tony. "Marcus Garvey, the Caribbean, and the Struggle for Black Jamaican Nationhood". In *Caribbean Freedom: Economy and Society from Emancipation to the Present*, edited by Hilary Beckles and Verene Shepherd, 364–68. Kingston: Ian Randle, 1996.
McClelland, David C. *The Achieving Society*. Princeton, NJ: Van Nostrand, 1961.
Menelik, Girma Yohannes Iyassu. *Rastafarians: A Movement Tied with a [sic] Social and Psychological Conflicts*. Munich: GRIN, 2009.
Mockler, Anthony. *Haile Selassie's War*. New ed. Oxford: Signal, 2003.
Moore, Brian L., and Michele Johnson. *Neither Led nor Driven: Contesting British Cultural Imperialism in Jamaica, 1865–1920*. Kingston: University of the West Indies Press, 2004.
Munroe, Trevor, and Arnold Bertram. *Adult Suffrage and Political Administrations in Jamaica, 1944–2002: A Compendium and Commentary*. Kingston: Ian Randle, 2006.
Murphy, Joseph M. *Working the Spirit: Ceremonies of the African Diaspora*. Boston: Beacon, 1994.
Murrell, Nathaniel Samuel. "Introduction: The Rastafari Phenomenon". In *Chanting Down Babylon: The Rastafari Reader*, edited by Nathaniel Samuel Murrell, William David Spencer and Adrian Anthony McFarlane, 1–22. Kingston: Ian Randle, 1998.
Nettleford, Rex M. *Mirror Mirror: Identity, Race and Protest in Jamaica*. 1970, Kingston: LMH Publishing, 1998.
Niaah, Jahlani. "Sensitive Scholarship: A Review of Rastafari Literatures". In *Caribbean Quarterly Monograph: Rastafari*, revised edition, edited by Rex Nettleford and Veronica Salter, 74–75. Kingston: Caribbean Quarterly, 2008.
Norris, Katrin. *Jamaica: The Search for an Identity*. New York: Oxford University Press, 1962.
Osborne, Francis J. *History of the Catholic Church in Jamaica*. 2nd ed. Chicago: Loyola University Press, 1988.
Owens, Joseph. *Dread: The Rastafarians of Jamaica*. Kingston: Sangster's Book Store, 1976.
Palmer, Colin A. "Identity, Race and Black Power in Independent Jamaica". In *The Modern Caribbean*, edited by Franklin W. Knight and Colin A. Palmer, 111–28. Chapel Hill: University of North Carolina Press, 1989.
Pankhurst, Richard. "The Political Image: The Impact of the Camera in an Ancient Independent African State". In *Anthropology and Photography, 1860–1920*, edited by Elizabeth Edwards, 234–41. New Haven, CT: Yale University Press, 1992.
Patterson, Orlando. *The Sociology of Slavery: An Analysis of the Origins, Development and Structure of Negro Slave Society in Jamaica*. Teaneck, NJ: Fairleigh Dickinson University Press, 1969.
Pettersburgh, Fitz Balintine. *The Royal Parchment Scroll of Black Supremacy*. Kingston: Headstart, 1996.
Post, Kenneth. *Arise Ye Starvelings: The Jamaican Labour Rebellion of 1938 and Its Aftermath*. The Hague: Martinus Nijhoff, 1978.
———. "The Bible as Ideology: Ethiopianism in Jamaica, 1930–38". In *African Perspectives:*

Papers in the History, Politics and Economics of Africa Presented to Thomas Hodgkin, edited by Christopher Allen and R.W. Johnson, 185–207. Cambridge: Cambridge University Press, 1970.

Price, Charles R. *Becoming Rasta: Origins of Rastafari Identity in Jamaica*. New York: New York University Press, 2009.

Ranston, Jackie. *Belisario: Sketches of Character; A Historical Biography of a Jamaican Artist*. Kingston: Mill Press, 2008.

Robotham, Donald. *The Notorious Riot: The Socio-Economic and Political Bases of Paul Bogle's Revolt*. Kingston: Institute of Social and Economic Research, 1984.

Rogers, J.A. *Sex and Race: A History of White, Negro and Indian Miscegenation in the Two Americas*. St. Petersburg, FL: Helga M. Rogers, 1994.

Rogers, Robert Athlyi. *The Holy Piby*. 1924. Reprint edited by Miguel Lorne. Chicago and Kingston: Research Associates School Times Publications and Headstart, 2000.

Royal Commission. *Report of the Jamaica Royal Commission, 1866, Part II: Minutes of Evidence and Appendix*. Shannon: Irish University Press, 1966.

Satchell, Veront M. "Colonial Injustice: The Crown v. the Bedwardites, 27 April 1921". In *The African-Caribbean Worldview and the Making of Caribbean Society*, edited by Horace Levy, 46–67. Kingston: University of the West Indies Press, 2009.

Sbacchi, Alberto. *Legacy of Bitterness: Ethiopia and Fascist Italy, 1935–1941*. Lawrenceville, NJ: Red Sea Press, 1997.

Schumpeter, Joseph A. *The Theory of Economic Development*. Cambridge, MA: Harvard University, 1934.

Selassie I, Haile. *Academic Honours of His Imperial Majesty Haile Sellassie I, Emperor of Ethiopia: A Commemorative Volume, 1924–1963*. Addis Ababa: University Office of Public Relations, 1964.

———. *My Life and Ethiopia's Progress, 1892–1937*, volume 2, *Addis Ababa, 1966 E.C*. Edited by Harold G. Marcus, Ezekiel Gebissa and Tibebe Eshete. East Lansing: Michigan State University Press, 1994.

Shepherd, Verene. *Transients to Settlers: The Experience of Indians in Jamaica, 1845–1950*. Leeds: Peepal Tree, 1993.

Sherlock, Philip. *Norman Manley*. London: Macmillan, 1980.

Sherlock, Philip, and Hazel Bennett. *The Story of the Jamaican People*. Kingston: Ian Randle, 1993.

Simpson, George Eaton. "Personal Reflections on Rastafari in West Kingston in the Early 1950s". In *Chanting Down Babylon: The Rastafari Reader*, edited by Nathaniel Samuel Murrell, William David Spencer and Adrian Anthony McFarlane, 217–30. Kingston: Ian Randle, 1998.

Smith, M.G., Roy Augier and Rex Nettleford. *Report on the Rastafari Movement in Kingston, Jamaica*. Kingston: Institute of Social and Economic Research, 1960. Reprint, Kingston: Department of Extra-Mural Studies, University of the West Indies, 1988. Also reprinted in *Rastafari: The Reports*, edited by Roy Augier and Veronica Salter, 1–45. Kingston: Caribbean Quarterly, 2010.

Spencer, William David. *Dread Jesus*. London: Society for Promoting Christian Knowledge, 1999.

Steer, George L. *Caesar in Abyssinia*. Boston: Little, Brown, 1937.

———. *Sealed and Delivered: A Book on the Abyssinian Campaign*. London: Hodder and Stoughton, 1942.

Stephens, Michelle A. *Black Empire: The Masculine Global Imaginary of Caribbean Intellectuals in the United States, 1914–1962*. Durham, NC: Duke University Press, 2005.

Stevenson, Howard, Michael Roberts and H. Irving Grousbeck. *New Business Ventures and the Entrepreneur*. Chicago: Irwin Publishing, 1992.

Stewart, Dianne M. *Three Eyes for the Journey: African Dimensions of the Jamaican Religious Experience*. New York: Oxford University Press, 2005.

Teelucksingh, Jerome. "The Immortal Batsman: George Padmore the Revolutionary, Writer and Activist". In *George Padmore: Pan-African Revolutionary*, edited by Fitzroy Baptiste and Rupert Lewis, 1–20. Kingston: Ian Randle, 2009.

Thompson, Robert Farris. *Flash of the Spirit: African and Afro-American Art and Philosophy*. New York: Vintage Books, 1984.

Thoywell-Henry, L.A., ed. *Who's Who and Why in Jamaica, 1939–40*. Kingston: Who's Who (Jamaica), 1940.

Timmons, J.A. *New Venture Creation: Entrepreneurship for the 21st Century*, 4th ed. Burr Ridge, IL: Irwin, 1994.

Turner, Mary. *Slaves and Missionaries: The Disintegration of Jamaican Slave Society, 1787–1834*. Kingston: University of the West Indies Press, 1998.

Van Dijk, Frank Jan. *Jahmaica: Rastafari and Jamaican Society, 1930–1990*. Utrecht: ISOR, 1993.

Veal, Michael. *Dub: Soundscapes and Shattered Songs in Jamaican Reggae*. Middletown, CT: Wesleyan University Press, 2007.

Vlach, John Michael. *The Afro-American Tradition in Decorative Arts*. Athens, GA: Brown Thrasher Books, University of Georgia Press, 1990.

Warner-Lewis. Maureen. *Central Africa in the Caribbean: Transcending Time, Transforming Cultures*. Kingston: University of the West Indies Press, 2003.

Williams, Eric. *Education in the British West Indies*. New York: A&B Books, 1994.

Zips, Werner. "'Repatriation is a Must!' The Rastafarian Struggle to Utterly Downstroy Slavery". In *Rastafari: A Universal Philosophy in the Third Millennium*, edited by Werner Zips, 129–68. Kingston: Ian Randle, 2006.

Journals and Review Articles

Alvord, Sarah H., L. David Brown and Christine W. Letts. "Social Entrepreneurship and Societal Transformation". *Journal of Applied Behavioral Science* 40, no. 3 (2004): 260–82.

Archer, Petrine. "Art and Emancipation in Jamaica". *Jamaica Journal* 31, nos. 1–2 (2008): 74–77.

Baumol, W.J. "Formal Entrepreneurship Theory in Economics: Existence and Bounds". *Journal of Business Venturing* 8 (1993): 197–210.

Bilby, Kenneth, and Elliot Leib. "Kumina, the Howellite Church and the Emergence of Rastafarian Traditional Music in Jamaica". *Jamaica Journal* 19, no. 3 (1986): 22–28.

Campbell, Carl. "Social and Economic Obstacles to the Development of Popular Education in Post-Emancipation Jamaica". *Journal of Caribbean History* 1 (1970): 57–88.

Charles, Christopher A.D. "Skin Bleaching and the Deconstruction of Blackness". *Ideaz* 2, no. 1 (2003): 78–105.

Chevannes, Barry. "Ships That Will Never Sail: The Paradox of Rastafari Pan-Africanism". *Critical Arts: South-North Cultural and Media Studies* 25, no. 4 (December 2001): 565–75.

Clayton, Anthony, K'adamawe KnIfe and Andrew Spencer. "Using Integrated Assessment to Develop Policy Options Trade, Land Use and Biodiversity: A Case of the Sugar Industry in Jamaica". *World Journal of Entrepreneurship and Sustainable Development* 8, nos. 2–3 (2012): 170–82.

Dagnini, Jérémie Kroubo. "Remembering Rasta Pioneers: An Interview with Barry Chevannes". *Journal of Pan African Studies* 3, no. 4 (December 2009): 17–26.

Dees, J., and J. Elias. "The Challenges of Combining Social and Commercial Enterprise". *Business Ethics Quarterly* 8, no. 1 (1998): 165–78.

Dunkley, D.A. "Hegemony in Post-Independence Jamaica". *Caribbean Quarterly* 57, no. 2 (June 2011): 1–23.

Eisenhardt, K.M., and C.B. Schoonhoven. "Organizational Growth: Linking Founding Team, Strategy, Environment, and Growth among U.S. Semiconductor Ventures, 1978–1988". *Administrative Science Quarterly* 35 (1990): 504–29.

Eyre, L. Alan. "Biblical Symbolism and the Role of Fantasy Geography among the Rastafarians of Jamaica". *Journal of Geography* 84, no. 4 (1985): 144–48.

Fiet, James O. "The Informational Basis for Entrepreneurial Discovery". *Small Business Economics* 8 (1996): 419–30.

———. "A Prescriptive Analysis of Search and Discovery". *Journal of Management Studies* 44, no. 4 (2007): 592–611.

Fiet, James O., Alexandre Piskounov and Pankaj C. Patel. "Still Searching (Systematically) for Entrepreneurial Discoveries". *Small Business Economics* 25 (2005): 489–504.

Fleegler, Robert L. "Theodore G. Bilbo and the Decline of Public Racism, 1938–1947". *Journal of Mississippi History* 68, no. 1 (2006): 1–27.

Hill, Robert A. "Dread History: Leonard P. Howell and Millenarian Visions in Early Rastafari Religion in Jamaica". *Epoché: Journal of the History of Religions* 9 (1981): 30–71.

———. "Leonard P. Howell and Millenarian Visions in Early Rastafari". *Jamaica Journal* 16, no. 1 (1983): 24–39.

Hoenisch, Michael. "Symbolic Politics: Perceptions of the Early Rastafari Movement". *Massachusetts Review* 29, no. 3 (1988): 432–49.

Hutton, Clinton. "The Creative Ethos of the African Diaspora: Performance Aesthetics and the Fight for Freedom and Identity". *Caribbean Quarterly* 53, nos. 1–2 (March–June 2007): 127–49.

———. "The Revival Table: Feasting with the Ancestors and Spirits". *Jamaica Journal* 32, nos. 1–2 (August 2009): 18–31.

Kirzner, I. "Entrepreneurial Discovery and the Competitive Market Process: An Austrian Approach". *Journal of Economic Literature* 35, no. 1 (1997): 60–85.

KnIfe, K'adamawe, Edward Dixon and Allan Bernard. "Marcus Garvey the Entrepreneur? Insights for Stimulating Entrepreneurship in Developing Nations". *Journal of Liberty Hall: The Legacy of Marcus Garvey* 2 (2011): 37–59.

KnIfe, K'adamawe, Andre Haughton, Edward Dixon and Allan Bernard. "Measuring Sustainability and Effectiveness of Social Value Creation by Social Sector Actors/Social Enterprises, within Developing Countries". Forthcoming, *Academy of Entrepreneurship Journal*.

Kuemmerle, Walter. "A Test for the Fainthearted". *Harvard Business Review* 80, no. 5 (reprint, May 2002): 122–27.

Mair, J., and I. Marti. "Social Entrepreneurship Research: A Source of Explanation, Prediction and Delight". *Journal of World Business* 41, no. 1 (2006): 36–44.

Mansingh, Ajai, and Laxmi Mansingh. "The Impact of East Indians on Jamaican Religious Thoughts and Expressions". *Caribbean Journal of Religious Studies* 10, no. 2 (1989): 36–52.

Martin, Roger L., and Sally Osberg. "Social Entrepreneurship the Case for Definition". *Stanford Social Innovation Review* 5, no. 2 (2007): 28–40.

Morris, M., D. Kuratko and M. Schindehutte. "Towards Integration: Understanding Entrepreneurship through Frameworks". *Journal of Entrepreneurship and Innovation* 2, no. 1 (2001): 35–49.

Patterson, H. Orlando. "Rastafari: The Cult of Outcasts", *New Society* 4, no. 3 (November 1964): 14–16.

Peredo, A., and M. McLean. "Social Entrepreneurship: A Critical Review of the Concept". *Journal of World Business* 41, no. 1 (2006): 56–65.

Post, Ken W. "The Politics of Protest in Jamaica, 1938: Some Problems of Analysis and Conceptualisation". *Social and Economic Studies* 8 (1969): 380, 195.

Robertson, James. " 'The First of August 1838, Never to Be Forgotten through All Generations': Recalling Emancipation in Spanish Town". *Jamaica Journal* 31, nos. 1–2 (2008): 44–52.

Russell, Horace. "The Emergence of the Christian Black: The Making of a Stereotype". *Jamaica Journal* 16, no. 1 (February 1983): 51–58.
Seelos, C., and J. Mair. "Social Entrepreneurship: Creating New Business Models to Serve the Poor". *Business Horizon* 48, no. 3 (2005): 241–46.
Shane, S., and S. Venkataraman. "The Promise of Entrepreneurship as a Field of Research". *Academy of Management Review* 25, no. 1 (2000): 217–26.
Simpson, George Eaton. "Political Cultism in West Kingston, Jamaica". *Social and Economic Studies* 5 (1955): 133–49.
———. "The Ras Tafari Movement in Jamaica: A Study of Race and Class Conflict". *Social Forces* 34, no. 2 (1955): 167–70.
———. "Religion and Justice: Some Reflections on the Rastafari Movement". *Phylon* 46, no. 4 (1985): 286–91.
Van Dijk, Frank Jan. "Sociological Means: Colonial Reactions to the Radicalisation of Rastafari in Jamaica, 1956–1959". *New West Indian Guide* 69, nos. 1–2 (1995): 67–101.

Dissertations

Albuquerque, Klaus de. "Millenarian Movements and Politics of Liberation: The Rastafarians of Jamaica". PhD dissertation, Virginia Polytechnic Institute and State University, 1977.
Chevannes, Alston Barrington. "Jamaican Lower Class Religion: Struggle against Oppression". MSc thesis, University of the West Indies, 1971.
———. "Social and Ideological Origins of the Rastafari Movement in Jamaica". PhD dissertation, Columbia University, 1989.
Homiak, John Paul. "The 'Ancient of Days' Seated Black: Eldership, Oral Tradition and Ritual in Rastafari Culture". PhD dissertation, Brandeis University, 1985.
Hutton, Clinton. " 'Colour for Colour, Skin for Skin': The Ideological Foundations of Post-Slavery Society, 1838–1865 – The Jamaican Case". PhD thesis, University of the West Indies, 1992.
Niaah, Jalani. "Rasta Teacher: Towards the Establishment of a New Faculty of Interpretation". PhD thesis, University of the West Indies, 2005.
Price, Charles R. "No Cross No Crown: Identity Formation, Nigrescence, and Social Change among Jamaica's First and Second-Generation Rastafarians". PhD dissertation, City University of New York, 2002.
Yawney, Carole. "Lions in Babylon: The Rastafarians in Jamaica as a Visionary Movement". PhD dissertation, McGill University, 1978.

Lectures, Symposia and Conferences

Chevannes, Barry. "Ambiguity and the Search for Knowledge: An Open-Ended Adventure of Imagination". Inaugural lecture, University of the West Indies, Mona, Jamaica, 2001.

Leonard Howell Symposium. Institute of Cultural Studies and Leonard Howell Foundation. University of the West Indies, Mona, Jamaica, 17–18 June 2011.
Morris, Michael, and Minet Schindehutte. "Teaching Entrepreneurship Students the Concept of a Business Model". Paper presented at Experiential Classroom XI, Oklahoma State University, 2011.
Ramirez, C., T. Hernandez, A. Cardenas, L.C. Calcedo and M.A. Gonzales. "Social Entrepreneurship Education for Engineers". Paper presented at the NCIIA 16th Annual Conference, 2012.
Yawney, Carole. "Don't Vex Then Pray: The Methodology of Initiation Fifteen Years Later". Paper presented at Qualitative Research Conference, University of Waterloo, Ontario, 15–17 May 1985.

Online Collections and Unpublished Papers

Brodber, Erna. "The Church of God and Saints of Christ: African American/African Jamaican Cooperation and Incorporation before Marcus Garvey's UNIA". Unpublished paper, 2010.
Dees, J.G. "The Meaning of Social Entrepreneurship". Draft report for the Kauffman Centre for Entrepreneurial Leadership, Stanford University, 1998.
The Marcus Garvey and Universal Negro Improvement Association Papers Project, James S. Coleman African Studies Center, UCLA. http://www.international.ucla.edu/africa/mgpp/intro01.asp.
Sarasvathy, Saras D. "What Makes Entrepreneurs Entrepreneurial?". Available at http://ssrn.com/abstract=909038.

Recordings

Bilby, Ken. Liner notes. *Bongo, Backra and Coolie: Jamaican Roots*. Volume 1. Folkways Records, 1975.
———. Liner notes. "From Kongo to Zion: Three Black Musical Traditions from Jamaica". *Kumina and Revival Selections*. Folkways Records, 1979.

Interviews

Downer, Gerald Lloyd, Alphanso Gallimore, and Florence Stewart. Interviewed by D.A. Dunkley, Tredegar Park, St Catherine, Jamaica, 24 April 2011.

CONTRIBUTORS

PETRINE ARCHER (1956–2012) was an art historian, lecturer and curator who taught at Cornell University. Her many publications include *Negrophilia: Avant-Garde Paris and Black Culture in the 1920s* and (with Kim Robinson) *Jamaican Art*.

MICHAEL A. BARNETT is Senior Lecturer, Department of Sociology, Psychology and Social Work, University of the West Indies, Mona, Jamaica. His publications include *Rastafari in the New Millennium*.

ALLAN BERNARD is a researcher in the field of violence prevention and human development, focusing on youth social participation, political culture and popular culture in Jamaica.

CHRISTOPHER A.D. CHARLES is Lecturer, Department of Government, University of the West Indies, Mona, Jamaica.

EDWARD DIXON is Research Assistant, Mona School of Business and Management, and Project Coordinator, Office of Social Entrepreneurship, University of the West Indies, Mona, Jamaica.

D.A. DUNKLEY is Assistant Professor, Department of Black Studies, University of Missouri, United States. His publications include *Readings in Caribbean History and Culture: Breaking Ground* and *Agency of the Enslaved: Jamaica and the Culture of Freedom in the Atlantic World*.

CLINTON A. HUTTON is Lecturer in Political Philosophy and Culture, Department of Government, University of the West Indies, Mona, Jamaica. His many publications include *The Logic and Historical Significance of the Haitian Revolution* and the *Cosmological Roots of Haitian Freedom*. He is also a noted painter and photographer.

I-NATION (KIRK SCARLETT) is a revolutionary literary advocate who sells black literature via his mobile book stall, I-Nation Books, in Kingston, Jamaica.

K'ADAMAWE A.H.N. K'NIFE is Lecturer, Mona School of Business and Management, University of the West Indies, Mona, Jamaica.

MIGUEL LORNE is a book publisher (Headstart Books) and a practising attorney-at-law.

LOUIS MOYSTON is a PhD candidate in the Department of Government, University of the West Indies, Mona, Jamaica, and a columnist for the *Observer* (Jamaica).

JAHLANI A.H. NIAAH is Lecturer in Cultural and Rastafari Studies, Institute for Caribbean Studies, University of the West Indies, Mona, Jamaica, where he also coordinates the Rastafari Studies Unit. His publications include *Let Us Start with Africa* (co-edited with Erin MacLeod).

JAMES ROBERTSON is Senior Lecturer, Department of History and Archaeology, University of the West Indies, Mona, Jamaica. His publications include *Gone Is the Ancient Glory: Spanish Town, Jamaica, 1534–2000*.

www.ingramcontent.com/pod-product-compliance
Lightning Source LLC
Chambersburg PA
CBHW021137230426
43667CB00005B/158